City of Flowers

....

City of Flowers

An Ethnography of Social and Economic Change in Costa Rica's Central Valley

SUSAN E. MANNON

New York   Oxford

OXFORD UNIVERSITY PRESS

Oxford University Press is a department of the University of Oxford.
It furthers the University's objective of excellence in research,
scholarship, and education by publishing worldwide.

Oxford   New York
Auckland   Cape Town   Dar es Salaam   Hong Kong   Karachi
Kuala Lumpur   Madrid   Melbourne   Mexico City   Nairobi
New Delhi   Shanghai   Taipei   Toronto

With offices in
Argentina   Austria   Brazil   Chile   Czech Republic   France   Greece
Guatemala   Hungary   Italy   Japan   Poland   Portugal   Singapore
South Korea   Switzerland   Thailand   Turkey   Ukraine   Vietnam

For titles covered by Section 112 of the US Higher Education
Opportunity Act, please visit www.oup.com/us/he for the
latest information about pricing and alternate formats.

Published by Oxford University Press
198 Madison Avenue, New York, New York 10016
http://www.oup.com

Library of Congress Cataloging-in-Publication Data

Names: Mannon, Susan E., author.
Title: City of flowers : an ethnography of social and economic change in
   Costa Rica's Central Valley / Susan E. Mannon.
Description: Oxford ; New York : Oxford University Press, [2017] | Series:
   Issues of globalization : case studies in contemporary anthropology |
   Includes bibliographical references and index.
Identifiers: LCCN 2015033238 | ISBN 9780190464431 (pbk. : alk. paper)
Subjects: LCSH: Social class--Heredia--Costa Rica--Case studies. | Economic
   development--Social aspects--Costa Rica--Heredia--Case studies. | Heredia
   (Costa Rica)--Social conditions--21st century. | Heredia (Costa
   Rica)--Economic conditions--21st century.
Classification: LCC HN140.H47 M36 2017 | DDC 306.097286/4--dc23 LC record
available at http://lccn.loc.gov/2015033238

Printing number: 9 8 7 6 5 4 3 2 1

Printed in the United States of America
on acid-free paper

For my parents

CONTENTS

LIST OF FIGURES AND TABLES

PREFACE

....

*C*ity of Flowers uses the country of Costa Rica to challenge how scholars study global economic change in the global South. In contrast to past studies of the global economy, which primarily focus on the market, the workplace, and the household, this book highlights the individual biography as a window into economic restructuring. Focusing on Heredia, a city in Costa Rica's populated Central Valley, and drawing on more than ten years of fieldwork, it examines how men and women in four different class locations negotiate the economic changes going on around them, constructing new worldviews and lifeways in the process. The book demonstrates that economic restructuring is experienced by most individuals in Heredia as a process of profound class and gender restructuring that has implications for individual consciousness, social relations, and political trends.

City of Flowers began in 2003 as a dissertation. But it has been rewritten many times as I have revisited the field to study the evolving political and economic climate in Costa Rica. This rewriting has occurred over a decade of teaching—years that I have struggled to find books for the classroom that are intellectually rigorous but also engaging to read. As such, I have tried to adopt a narrative style that befits the classroom. In general, the book may be used to guide classroom discussions of the global economy, the country of Costa Rica, and/or the ethnographic encounter. It is meant to be read as a rich narrative—an engaging story about social and economic change in one country. Hence, quantitative figures and theoretical debates have been minimized or relegated to notes. Because this book is intended for readers who may be unfamiliar with many terms in the study of economic change (e.g., neoliberalism), the book goes to great lengths to use basic language and to define key terms. Given my narrative approach, however, I do not want the book to be read as a traditional text, with key terms in bold and discussion questions following each chapter. Thus, a companion website provides many of the features that would be found in a traditional textbook.

Readers will find in the pages that follow an introductory chapter that provides a brief history of neoliberal economic restructuring, especially as it has occurred in Latin America. This history is followed by an overview of the ways in which scholars have conceptualized economic change and how I approach this subject in the book. Chapter 2 provides an historical overview of Costa Rica and the city of Heredia so that readers might better understand how and why individuals from different class locations respond to and experience economic change in the ways that they do. Included in this history is a brief discussion of my relationship to this city and one lower middle-class family in it so that I can situate the ethnographic research that follows.

Chapters 3 through 6 form the empirical thrust of this book. Each chapter corresponds to one particular social class: Chapter 3 the new professional class, Chapter 4 an older middle class, Chapter 5 the formal working class, and Chapter 6 the impoverished informal class. Within each of these class locations, I highlight individuals with very different backgrounds and occupations. What unites the individuals in each group is a general class milieu that guides their understanding of and responses to the changes occurring in the larger economy. Thus, although I provide biographical portraits of specific individuals, the biographies in each chapter are meant to paint a collective picture of the lifeways and worldviews that are emerging in specific classes. Chapter 7 concludes by exploring Costa Rica's storied "exceptionalism" and the social dynamics that are playing out in a reconfigured economy.

ACKNOWLEDGMENTS

....

In the pages that follow, I introduce the idea of a "book of one's own," which refers to the importance of taking a biographical, or life history, approach to the study of economic change. The idea of a "book of one's own," however, has another, much more personal meaning. For years, I have struggled to complete this book—a book of *my* own. It seemed as if, at every turn, there was some obstacle in my way. In my first job as a tenure-track professor, books "counted" about as much as journal articles in the tenure process. So I had little incentive to invest my time in writing this book. Instead, I churned out research articles, working on the book in stolen moments at night when the work of the day was complete.

Every few years, I applied for funding to revisit Heredia, lest the city change before I could complete the book. After my second revisit to Heredia in 2006, I encountered another obstacle: I became pregnant with my first daughter, Rosemary. It was a bit of a surprise, and my circumstances were hardly ideal. I was living in Utah while my husband, Bart, was living in Wyoming and preparing to move to take a job outside of Sacramento, California. And so, the day after I received tenure, I resigned from my job, sold my house, packed up my belongings and moved to California to be with him. The pages of the manuscript languished in cardboard boxes as I set up a new household, raised my baby daughter, and struggled to find part-time teaching jobs in the area. During the next five years, I taught as an adjunct at five different universities; I gave birth to another daughter, Liberty; and I tried my best to nurture my young family and marriage. My book, arguably my first "baby," was last on a long list of priorities.

When I was offered another tenure-track job at the University of the Pacific in Stockton, California, I figured I had one last chance to complete the book. During the next two years, I revisited Heredia to collect more data, I rewrote the entire manuscript, and I sent the manuscript to any editor who might be interested. A few were, among them a senior editor at Oxford University Press named Sherith Pankratz. For the sake of transparency, Sherith is not just an editor to me; she has been the best friend of my older sister, Sarah, since they were little girls in Greencastle, Indiana. My dearest (and most useful) memory of her is going up the stairs in her old, creaky house after the electricity had gone out. I was just 4 years old and terrified of the darkness. "You just have to sing Christmas carols at the top of your lungs," she advised. So I did, and still do to this day when I'm scared. Sherith happened to go into book publishing in subject areas that I would later study—anthropology and sociology. So it was by pure coincidence that when I was putting the final touches on my manuscript, she, a dear friend, was in the position to take a look at a chapter and suggest a few presses to which I might submit the manuscript. Her husband, Steve Rutter, was also a senior editor in the area of sociology at Routledge. Both of them had been sending me a steady stream of freelance editing jobs in the years that I was without full-time work. They sustained me for many lean years with work, support, and advice.

Sherith asked if she might share my sample chapter with one of her series editors, Carla Freeman, who just happened to be the author of one of my favorite books in graduate school. *High Tech and High Heels in the Global Economy* described the changes in work life and identity among women in Barbados. It was precisely the kind of ethnographic work I had always hoped to do. So it was with some intimidation that I agreed to have Sherith send it to her. As it turned out, Carla thought my book would be well suited for the series she was editing for Oxford called Issues of Globalization. When Sherith e-mailed to tell me that Carla was interested in the book, it was more surreal than joyful. Even as I write these acknowledgments, the idea of this "book of my own" feels unreal. But this moment is undoubtedly one of the most exciting of my life. I share all this information because I want to suggest that writing a book is a bit of a tortuous journey. It takes tremendous grit and a heavy dose of luck for a story to make it into the pages of a book. And I have had both. I also share this story because I want my first acknowledgments to go to Sherith and Steve, who have been the biggest supporters of my writing. I cannot overstate the help they have given me and, for this, I thank them.

There are, of course, many other sources of support that I would like to acknowledge. In that I have been working on this project for many years, I have had different sources of financial support. My initial fieldwork was funded by a Fulbright grant administered by the Institute of International Education for the US Department of State. One of my subsequent revisits was funded as part of an Undergraduate International Studies and Foreign Language Grant awarded to Utah State University by the US Department of Education. My most recent revisit in 2014 was funded by the College of the Pacific at the University of the Pacific, where I am now an Associate Professor. This book began as a dissertation in the Department of Sociology at the University of Wisconsin–Madison. As such, its earlier renditions owed a great deal to the careful guidance of my dissertation committee: Gay Seidman, Gary Sandefur, Jane Collins, Florencia Mallon, and Francisco Scarano. I will forever be indebted to Gay Seidman, my advisor, for not simply mentoring me but helping me endure the emotional roller coaster that is graduate school. She also humored and honored my struggle to find a "voice" in my writing.

Although he was not my official advisor, Gary Sandefur was in many ways so much more. He was, first, my benefactor, offering me office space and a steady stream of work as a teaching and a research assistant. He was also my mentor in the truest sense of the word. He counseled me on how to deal with others in a professional setting, he shoved money in my hand with orders to buy food when it was obvious I had not eaten in days, and he had a huge book shelf in his office that he let me peruse and steal from on a regular basis. But more than a benefactor and mentor, Gary was and is a dear friend. To put it simply, I would not have made it through graduate school, and I would not have become the person I am today, without Gary's help. Special thanks also to my dear friends in graduate school who helped me not take it all too seriously: Molly Martin, Arthur Scarritt, Monica Erling, Jennifer Eggerling-Boeck, Jeff Rickert, Jeff Rothstein, and Dana Fisher.

As I left graduate school and took my first job at Utah State University and my second job at the University of the Pacific, I accumulated a network of wonderful colleagues whom I would like to recognize. Rick Krannich, Eddy Berry, and Mike Toney at Utah State led me through the tenure process and ushered me into and through my early career as a sociologist. They also forgave me when I left Utah State. Christy Glass and Peggy (Peg) Petrzelka, also at Utah State, became not simply colleagues but close friends. Both are brilliant, with an adventurous spirit and emotional depth that makes spending time and doing research with them rich and rewarding. Special thanks are owed to Peg, now the godmother of my second daughter, who moved quickly from "that professor who never talks to me" to my "best friend in the whole wide world." Without her emotional support and friendship, I doubt I would have survived those early career years or my life now.

Finally, I would like to thank some of my newer colleagues at the University of the Pacific, who have embraced me and cheered me on through the publishing process: Ethel Nicdao, Marcia Hernandez, Alison Alkon, Joan Meyers, Greg Rohlf, and, especially, Kris Alexanderson. In the very final stages of preparing this book for publication, I started the "Faculty Bootcamp," which is an intensive program run by the fabulous National Center for Faculty Development and Diversity (NCFDD) to help scholars improve their productivity and achieve work-life balance. Given that this program has helped me reach the "finish line," I would like to acknowledge the program, my coach David Cook-Martin, and the other members of my group: Courtney Quaintance, Sylvia Martin, and Magdalena Barrera. Also crucial in this final stage were the incredibly helpful reviewers who read the manuscript and provided valuable feedback: Allison Alexy, University of Virginia; Donald Anderson, Pima Community College; Lowell Gudmundson, Mount Holyoke College; Catalina Laserna, Harvard University; Monica Ricketts, Temple University; and one anonymous reviewer.

I have saved the most important acknowledgments for last. First, thanks to Molly Lambert and all my friends at Pro-English in San José who helped make my year in Costa Rica a wild adventure. Special thanks, too, to Anne Snouck-Hurgronje, my oldest and dearest friend, who moved down to Costa Rica with me in 2001. Anne not only helped me survive the ups and downs of fieldwork, she literally helped me with my research— entering and coding data on my sample and helping me keep track of important social and economic developments in Costa Rica. I owe everything, of course, to the people of Heredia, who sat for hours while I asked them endless questions about their lives. Without them, I would have no story to tell. It pains me that I cannot mention my Costa Rican family by name since they were among my "research subjects." But "Margarita," "Ricardo," "Violeta," and "Cecilia" became truly a second family to me. My relationship with "Margarita" has especially helped me become a better wife, mother, and friend. Although she has always been frustrated by my inability to learn how to cook from her, she and I both know that I have learned so much more from her, especially how to open my heart to the loving chaos of having my own family.

Thanks to the many incredible friends who have sustained me over the years: Anne Snouck-Hurgronje, Mary Broz, Justine Sarver, Claudia and John Graver, Molly Martin, Monica Erling, Arthur Scarritt and Jill Lawley, Peg Petrzelka, and Lisa Miller. Special recognition goes to two dear friends—Erica Lipman Lopez and Jeff Rickert—both who died during the years it took to write this book. Finally, I want to express my abiding love and deep appreciation for my family. My husband, Bart McDermott, and my two daughters, Rosemary and Liberty, sacrificed much as I buried myself in my home office to write this book. Having my own family has always been my greatest hope and accomplishment, and every day I wake up to them, I am thankful to be alive. My big sister, Sarah Hanly, has always been my biggest supporter. Together, she and I have endured our parent's divorce, long years of university training, and the struggle to bring children into the world. Without her, life would have been much lonelier and, of course, much less fun. Thanks also to my brother-in-law, Paul Hanly, who is probably the only sane person in my family.

I have dedicated this book to my parents—Molly Mannon and Jim Mannon—because I owe my greatest thanks to them. Parenthood, as I now know, is a long and difficult journey. You never feel confident and you certainly never feel as if your work is done. In fact, it is a lot like fieldwork. Now that I know how very hard it is to be a parent, I appreciate all the more how incredible they are. Always supportive but never intrusive, they somehow walked the fine line between being there for me and nurturing my independence. From them, I got my love for writing and my confidence as a writer. From them, I also got to enjoy having two incredible people in my life—my stepmom, Sue Rice, and my stepfather, Bob Herman—who themselves nurtured and mentored me as a child and as an adult. Sue embodied the spirit of social justice and charity and Bob the beauty and power of raw intellect. They left an indelible mark on my life. During the writing of this book, both Sue and Bob died from cancer. But their spirit and their impacts on me and this world endure. Many thanks, too, to my father's new wife, Karen, who has helped keep him happy and healthy. Together, all of them have created a constellation of love and support that has made all the difference in my life.

CHAPTER 1

A Book of One's Own

December in the Costa Rican city of Heredia is delightfully tropical, if a bit disconcerting. Accustomed to the bitter wind and freezing temperatures of Madison, Wisconsin, I amble about town in summer dresses, marveling at Christmas decorations set against green foliage and trees bursting with bright red coffee beans. Given Heredia's location in the country's central highlands, temperatures remain at a temperate mid-70s year round. But December ushers in what is considered "summer"—a stretch of months in which the tropical rains of "winter" disappear and a hot sun becomes a fixture in the sky. Eager to get out of the afternoon heat, I trot up the cement stairs of an urban shopping plaza in search of an Internet café owned by Rafael. I find the café empty, save for the eight computers lining the room's perimeter. By 2014, most Internet cafés such as these would be long gone as homes in Costa Rica's Central Valley became connected to the Internet. But in 2002, they are popular throughout Heredia as an inexpensive means to access the Internet. As I stand in the empty room considering my next move, the door swings open and a handsome young man with dyed platinum hair walks in. He looks expectantly at me, and I introduce myself as a sociology doctoral student from *Los Estados Unidos* (the United States) here to ask him questions about his life, his ambitions, and his country.

Three hours later, I close my notebook, my head swirling with more questions than answers. Rafael has just finished telling me his life story:

twenty-eight years of hard work and unrelenting ambition. Save for a newspaper route at age 12, Rafael's work history began at age 15, when he took a job at a factory, attending school at night so he could work during the day. He managed to finish high school—but just barely. In addition to his job manufacturing custom rubber moldings, he busied himself with various sideline businesses such as selling perfume. "I've always been something of an entrepreneur," he explains. After eight years at the factory, he developed chronic asthma due to chemical exposure at the plant. He was forced to quit but was given some severance money, which he invested in a clothing store in the center of town. By then, he had married his high school sweetheart. Their marriage—and his business—lasted just four years. Divorced and distraught, but still determined, he used what money he had left to travel to the United States on a tourist visa. After a brief visit with family friends in Houston, he made his way to Miami, where he bought fake documents from a Colombian. Within a week, he found a job doing hotel maintenance. He worked in Miami for a year before returning to Costa Rica with some $15,000 in savings. "I hated Miami and every arrogant Latino in that city," he laments.

As the interview comes to a close, Rafael pushes his designer glasses further up the bridge of his nose and leans back. I study him—his brand-name sneakers, stylish goatee, and neatly trimmed nails. "You have been busy," I finally say with a small laugh. "Busy?" he says with a surprised smile. "Yes. Yes, I have." We sit for a moment in silence as I scribble some remaining notes in a notebook already crammed with my hurried observations. "You know," he ponders out loud, "you could write a whole book about me." I consider the statement for a moment before responding. Is this arrogance, I wonder silently, or just honesty? Neither, I finally decide. It is an ethnographic truth. In this one life, we see something remarkable about the evolving opportunity structures in Costa Rica; the emerging lifeways taking shape in the country's Central Valley; and the ways that gender, class, and nationhood shape both. But we also see a person—a human being whose life is noteworthy and meaningful. Rafael's life, I conclude, *is*, in fact, worthy of a book of its own.

Rafael would be the first to say this to me during the course of my dissertation fieldwork—but not the last. Andrés, an orphan at age 6 who was struggling to make something of himself, also mentioned that a book could be written about his life. So, too, did Jesús, a Nicaraguan drug addict turned evangelical proselytizer. The women were more self-deprecating, but their lives were no less worthy of books of their own. There was Rosario, the 80-year-old mother of 12 who spent her entire adult life pregnant, cooking, and washing clothes. "Now *her* life—that's a story!" said her daughter. Each life history I collected in Heredia was supposed to provide me bits of data on one city's evolving class structure and culture. Instead, they provided me rich stories whose integrity I could not bring myself to compromise. Thus, the idea of a "book of one's own" was an interesting point of departure for me, an ethnographer studying global economic change in Central America. It captured the tension, often facing ethnographers, of how to balance representations of the human condition with analyses of larger social patterns.

The idea of having a book of one's own is not an easy one to reconcile with the social science tradition, which encourages scholars to look beyond the minutiae of individual lives and to generalize and make abstract all that is personal. Given the imperative to generalize and theorize, scholars of global economic change generally skirt around real people. They focus on macroeconomic policies, a changing workplace, and household livelihood strategies. No doubt, real people are implicated in each case. Somewhere in the world is a farmer who cannot compete when free-trade agreements usher in a flood of inexpensive imports, somewhere is a young woman who works a ten-hour factory shift so that she might send money home to her family, and somewhere is a young boy from a poor household who thinks of migrating abroad to achieve some semblance of mobility. But their faces, their names, and their biographies are lost in many contemporary studies of globalization. It is difficult, then, for readers to see economic change as anything but a kind of tsunami that wipes out all individual history, action, and meaning.

For two decades, I have studied Heredia's experience with rapid social and economic change—how it has gone from a sleepy town with a long history of coffee farming to a bustling city with manufacturing plants, call centers, and shopping malls. I have collected 100 life histories of residents of the city, studied the city's history, and observed social life over time to get a handle on how individuals understand and respond to an economy that has been restructured in significant ways. In this book, I will give you my observations of how this city and its residents have changed as Costa Rica has become incorporated into a twenty-first-century global economy. My hope is that you will learn something about large scale shifts in the economy and how they are affecting the population living in Costa Rica's Central Valley. But what I most want you to grasp is that the macro level processes that we understand under the rubric "global economic change" are not abstract. They are "lived"—enacted and negotiated by real people who matter. Until we, as scholars, consider more compelling representations of economic change, we may miss the fundamental point that Rafael and others are trying to make: these peoples' lives are not simply pieces of data but meaningful stories of their own.

A Brief History of Neoliberalism

What exactly are these large-scale economic changes that I have been mentioning? Broadly speaking, I am referring to the emergence and evolution of a global capitalist economy, which, since the collapse of the Soviet Union in 1991, has incorporated almost every corner of the globe. I use the term "economic change" because change is endemic to global capitalism. Under global capitalism, businesses rise and fall, new markets are discovered and exploited, and technologies change and alter production. Such change has not simply occurred over the long span of capitalism's history, which we can trace back to the sixteenth century. It has occurred in shorter spans of time, such as a few decades or even years. For example, in my lifetime, some 42 years as I write this, considerable economic change has occurred. Within months of my birth in 1973, oil prices skyrocketed, the stock market crashed, and major shifts in business strategy and economic policy took place. In a broad departure from an era in which businesses conceded relatively high wages to workers, governments took steps to protect citizens, and most households enjoyed an increased standard of living, the 1970s marked a turn toward more competitive business strategies, a retraction in state protections and services, and diminishing job opportunities and wages. Not to put too fine a point on it, the party ended in the 1970s.

On the whole, the global economic changes that began in the early 1970s emphasized less state intervention and more market freedom. The philosophy that came to reign—and that continues to reign today—is that, to maximize prosperity for everyone, businesses should be allowed to compete without government intervention. To capture this broad shift in economic philosophy and direction, scholars have used many terms. The term "economic globalization" captures this shift, because the freeing up of markets has allowed businesses to expand their operations overseas, where wages are lower and new markets are emerging. In the history of capitalism, businesses have always experimented with different sources of labor and expanded into new markets. However, new communications and transportation technologies have allowed businesses more facility in organizing production across borders. Money, goods, and people are now crossing borders at such a rapid pace that the nation-state seems almost passé. As a result, economic, political, and social life is today deeply global.

As corporations have internationalized production, governments around the world have reduced their role in economic life. The philosophy behind small government is known as "economic liberalism." Again, there is nothing new about this philosophy. It has been alive and well since

Adam Smith first laid the foundations of classical economics in the latter half of the 1700s. His philosophy was that open markets, freer trade, and fewer regulations would expand profits, productivity, and prosperity for all. However old these ideas, they ran counter to the philosophy, known as "Keynesian economics," that emerged in the aftermath of World War II. At the end of the war, political leaders in advanced, industrial countries advocated macroeconomic interventions by the government to prevent the kind of economic crisis that free and unfettered capitalism had caused during the Great Depression. In many parts of the so-called "Third World,"[1] government policies were put in place that protected domestic industries, created state enterprises, and ensured social welfare.[2] But the squeeze on corporate profits that occurred in the 1970s made capitalists less accommodating toward such government interventions. The new assumption (or old assumption, depending on your reference point) was that the "invisible hand" of the free market would regulate economic activity better than any government could.

Of the terms used to describe the economic changes we have seen over the past four decades, I prefer the term "neoliberalism." Like the term "economic liberalism," neoliberalism refers to a process of economic restructuring that favors free-trade policies, private sector investment, and reduced government intervention in the economy. But what I like most about the term is that it captures not just the philosophy behind economic liberalism but the political and class-based project of institutionalizing this philosophy in countries around the world. The return to economic liberalism did not occur naturally; it was encouraged, pushed, and even forced on countries by elite economic and political interests. When I use the term "neoliberalism," then, I mean to capture and portray this form of economic restructuring as a method of reasserting and preserving capitalist interests. At the helm of this project was a set of conservative thinkers and business-friendly politicians, such as Margaret Thatcher (Prime Minister of the United Kingdom from 1979 to 1990) and Ronald Reagan (President of the United States from 1980 to 1988). In Latin America, the neoliberal turn began in the 1970s under the administration of Augusto Pinochet in Chile. Having overthrown the democratically elected president Salvador Allende, Pinochet tapped into a group of Chilean economists known as the Chicago Boys, so-called because they had studied at the University of Chicago and were deeply influenced by the free market principles espoused there. Under Pinochet, the Chicago Boys devised and implemented one of the most aggressively liberal approaches to economic development seen in Latin America in modern times.

Outside of Chile, international lending institutions such as the World Bank and the International Monetary Fund (IMF) began imposing free-market reforms on developing countries in the 1980s with the onset of the "Third World" debt crisis. The roots of the 1980s debt crisis were laid in the 1970s, when low interest rates encouraged high levels of borrowing among developing countries. When those interest rates skyrocketed in the late 1970s, loan repayment became unsustainable. Country after country defaulted on loan repayments—or came dangerously close. This created an opportunity for international banks, as representatives of global capitalist interests, to intervene and restructure developing economies along liberal lines. As a precondition for both bailout funds and future loans, the World Bank and the IMF required that developing countries adopt neoliberal reforms known as "structural adjustment policies" because their purpose was to structurally adjust the economies of developing countries. In the late 1980s, these policies became codified in a standard package of policy reforms known as the "Washington Consensus" (Naim 2000; Rodrik 1997; Stiglitz 2002; Williamson 2004).

Generally speaking, structural adjustment policies advocated a free-trade, free-market, and free-enterprise model that left little room for state involvement in the economy. Reforms dictated the privatization of state enterprises and services, the downsizing of the public sector workforce, and the reduction of state welfare spending. They also mandated that developing countries open up to international trade through the lifting of import and export restrictions. Developing countries were encouraged to participate in the world market through the export of diverse commodities for which each country was comparatively advantaged. Low wages constituted a unique comparative advantage for low-income countries, and many developing countries exploited this niche by promoting the low-wage manufacturing of apparel and electronics exports. Over time, this export repertoire expanded to include fresh produce, auto parts, medical equipment, and other products and services. As a result, plantations, factories, and call centers have sprouted up and around countries such as Mexico, China, and India, producing everything from blue jeans to fresh flowers to technical advice. In many countries, this labor-intensive production became concentrated in industrial export complexes known as "export processing zones" or "free-trade zones," wherein companies enjoy special tax breaks and exemption from many labor and environmental regulations.

In Latin America, as in most regions of the developing world, neoliberal restructuring reconfigured the social and economic landscape. According to neoliberalism's proponents, private investment and free trade will generate economic growth, which will "trickle down" to workers through job creation and low-priced goods. But the evidence suggests that economic growth can (and does) coexist with economic inequality and poverty. Historically, Latin America has featured some of the highest levels of inequality in the world. For this reason, Hoffman and Centeno (2003) refer to the region as "the lopsided continent."[3] Notwithstanding variations within the region, Latin America has been characterized by a small but exceedingly wealthy class and a large impoverished class. Research suggests that the neoliberal turn of the 1980s did nothing to lessen this inequality and, in fact, may have exacerbated it (Babb 2005; Hoffman and Centeno 2003; Lustig 1995; Portes and Hoffman 2003). Due in part to these problems, many Latin American countries have begun looking again to the state to soften the effects of the free market (Grugel and Riggirozzi 2009; Panizza 2009). Leaders such as Hugo Chávez in Venezuela and Evo Morales in Bolivia have pursued policies that allowed the state a more prominent role in regulating the economy and extending social welfare. This trend has led many scholars to call this a *post*-neoliberal moment in Latin America (Burdick, Oxhorn, and Roberts 2009; Grugel and Riggirozzi 2012; Macdonald and Ruckert 2009).[4]

One manifestation of this post-neoliberal turn is a slew of social programming to combat poverty in the region. Most of these programs resemble some form of "conditional cash transfer," in which governments provide subsidies to poor families on the condition that parents—mostly mothers—send their children to school and, in many cases, for health checks.[5] These "pro-poor" policies have helped produce a considerable decline in inequality in many parts of Latin America over the past decade (Lustig, Lopez-Calva, and Ortiz-Juarez 2012). Even so, it is clear that the neoliberal project has not vanished. Indeed, Grugel and Riggirozzi (2012:5) describe the post-neoliberal turn as fitting within the "grain of a liberalized global economy." For example, the purpose of the conditional cash transfer programs is not simply to eradicate poverty but to increase a country's stock of human capital and attract foreign investment (Molina and Fallas 2009).[6] In short, these post-neoliberal tendencies have yet to resolve any of the class contradictions brought on by neoliberalism.

Globalization and the Ethnographic Imagination

The rise of the neoliberal project has sparked a number of debates about economic growth and social inequality (Gereffi and Korzeniewicz 1994; Hoffman and Centeno 2003; Korzeniewicz and Smith 2000; Portes and

Hoffman 2003). These debates generally focus on economic indicators and do not provide a sufficient feel for how everyday people experience global economic restructuring. For these experiences, we must turn to a rich ethnographic tradition in the study of globalization. Take as a whole, this research has two broad foci: the changing workplace and the strategizing household. Both of these are implicated by neoliberal policies. The freeing up of markets, for example, encourages foreign investment in countries where wages are relatively low, with the result that global manufacturing becomes concentrated in the developing world. In turn, reduced state funding has transferred the responsibility for social welfare from the public to the private sector, where individuals, families, and communities must assume greater responsibility for survival and welfare.

As scholars have shown, these trends have particular relevance for women, because women have become a preferred source of low-wage labor and a foundation on which household survival rests. Indeed, one of the first things that ethnographers noticed when they began studying global factories in the developing world was that their workforces were predominantly female (Elson and Pearson 1981; Fernandez-Kelly 1983; Safa 1981).[7] Standing (1999) explains this trend as part of a larger process in which labor is becoming "feminized." By this, he means that women are entering and remaining in the workforce and that jobs for both women *and men* are becoming less secure and less well paid. By putting a premium on "cost-cutting competitiveness," global economic restructuring has led to employer preferences for workers who are willing to take low-wage jobs (Standing 1999:585).[8] Relocation to the developing world and recruitment of economically vulnerable women, then, are understood as profit-maximizing strategies on the part of corporations. In large part, the governments of developing countries condone these strategies and further them by helping to draw women into the global assembly line and discipline them into low-wage factory work (Fernandez-Kelly 1983; Lee 1998; McKay 2006; Ngai 2005; Ong 1987; Salzinger 2003; Tiano 1994).

Just as there was a new demand for low-wage female workers with neoliberal restructuring, there was an increased supply of women looking for work. Economic crisis and restructuring pushed households to deploy more family members into the world of work to make up for declining real wages and increasing unemployment (Benería and Roldán 1987; Cerrutti 2000; González de la Rocha 1994; Wolf 1992).[9] Many of the individuals newly deployed into the labor force were previously economically inactive women or women who, in earlier generations, would have married rather than gone to work (Garcia and Oliveira 1994; González de la Rocha 1994;

Safa 1995). As these women transgressed existing gender norms to become wage earners and not just caregivers, a number of generational and marital conflicts ensued (Benería and Roldán 1987; González de la Rocha 1994; Wolf 1992). These conflicts were exacerbated by cutbacks in government spending, which burdened women with more caregiving responsibilities at precisely the same moment when they were going out and into the world of paid work. Indeed, recent research suggests that neoliberal reforms have stretched women's labor to the point of exhaustion, eroding the efficacy of household survival strategies in the process (González de la Rocha 2000, 2001).[10]

In sum, global economic change has brought about not simply a change in economic philosophy and policy (again—more market, less state), but also a reconfiguration of social classes and gender relations in the global South. But we get only a partial view of this class and gender restructuring in the existing ethnographic literature. For one, the literature tends to be overly focused on the working poor. Yet one of the most critical trends associated with economic restructuring since the 1980s is the erosion of the middle class in regions such as Latin America (Hoffman and Centeno 2003; Minujin 1995; O'Dougherty 1999). The literature also tends to be preoccupied with the situation of women, leading to what Chant (2002:555) has called a "female bias" in the study of global economic change. As Hite and Viterna (2005:78) have argued, "the most important changes in the Latin American class structure in the last two decades appear to have been in the situation of male, and not female, workers." Although there is a growing body of research on men and masculinity in Latin America (Chant 2000; Chant and Gutmann 2001; Guttman 1996, 2003; Menjívar 2010; Sandoval-García 2007; Sweetman 2001),[11] the insights from this research need to be in deeper conversation with discussions of economic and class restructuring.

What is perhaps most limiting about the otherwise fascinating ethnographies written about globalization over the past three decades is that we get mere glimpses of the everyday people who are implicated by macro level changes to the economy. Descriptively rich accounts of everyday life serve primarily to bolster theoretical discussions of economic restructuring—not to provide a window into how real people develop new livelihoods and lifeways in the context of this restructuring.[12] And this shortchanges the debate about neoliberalism, which has narrowly been cast as a question of "winners" and "losers." By taking a snapshot of economic change from assembly lines and kitchen tables, scholars have suggested that individuals in most parts of the developing world have "lost" something consequential, namely the security of a living wage and the ability to formulate effective survival strategies. No doubt they have. But this approach tends to negate the role that everyday people play in negotiating, resisting, or accommodating the powerful economic forces affecting their lives.[13] What is needed, then, is an ethnographic imagination that captures neoliberalism not simply as an economic force imposed from above but as a lived experience of profound social change.

Economic Change as Biography

In the previous section, I suggested that important stories have yet to be told about the lived experience of neoliberal restructuring. Ethnographers are uniquely positioned to tell these stories. They have the training to investigate the social world, and they spend considerable amounts of time with everyday people as they grapple with larger economic forces. But I argue that ethnographers have been tugged in a more theoretical direction that obscures, rather than elucidates, these stories. Most ethnographic discussions of economic restructuring are far more likely to feature complicated theoretical discussions than deeply descriptive accounts of changing lifeways. During my fieldwork, I became quite frustrated in this regard, because I myself struggled to view people's lives as data from which I might develop similar theories. What interested me were people, not data. More than once, I decided that I was an ethnographic and sociological failure. My father, himself an ethnographer, kept me in line. Constantly reminding me that fieldwork was a journey with detours and doubts along the way, he assured me that "feeling like an idiot" was part of the process. He also suggested I go back and reread some of the writings of one of sociology's most renowned scholars—C. Wright Mills. This, it turns out, made all the difference.

Although he has been dead for more than fifty years,[14] Mills is a popular figure in many sociology classrooms today and for good reason: he was a good sociologist and an even better writer. Interestingly, he was quite marginal to the sociological mainstream when he was alive. In fact, given that he harshly critiqued the sociology of his day, he was reviled by many sociologists. In his 1959 book *The Sociological Imagination*, he lambasted the sociological establishment for being overly preoccupied with theorizing. In his estimation, such theorizing did not capture the important trends of the day and was written in such an obtuse, jargon-filled manner that it was inaccessible to most readers. Mills called for lucid writing, urging scholars to oscillate between the intimate realm of personal troubles and the public realm of social forces to grasp how social change translates into everyday life and is brought about by everyday people. As he explained, "The facts of contemporary history are also facts about the success and failure of individual men and women . . . When classes rise or fall, a man is employed or unemployed; when the rate of investment goes up or down, a man takes new heart or goes broke. When wars happen, an insurance salesman becomes a rocket launcher . . . Neither the life of an individual nor the history of a society can be understood without understanding both" (Mills 1959:3).

The relationship between biography and social change was best captured, according to Mills, by a well-developed sociological imagination, which "enables its possessor to understand the larger historical scene in terms of its meaning for the inner life and the external career of a variety of individuals" (Mills 1959:6). Borrowing from Mills, I have come to think of an "ethnographic imagination." The ethnographic imagination combines descriptive writing, rich storytelling, and social analysis to make the connection between larger historical forces and individual biographies in particular places and times. The purpose of this book, then, is to show in broad brush strokes how macroeconomic forces have realigned social classes in one Costa Rican city and how, within that realignment, new cultural lifeways and forms of consciousness have developed. Heeding Mills' call to take a more journalistic and literary approach to sociology, I elucidate particular biographies to describe these complicated processes.

One way to clarify my approach is to draw upon the distinction that Carol Heimer makes in her 2001 essay on cases and biographies. Heimer was not at all attempting to trace a new ethnographic or sociological paradigm. On the contrary, she was comparing how medical experts conceive of an infant in a neonatal intensive care unit versus how parents conceive of the same infant, their child. Heimer describes (2001:52) the different analytical approaches this way. "Poring over medical records and engrossed in discussions with colleagues, [physicians] may scarcely glance at the patient. In contrast, parents spend little time with the numbers and many hours with the baby. Not knowing the contents of the medical record and unable to interpret test results, their best hope is to develop a parallel analysis . . . structured less by a medical conceptual scheme than by an evolving understanding of the child." According to Heimer, physicians focus on symptoms, comparing one infant to other patients with similar diagnoses (2001:52). Parents, in contrast, refer to their child by name, making comparisons of the baby's progress over time (Heimer 2001:52).

The similarities between physicians and ethnographers are striking. Where the physician focuses on particular features of multiple patients, the ethnographer focuses on particular variables of similar units of analysis.

The purpose of both is to "eliminate the noise" from other variables, to discern the general processes at play, and to generalize and make abstract from particular cases (Heimer 2001:48). Like the physician, the ethnographer views the object of study as something passive—an object that lacks a personhood, a past, and a future. It sits still in time long enough for the "expert" to understand its reactions to external stimuli and influences. But what might an ethnographic analysis look like if the ethnographer was more like a parent than a physician? In this case, the analysis would be "more likely to focus on how the object acts on and shapes the world than on how external forces have acted on the object" (Heimer 2001:58). By assigning a personhood to the subject, such biographical analysis would elicit compassion on the part of the ethnographer in much the same way that constructing a personhood for critically ill infants generates devotion on the part of parents (Heimer 2001:58). I am not suggesting here that a study of "cases" be rejected, or that a study of "biographies" is the better of the two. In my own work that follows, I jostle between the ethnographer-as-physician and the ethnographer-as-parent, exploring patterns and processes at the same time that I attempt to construct a personhood for people that are viewed too clinically through the ethnographic lens.

In writing about how economic change is lived, I start with one key assumption, namely that economic forces are not the only influence on individuals' lives. Broader regional histories, cultural repertoires, and class and gender dynamics also play a role. Combined, all these factors constitute the ingredients of an evolving self-consciousness and biographical trajectory. Theoretically, these new forms of consciousness and individual trajectories will feed back into the social structure, putting their own signature on larger historical forces. But this theoretical framework should not be confused with some hard and fast causal model. This is simply my broad understanding of how social and economic change occurs—a dynamic much too messy to capture in simplified diagram form. Thus, rather than start with hypotheses or models of economic change, I start with two basic research questions. How does neoliberal restructuring "fit" into the story of an individual life? And how do individual lives "fit" into the story of neoliberal restructuring? These are the questions that are at the heart of this book.

An Introduction to the Study

Since my first visit in 1994, I have been particularly interested in Costa Rica (see Figure 1.1). As with most Latin American countries over the past thirty years, Costa Rica has experienced a long, drawn-out process of

FIGURE 1.1 Map of Costa Rica

neoliberal restructuring. It was one of the first countries in Latin America to default on its debt payments in the 1980s, due in part to the declining revenues of its two traditional exports: coffee and bananas. At the same time, Costa Rica is a unique case. To begin, it has long been seen as an exceptional country in Latin America and, indeed, the world. Known as the "Switzerland of the Americas," it has a long-standing social democracy with a remarkable record in human development, made possible in part by the fact that it has no standing military. It has also been considered a unique case of neoliberal restructuring because it has taken a gradual and arguably gentler approach to economic reform (Clark 2001). In particular, policy makers in Costa Rica have been far more aggressive in promoting foreign investment and free trade than they have been in reducing social spending or privatizing the public sector. But what makes the Costa Rican case increasingly more interesting is that, in spite of the country's history of moderate politics and its softer version of neoliberalism, it is here where neoliberal restructuring has faced some of its greatest opposition.

Heredia, popularly known as the City of Flowers, is emblematic of the larger country and the changes it has gone through over the course of its history. Historically, the city was one of four main centers of population and coffee production in Costa Rica's Central Valley. Over the past two decades, it has become one of the prime investment sites for some of the country's newer industries in high-tech manufacturing and global services. To capture the human story of economic change in Heredia, I conducted an ethnographic study of life in this city between 2001 and 2002, revisiting the study site at various times thereafter to follow up on individuals and trends. For my study area, I focused on eleven administrative districts in the province of Heredia that radiate out from the city center and that reflect diverse neighborhoods and populations (see Figure 1.2).[15] Between 2001 and 2002,

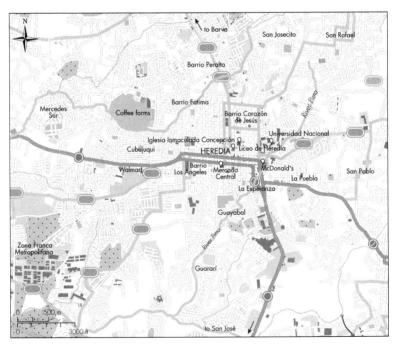

FIGURE 1.2 **Map of the Study Area**

I lived in one of these districts with a lower middle-class family that I have known since 1994. As with most ethnographic research, systematic and in-depth observations constituted the bulk of my data. I chose settings for my observations (e.g., households, markets, and schools) that would provide a window into the lives of individuals at different ages and socioeconomic levels. Written notes from all these observations were typed up and then coded for basic themes (e.g., neighborhood networks, sideline economic activities, parent-child relations).

While living in Heredia, I also collected 100 life histories of residents age 15 and older to explore how individuals from different social classes negotiated economic change. A table in the appendix gives the basic demographic characteristics of this group. In this portion of the study, I used a snowball sampling technique, starting from personal contacts (e.g., neighbors and friends) and organizational contacts (e.g., teachers of adult education classes and community leaders). Because of the nature of this data collection technique, I cannot generalize from the data to the population living in Heredia. As such, I understand the data to be *suggestive* of larger trends. All interviewees were at least 15 years of age and residents of one of the eleven administrative districts that made up my study area.[16] Interviews took place in Spanish, and they occurred in a variety of settings, such as public plazas, private homes, and school classrooms. For these interviews, I used a very informal interviewing style and made written notes (including quotes) on a notepad. All notes were typed up immediately after the interview, and interviewees were contacted at later times to confirm and validate information that they provided. Throughout the book, I use pseudonyms for the people I interviewed. All place names are real, with the exception of Pueblo Tico, the neighborhood in which I lived. I have chosen this pseudonym to protect the privacy of the family with whom I lived.

Unlike quantitative social scientists, qualitative researchers leave the office and travel to a site often far from their own home, collecting information that is not so much "data" as a series of relationships and situations that shed light on various phenomena. Field workers return with an archive of these experiences, which they then must analyze and share in some polished form. The onus on ethnographers is to be truthful, to shed light on how they collected the material, and to be honest about how valid they think their interpretations are. Although the interpretations I present in this book are both plausible and credible, they are undoubtedly shaped by my own history and relationship to my research "subjects." My being a woman resulted in a more intimate relationship with the women featured in this study, which explains why my data on women are far richer than they are for men. Interestingly, my being white and middle class provided a kind of entrée into parts of the community because Costa Rica has long constructed itself as a white, middle-class nation.[17] But being North American and non-Hispanic marked me as an "outsider" to this community.[18] To the extent that I was living and participating in the community, I was what one might call an "empathetic outsider."

Because I want to capture neoliberalism as a process of gendered class restructuring, the chapters that follow are loosely organized by the major social classes that can be found in Heredia. Borrowing from Portes and Hoffman (2003), I identify four class categories: (1) professional workers,[19] (2) middle class workers, (3) formal blue-collar and pink-collar workers, and (4) informal workers.[20] Table 1.1 illustrates the breakdown of my sample into these different class categories.[21] Chapter 3 corresponds to the professional class, Chapter 4 to the white-collar middle class, Chapter 5 to the formal working class, and Chapter 6 to the informal class. To be clear, none of these groups is perfectly delineated. Rather, the groups are very loose categories to which most of the biographies conformed. Thus, within each of these class categories was a diverse set of individuals who had different backgrounds and occupations. But there was also a general milieu in which these diverse individuals intermingled. To help keep track of the different individuals and occupations, each chapter includes a table detailing the characteristics of the study participants that are categorized in each class location.

In that I want to explore economic, class, and gender dynamics at an experiential level, I begin each chapter with a particular biography that illuminates a class- and gender-specific experience with economic restructuring. Taking my cue from C. Wright Mills, I then move outward from these personal "troubles" to describe the larger social forces that are

TABLE 1.1   Research Subjects by Class

	MEN	WOMEN	TOTAL
Professional class	7	8	15
Middle class	6	8	14
Working class	15	18	33
Informal class	12	11	23
Retired/not included	12	3	15
Total	52	48	100

shaping this and other biographies in the chapter. Each chapter proceeds from here to describe the kind of lifeways that are emerging for men and women in this class location, drawing on particular life histories to highlight. Of the 100 *Heredianos* I interviewed for this project, not all were people I knew on a personal level. The people I knew most intimately were the members of an extended family with whom I lived during the course of my fieldwork. As with most families, the members of this extended family straddled many different class locations, which gave me a more intimate understanding of economic, class, and gender restructuring from their perspective. Thus, toward the end of each chapter, I include an indepth exploration of the lives of one or more members of this family to bring the discussion back to the intimate details of contemporary life in Heredia.

One final precaution is in order before proceeding. There are many "characters" in this book. As Rafael reminds us, they each deserve books of their own. But for the purpose of this study, I would like their stories to be read collectively to understand a particular gendered class experience with economic restructuring. My suggestion, then, is to read each chapter from beginning to end with an eye on the overall class milieu I describe so that you might understand economic change as an experience that transforms class and gender consciousness. This will provide a kind of collective biographical portrait of economic change as seen from within different class locations. Before I can sketch out these collective biographies, however, I must begin with a larger history—a past in which these biographies are embedded. The next chapter lays out the historical background to the town of Heredia and Costa Rica's Central Valley more generally. In that my methodological approach is ethnographic in nature, I also provide a history of my place in this city so that I might locate my own position in the analysis that follows.

CHAPTER 2

A Nation Born and Transformed

In mid-March of 2002, Costa Rica's dry season is at its peak, bringing a thick blanket of heat and an exceedingly bright lamp of sunlight in the sky above. A peach-colored hotel on Heredia's east side offers a reprieve from the oppressive heat: a crisp, air-conditioned lobby with freshly polished tile floors. I sit with Luisa in a vacant hotel room on the second floor, talking while she is on duty as a cleaning woman. We lounge on the scratchy surface of a polyester bedspread, Luisa kicking her dirty white sneakers off to massage her callused feet, I unbuttoning the top of my cotton slacks so that the air conditioning can cool my waist. It is a Tuesday morning, and we are discussing Luisa's life story. Having been born in Heredia in 1948, the year of Costa Rica's civil war and the beginning of its Second Republic, Luisa's life encapsulates the incredible social, economic, and political transformations that have ushered the country into the modern era.

A child of mid-twentieth-century Costa Rica, Luisa's work history began at age 12, when she started collecting coffee during the annual harvest. That same year, her father died, and her mother would die just four years later. It was after her mother's death that Luisa's seven older siblings pooled their money to keep Luisa in school. The second youngest in a family of nine children, Luisa became the only child in her family to finish secondary school. The educational opportunities of the day allowed Luisa to go on to attend one of Costa Rica's public universities, where she studied for two years to become a librarian. During her first year at the university, she became pregnant with the child of her then boyfriend. They never married, and Luisa would raise this daughter and another daughter born just one year later on her own. Thus, when she finished school and began a career as a public librarian, she was already heading a household of two small children. Many years later, at age 33, Luisa would meet another man and bear him two more children, both sons. They never formally married, although they lived together in a *unión libre* (cohabitating union).[1]

When Luisa was age 43, the restructuring of Costa Rica's public sector pushed her to take an early retirement. She was given a severance package, which she used to buy a house in a working-class housing development on Heredia's east side. That same year, her *compañero* (partner) abandoned her and her four children. Economically stretched with the buying of her house and the abandonment by her *compañero*, not to mention being out of work, Luisa took a job at a new electronics factory in town, working on the assembly line 48 hours per week. Three years before my interview with her, the factory closed, and she took a job as a cleaning woman at a hotel near her home. She found out about the job from the hotel's security guard, whom she greeted each morning on her way to the corner grocery store.

Luisa's story brilliantly illustrates how Costa Rica's changing economy translates into the individual lives of everyday *Heredianos*. In her biography, we see the restructuring of the country's coffee industry and public sector. We also see the rise and precarious evolution of the country's manufacturing and tourist sectors, which have become two important segments of this small economy. Of course, what is striking about Luisa's story is that what punctuated her life narrative as told to me in 2002 were *not* the changes in the Costa Rican economy but the intimate details of her personal life during these times of economic change. Her first work experience collecting coffee was a story of her father's early death from a "mysterious" and "unbearable" pain in his stomach.[2] Her education and rise to obtain a much-coveted public sector job was a testament to her older siblings, who worked together to give Luisa what they themselves did not have. Her entrance into the public sector was defined by the birth of her two daughters, whose survival rested entirely on Luisa. Finally, her early retirement and subsequent factory work was a bitter tale of abandonment by her *compañero*. In fact, Luisa's biography was actually two stories in one: a personal biography marked by tragedy and joy plus an economic and social history of a country.

That there is a relationship between Luisa's life trajectory and the history of Costa Rica would be of no surprise to C. Wright Mills who, again, urged us to connect biography and history to understand both. But to make this connection, we need to know something about how Costa Rica has been inserted into the global economy, how its class structure and cultural identity have evolved, and how it has been transformed economically and socially in recent decades. In this chapter, I want to provide some historical scaffolding for the empirical analyses that follow. An historical overview is standard fare in any ethnography. But it is particularly important in this study because I want to show how social and economic change unfolds across the life histories of a variety of groups in Heredia. That unfolding can only be captured by a careful analysis of how economic forces, regional histories, class structures, and gender dynamics shape and are shaped by the collective consciousness of various peoples. By "collective consciousness," I am simply referring to how groups of people see the world and their place in it. To understand Luisa's story, then, we must understand the history of this small Central American country. And to understand the present history of Costa Rica, we must understand how millions of Luisas are reimagining the Costa Rican nation and its location in the world.

It is not hard to find an entrée into the history of Costa Rica. Heredia itself is awash in its far distant past. *La Inmaculada Concepción*, the main Catholic Church that sits at the heart of the city, is itself one of the oldest churches in Costa Rica. Although the town's Central Plaza has undergone many changes since it was first established in the 1700s, its cobblestone floor is littered with the footsteps of residents past. But Heredia is also a city that is rapidly changing. Everywhere, old adobe homes are being torn down to make way for air-conditioned grocery stores and cramped parking lots. It is, in short, a place where the past and present interpenetrate and collide. This interpenetration is not simply physical but ideological. Historical ideas creep into the present and frame current events in terms of a story of national becoming. That Costa Ricans are descended from Europeans and thus racially distinct from Central America, that Costa Rica is rooted in a small farming culture and thus egalitarian, that Costa Rica is "exceptional" in its standard of living and democratic principles— these deeply rooted ideas give contemporary economic and social change a particular meaning in this country. In the sections that follow, I pay attention not simply to what has happened in this nation over time but to how those events became part of a national narrative and collective identity. The first section provides a cursory review of pre-1917 Costa Rica, or all that came before the birth of the oldest person in my sample. I then go on to paint a picture of twentieth-century Costa Rica at two moments of redefinition. In all cases, I draw not simply on the written scholarship about Costa Rican history, but the memories of an earlier Costa Rica that the fifteen retired individuals in my sample shared. Some basic characteristics of these fifteen individuals can be found in Table 2.1.

TABLE 2.1   Retired Research Subjects

	YEAR OF BIRTH	PLACE OF BIRTH	CIVIL STATUS	NO. OF CHILDREN	LEVEL OF EDUCATION	FORMER OCCUPATION
Antonio	1928	Heredia	Married	12	Some primary	Store owner
Armando	1928	Heredia	Divorced	3	Primary	Store assistant
Cleto	1931	Heredia	Single	2	Secondary	Merchant
Edgar	1937	Heredia	Married	6	Secondary	Government worker
Francisco	1936	Heredia	Remarried	5	Secondary	Cook
Graciela	1927	Heredia	Single	0	Some primary	Washer woman
Gustavo	1928	Heredia	Married	2	University	Public school teacher
Herminio	1917	Limón	Widower	4	Some primary	Factory worker
Humberto	1925	Heredia	Single	0	Some primary	Government worker
Reynaldo	1933	Heredia	Married	3	Primary	Furniture maker
Rodolfo	1936	Heredia	Married	3	Secondary	Government worker
Rodrigo	1928	Heredia	Single	0	Primary	Shoemaker
Rosario	1921	Heredia	Widow	11	Some primary	Housewife
Ruben	1937	Heredia	Married	3	Some secondary	Government worker
Virginia	1928	Heredia	Single	0	Some primary	Factory worker

A Coffee Culture Constructed

The geographic territory that we today refer to as the Republic of Costa Rica did not even exist 5 million years ago. At that time, a series of volcanic peaks poked out of the ocean's surface between Central and South America. As layers of cooling volcanic material collected around the slopes of these volcanoes, a bridge emerged connecting two land masses. Costa Rica's position as a land bridge accounts for the country's renowned biodiversity, because it became a site where plant species from north and south intermingled. The country's volcanic origins also help explain the country's varied topography, which is characterized by eastern and western coastal lowlands that rise up to form a rugged central plateau, known as the *Meseta Central* (the "Central Table").[3] Costa Rica's unique position between Central and South America also meant that the area once served as a buffer zone of sorts between two indigenous cultural complexes: a Mesoamerican cultural system in the north and an Andean cultural complex in the south (Creamer 1987).

The oft-cited idea that Costa Rica's unique small-farming culture emerged due to the paucity of indigenous labor, although true, gives the impression that the territory was relatively uninhabited when Christopher Columbus "discovered" the area in 1502. We know this to be false. On the eve of the Spanish conquest, the indigenous population of Costa Rica numbered around 500,000 and concentrated in the Pacific northwest and the Central Valley (Molina and Palmer 2000:13). Costa Rica's lack of indigenous peoples came *after* European contact, which reduced the population to 10,000 (Molina and Palmer 2000:19; Newson 1987:336).

The decline of the indigenous population, the distance from the Central American colonial capital in Guatemala, and the lack of precious metals explain in part Costa Rica's unique colonial history.[4] It did not have the characteristics that led to a dynamic, if exploitative and brutal, colonial economy that emerged in such places as Guatemala and Peru. The Spanish eventually settled in the central highlands, establishing the colonial capital in the city of Cartago in 1564. As colonial settlers struggled to build a viable economic base, labor scarcity was a major problem. After repeated failures before 1750 to bring the remaining indigenous populations into the fold of the *encomienda* system, which gave colonial settlers the legal right to exploit indigenous labor, the colonial government began to import African slaves (Alvarenga 1997:18). In 1611, these slaves and their descendants made up some 8 percent of the country's population (Melendez and Duncan 1977:42–3). Over time, this population was assimilated into village society through *mestizaje*, or racial mixing. Indeed, the purchase of freedom, manumission, and racially mixed unions were relatively common (Gudmundson 1984; Molina and Palmer 2000). This is not to say that colonial Costa Rica was not strictly segregated by race, which it was (Gudmundson 1986). But by 1750, labor systems based on slave labor gave way to limited wage labor and subsistence production (Molina 1995).

Costa Rica's early population and its descendants concentrated in the temperate central highlands. Most practiced small-holding agriculture, and they eventually expanded outward from Cartago as land around the colonial capital became exhausted. It is here, in the early eighteenth century, that Heredia becomes part of our story. The migration of small farming families out of Cartago and into the remaining land in the Central

The cities of Heredia, San José, and Alajuela were all founded in the 1700s as land was exhausted around the colonial capital of Cartago. Small farming families moved into the remaining land in the Central Valley, establishing new centers of population and coffee production. The original settlement of Heredia was established in 1706. The settlement moved to what is today Central Heredia in 1717. Pictured here is *La Inmaculada Concepción*, the main Catholic Church that sits at the heart of the city. The church is one of the oldest in Costa Rica.

Valley happened east to west, with the establishment of Heredia (*Villa Vieja*) in 1706, San José (*Villa Nueva*) in 1736, and Alajuela (*Villa Hermosa*) in 1782.[5] What would become the four main centers of coffee production, and the four most populated provincial capitals in modern Costa Rica, began as sparsely populated villages where colonial families migrated in search of land. The original settlement of Heredia was located on a site in Barreal, Heredia. In 1717, the village was moved to what is today Heredia's city center, known then as Cubujuquí. Heredia had a population of 2,030 at this time (González 1997:22).

If the early 1700s signifies the beginning of Costa Rica's modern cities, it also marks the starting point of the country's official mythology, what Lowell Gudmundson calls "the most attractive and widely disseminated

[myth] . . . of any Latin American nation" (1986:1). In *Historia de Costa Rica* (1980), Carlos Monge Alfaro argues that the country's democratic nature can be traced back to its isolation and poverty during the late colonial period. He was the first to articulate a particular image of Costa Rica, one dominated by subsistence farmers living "in humble huts of straw and in primitive shacks of mud" (reprinted and translated in Edelman and Kenen 1989:11). In short, the heart of Costa Rican exceptionalism and the country's "myth of rural democracy" was the small farmer, who struggled to subsist but who was more or less on equal footing with others. Later historians challenged this view, arguing that Costa Rica's colonial class structure was not strictly egalitarian. Stone (1989), for example, points to the concentration of power in just a few Central Valley families who traced their lineage to the original Spanish conquistadors and who owned haciendas and plantations in the northwest and along the Atlantic coast. Perhaps the sharpest critic of the "myth of rural democracy" is Lowell Gudmundson. In *Costa Rica Before Coffee*, Gudmundson provides a meticulous analysis of census data to show that late-colonial Costa Rica was characterized by considerable inequality. Rather than producing for subsistence in isolated households, most people were part of an expanding village economy that consisted of elite families, small farmers, and wage workers (Gudmundson 1986).

When Costa Rica won its independence in 1821, it was, in the words of Molina and Palmer (2000:51), "not so much a country as it was a territory ruled by four affiliated but rival towns: Cartago, Heredia, San José, and Alajuela." Politically, the territory was organized under *cabildos*, or town councils, which gave each town an identity stronger than any feeling of nationhood. The lack of a clear sense of national identity at the time led to more than a few struggles to plot a path for the future of the territory. After twenty years of conflict, the Republic of Costa Rica was born, with a newly established capital in San José. The remarkable changes occurring at the political level at this time were matched by equally spectacular economic changes. In 1843, everything marginal about this country was to be swept aside by the introduction of an overseas trade in coffee. The cultivation of the "golden bean" began on a limited number of farms in San José. It spread quickly, however, in response to remarkable international demand. There is much debate about coffee's early effects on Costa Rican society. Seligson (1980) and Samper (1978) argued that coffee brought about proletarianization, forcing farmers off their land and into wage work. In contrast, Hall (1976) contends that small farmers persisted. According to Gudmundson (1986) and the more recent work of Samper (2003), the truth is somewhere in the middle. Over time, proletarianization *did* come about, but the process was slow and stalled by the migration of small farmers into new areas of the Central Valley (Gudmundson 1986:110). That many families were able to continue farming does not mean that coffee's expansion was not associated with growing inequality. The merchant families of the late colonial period combined coffee production with a growing monopolization over credit, processing, and marketing (Molina and Palmer 2000: 49–50). Their *beneficios*, or processing plants, soon dotted centers of coffee cultivation in the Central Valley.

By 1880, Costa Rica's agro-export model was solidified, and efforts were made to harness the economic growth of the period to create a modern nation-state. In 1883, Minor Keith, a North American entrepreneur, funded the construction of the country's railroad, which connected the Central Valley's coffee industry to the Atlantic port of Limón. In exchange for constructing the railroad, Keith was granted a tract of land in the Atlantic lowlands that amounted to a full 7 percent of the national territory. The multinational corporation United Fruit was established shortly thereafter, initiating Costa Rica's long-standing export trade in bananas. The construction of the railroad and the banana industry was based in large part on immigrant labor and resulted in the migration of Jamaicans, Italians, Nicaraguans, Chinese, and many others to Costa Rica. By the turn of the twentieth century, banana exports became the second most important foreign exchange earner, and the industry provided a steady supply of jobs for those Central Valley residents less fortunate in the coffee boom.

The enormous growth of the economy at this time produced an elite class that was intent on establishing Costa Rica as a progressive and modern nation. Like the elite in other Latin American countries during this period, this class strove hard to rub clean the stain of Costa Rica's multiethnic and multiracial society (Stepan 1991). Ideological whitening allowed *mestizos* (persons of mixed race) in the Central Valley to see themselves as European descendants. The association between coffee, economic progress, and whiteness tended to divide the country geographically along socioracial lines. In the northwest, for example, *maiceros* (maize growers), were seen as economically backward in their subsistence production of basic grains (Edelman 1992:127–8). But the stigma had as much to do with the indigenous and African heritage of the population in this region. This modernizing discourse also entailed an elite-based model of a monogamous and harmonic family, which was seen as critical in promoting economic development and social progress (Rodriguez 2000). This, then, is a snapshot of Costa Rica just before the birth of the oldest person in my study.

Birth of the Second Republic

In 1917, in a small village called El Cairo, a young couple welcomed their first born, a boy they named Herminio. In 2002, at age 84, Herminio became the oldest participant in my research project. That he defines the beginning of my sample's historical record is telling. Herminio was neither born in the Central Valley nor involved in coffee cultivation. Of perhaps greater interest is the fact that Herminio does not descend from the early European settlers or the West Indian immigrants who populated the tropical Caribbean lowlands where El Cairo is located. Rather, Herminio was born to an indigenous woman and a Chinese immigrant, and he grew up speaking Cantonese, not Spanish, in his home. His early family life centered on a small *cantina* (bar) that grew up with the railroad and that his father ran after migrating to Costa Rica in the late 1800s. Herminio would go on to marry and have three children of his own. In middle age, after his wife's death, he would migrate to the Central Valley to live with his daughter, then starting her own family. He would work at a factory in Heredia until retiring at age 68.

Herminio's year of birth and his origins are of interest for two reasons. First, his case provides a compelling reminder that if Heredia's history is one defined by coffee cultivation and *mestizo* farmers, the history of its residents is not necessarily defined as such. Some older residents in my sample did in fact grow up on coffee farms. Others, such as sisters Virginia and Graciela, came from families that were already landless. They grew up working as laundresses and early factory workers. Other important segments of the town's current population migrated from war-torn Central America, port cities along Costa Rica's Pacific and Caribbean coasts, and plantation towns in the coastal lowlands. Herminio's year of birth also marks the first of many coffee crises that occurred in the first half of the twentieth century. After the closing of European coffee markets during World War I, then Costa Rican President Alfredo Gonzalez Flores, himself a prominent *Herediano*, established a tax on coffee to weather the crisis. The coffee elite revolted in 1917, supporting a coup d'état by the president's own army chief. These events signaled the beginning of a long crisis and the start of an important stage in Costa Rican nation-building.

To review, Costa Rica was a relatively young nation at this time, with an economy almost completely dependent on the export of coffee and bananas. We can identify three basic social classes within the coffee economy of the Central Valley: elite coffee processors and estate owners, small coffee farmers, and wage workers (Gudmundson 1995:120). At the household level, there was much fluidity between these social classes. Analyzing landholding data from this period, Paige (1997) finds that the largest group of coffee farmers had farms too small to support a family on coffee growing alone. These families were forced to deploy at least part of their household to work for wages on large coffee estates. The relationship between farmers and workers was paternalistic in nature, particularly because the latter were often extended family members who worked on a seasonal basis. Towns such as Heredia also witnessed a growing artisan class in the late 1800s and early 1900s. The wage workers employed in this sector were not factory workers per se but craftsmen who began in small workshops as apprentices, often working for the same workshop throughout their career. In this sector, there was a notable division of labor by gender; men worked as furniture makers, tailors, and shoemakers, and women worked as seamstresses, cooks, and cigar rollers (González 1997).

Although working-class communities intermingled with the elite in central plazas, where outdoor concerts by military bands became a popular form of entertainment on Sundays, the working class developed its own particular subculture at this time. Politically, this urban working class culture was rooted in Costa Rica's Communist Party, established in 1931 under Manuel Mora. The Party's base included political militants, radical intellectuals, and artisan workers. One of the party's major feats was helping to lead a successful strike of banana plantation workers against United Fruit in 1934—one of the largest strikes ever in Latin America against a North American company.[6] But if militancy was the defining characteristic of the banana plantation workforce, it was cooperation that defined coffee's workforce. This is not to say that there were not tensions in the coffee industry at this time. When the Depression occurred, small farmers were hit the hardest, because large estate owners and processors were able to pass on their losses to them (Paige 1997:129). In response, small farmers staged a number of protests against the pricing policies of the beneficios, which compelled the government to intervene to regulate coffee prices in 1933. But aside from this antagonism, tensions did not escalate (Paige 1997). Indeed, government regulation of the coffee industry acted to diffuse tension between these two classes.

In the absence of class antagonism, the Communist Party became increasingly reformist. By the late 1930s, Mora was articulating Costa Rican–style communism, which combined reform and nationalism with communism's more orthodox commitment to workers and the economically disadvantaged. In 1945, Mora went even further in declaring that class collaboration had replaced class struggle as the main thrust behind

Costa Rica's Communist Party. What accounts for this political shift within the Party can be explained in part by the way that class relations had evolved in Costa Rica. But it can also be explained by the maneuvers of one section of the elite during the 1940s. In 1940, Rafael Angel Calderón Guardia, representing a reformist segment of the coffee elite, was elected president. Calderón was both paternalistic and progressive, and he went on to institutionalize many reforms pushed for by the Communist Party, including the establishment of the social security system (1941), a social bill of rights (1942), and the national labor code (1942). Calderón's reforms angered a powerful segment of the coffee elite, which alienated him from his elite base of support. In an unprecedented move, Calderón formed an alliance with the Communist Party in 1942 to bolster his popular support. Calderón's embrace of the communists solidified a crisis in elite ideology. At the margins of the crisis, but soon at the center, was a man by the name of José Figueres, whose criticism of Calderón had landed him in exile in Mexico. Figueres was part of a loose coalition of elites who opposed Calderón—everyone from coffee barons to small businessmen (Paige 1997:145). In the 1948 presidential elections, this group threw their support behind Otilio Ulate. Officially, Ulate won the elections; but charges of voting irregularities were strong. Regardless, those loyal to Calderón won the legislative assembly, and Calderón used his power there to overturn the election results and declare himself president. Figueres, in turn, used the disputed elections to launch an armed offensive from exile in Mexico.

Costa Rica's civil war began on March 11, 1948. Although it lasted just five weeks, 2,000 men died, and everyday life was disrupted for more than a year. One *Herediano* recalls such challenges: "I don't remember how we ate or how we managed the household expenses . . . probably other family members or neighbors helped us" (Cambronero 2001:865, translation my own). If social cohesion permitted households to get through the conflict, it was also torn apart in some cases as a result of the war. "Everything in our pueblo changed," explains Herrera (2001:879) in his recollection of the conflict (translation my own). Families were forced to stay indoors, neighbors on opposite sides of the conflict became enemies, and many households moved following the conflict due to neighborhood harassment (Herrera 2001:879–80). Among the *Heredianos* I interviewed, two were ardent *Calderónistas* who found themselves on the losing end of the war. One woman in my sample, Rosario, expressed respect for Calderón and communism, but lacking an education she never felt that she had the right to call herself a communist. Her role in the war was limited to figuring out how to make meager supplies stretch across her large family.

On April 19, 1948, the Pact of the Mexican Embassy ended the war in favor of Figueres, who had promised Mora that he would carry on with the reforms initiated by Calderón and respect the rights of the communists to organize. Indeed, he instituted a 10 percent tax on wealth, institutionalized labor rights, and abolished the nation's army.[7] But Figueres did not keep all of his promises. In late 1948, he banned the Communist Party.[8] Mora was sent into exile, and many other communists were killed or otherwise ostracized from political, social, and economic life. In general, Figueres and his administration effectively buried the communist narrative, leaving communist ideology "without a place in . . . official histories [and] popular ideologies" (Paige 1997:101). The irony, of course, was that Figueres, an avid anticommunist, instituted and furthered the reforms pushed for by the Calderón-Communist alliance. Paige (1997) argues that this move was more strategic than reformist. Figueres' administration reconfigured elite control in the country, which meant sweeping aside the power of the producer-processor class of coffee farmers and making room for a new elite class of agro-industrialists. Although this class at first opposed the social welfare reforms that Figueres implemented, Figueres was able to package these reforms as an elite project, highlighting how they would suppress popular discontent and increase worker productivity.

Within the first few years of Costa Rica's Second Republic, the government established a national healthcare system, nationalized the country's banking and electrical systems, extended voting rights for all women and Afro–Costa Ricans, and institutionalized a public education system that was compulsory from 6 to 14 years of age. There is no doubt that these state interventions had a profound impact on Costa Rican society. The percentage of the population living in poverty declined from 50 percent in 1961 to 20 percent in the mid-1970s. By 1978, 90 percent of the population was literate and life expectancy stood at 70 years (Clark 2001:32, 40). The bureaucratic structure that supported this welfare state not only raised the standard of living. It also created a vast public workforce rooted in the country's increasingly urban Central Valley. Between 1950 and 1970, state employees tripled to 51,000, or 10 percent of the workforce (Molina and Palmer 2000:103). It was this public sector workforce that accounted for much of the growth in the country's urban middle class during this period. One of the key features of this middle class was its ability to achieve upward social mobility, using the public educational system as its main vehicle in doing so (Molina and Palmer 2000:103–4).[9]

If the agro-industrial elite and the urban middle class prospered during this time, many other groups were less fortunate. Rural landlessness, for

After a brief civil war in 1948, Costa Rica settled into a long period of political reform and economic growth. The government abolished the military, nationalized healthcare, and universalized public education. These and other government interventions had a positive impact on Costa Rican society, helping to reduce poverty and increase life expectancy. During this "golden era," an urban middle class emerged and prospered in towns such as Heredia, seen here in 2001.

example, skyrocketed after 1950, forcing many families from the coastal lowlands to migrate into the Central Valley in search of work and housing.[10] Urban workers also suffered under the Second Republic. After 1950, craft workshops slowly gave way to factories, which had little connection to the country's radical labor history, resulting in a drastic decline in union membership (Molina and Palmer 2000; Yashar 1995).[11] Figueres encouraged this decline, promoting a unique form of company unionism called *solidarismo*.[12] The *solidarista* association acts as an employee savings fund of sorts, to which both labor and management contribute. This fund finances benefits, with the goal of limiting class confrontation, and more specifically, strikes.[13] The decline in labor militancy and the rise of middle class values created an urban culture in Costa Rica's Central Valley that contrasted sharply from the preceding era. The militant working-class *barrios* that revolved around workers' centers and soccer fields were replaced in part by schools and suburban developments. To be sure, radical currents did not cease to exist. The growth of public universities, for example, created fertile ground for radical student movements in the 1960s. These movements, however, were contained by the conservative middle-class thrust of Costa Rica at this time.

If Costa Rica's culture was conservative and conformist at this historical juncture, its economy was dynamic and growing. But in the 1970s, a number of factors combined to put a break on this growth. To begin, world market prices for coffee and bananas, Costa Rica's main sources of revenue, began to decline. To exacerbate the situation, public spending continued to rise (Molina and Palmer 2000:117). As a result, Costa Rica saw a troubling rise in its foreign public debt, from $164 million in 1970 to more than $1 billion in 1978. In 1981, this financial crisis came to a head as Costa Rica's economy collapsed and the country became one of the first Latin American countries to default on its debt (Clark 2001:43). As it turned out, socialist revolution broke out in Nicaragua at the same time, leaving the United States poised to provide funding to any Central American country that might help stave off revolution in the region. Costa Rica became, for a time, the ideal recipient.

Economic Crisis and Transformation

In 1982, just one year after Costa Rica defaulted on its external debt, a young woman named Sylvia was born. The year was not exactly an auspicious one, and Sylvia's life reflected this. Her mother was a migrant from Costa Rica's northwestern province of Guanacaste who had traveled to San José to work as a domestic when she was a teenager. There, she met another migrant from Costa Rica's Atlantic coastal province of Limón. Together, they would have four children. Sylvia was their third. When Sylvia was 6 years old, her father abandoned the family. Struggling to support her four children, Sylvia's mother moved them to a slum on Heredia's southern perimeter. She took a job at a Colgate factory in San José while Sylvia and her siblings worked part-time at clothes stores in town. The factory job proved unstable, and Sylvia's mother eventually settled into a job at a Payless Shoe Store, newly built on the highway between Heredia and San José. Sylvia, in turn, found work at a nearby Hanes factory, attending secondary school at night.

The year of Sylvia's birth marked a very important transition in the Costa Rican economy, a point at which structural problems brought the country's economy to a standstill. The immediate result of the debt crisis was a serious cash flow problem in most Costa Rican households, middle and working class alike. In just one year, real salaries plummeted by 40 percent and inflation fluctuated between 80 and 100 percent (Molina and Palmer 2000:119). The average Costa Rican had less money to purchase basic goods, whose prices simultaneously skyrocketed. To aggravate matters, high employment sectors, such as the banana industry, began a series of layoffs that had real effects on the livelihoods of the population during the 1980s. One of the consequences was rapid migration to the metropolitan area of San José, where people flocked in search of work. Most of this urban growth was unplanned and chaotic, creating slums of migrant families that were more typical of other Latin American urban areas.

In response to Costa Rica's economic crisis, the World Bank and International Monetary Fund imposed a set of economic reforms, again, known as structural adjustment policies (SAPs).[14] These reforms were neoliberal in nature and mandated that the country cut costs and increase revenues. More specifically, SAPs demanded cuts in public spending, principally through privatization of state industries, elimination of state subsidies, and reduction of social spending. Industries, in turn, were to be given more freedom in a liberalized trade and financial environment to develop a variety of new exports, loosely labeled "nontraditional exports" because they departed from the traditional export base of coffee and bananas. Although most Latin American countries eventually adopted these neoliberal reforms, Costa Rica became a rather unique case of neoliberal restructuring. That the rest of Central America was torn by revolution during the 1980s meant that Costa Rica became a key strategic spot for the United States and a major recipient of US development assistance (Clark 2001). This was no small matter. Between 1982 and 1984 alone, the US Agency for International Development (USAID) funneled $530 million into the Costa Rican economy (Molina and Palmer 2000:121).[15] Costa Rica's experience with structural adjustment was also unique in that its democratic tradition made for a more gradual process of neoliberal reform, contrasting sharply to those countries implementing a "shock therapy" approach (Clark 2001).

Clark (2001) distinguishes between an "easy" phase of structural adjustment in Costa Rica in the 1980s and a more difficult phase of adjustment in the 1990s. During the "easy" phase, Costa Rica enjoyed the injection of enormous sums of US financial aid, not to mention special trade status with the United States. The Caribbean Basin Initiative (CBI), implemented by the Reagan administration in 1982, was established to stabilize the region politically by promoting capitalist economic development. Between 1984 and 1995, the CBI allowed for the duty-free entry into the US market of such nontraditional exports as vegetables, fruit, flowers, and labor-intensive textiles and electronics. Once the CBI was implemented, the USAID intervened to restructure the Costa Rican economy so as to meet the new market opportunities. In 1983, it set up and began financing an organization called the Coalition of Development Initiatives (CINDE in Spanish), which acted as an investment promotion center. It was not difficult to convince foreign companies to invest in Costa Rica, whose highly educated workforce, political stability, and proximity to US markets made this country an ideal site for multinational corporate investment. Export production became concentrated in *zonas francas*, which are territorially bound industrial parks, where companies enjoyed fiscal incentives and proximity to urban labor markets.[16] In 1997, Intel, the world's largest maker of microprocessors, chose the country as the site of its newest assembly plant. Following this move, the country's economy became tied largely to the economic fortunes of Intel, whose exports became the leading commodities from the country.[17]

The socialist electoral defeat in Nicaragua in 1990 and international developments elsewhere led to decreased attention to Costa Rica by the United States. As a result, USAID funding began to dry up in 1991. By 1995, it had dropped to $6 million from its peak of $219 million in 1985 (Clark 1995, 1997). At this time, the country entered a second, more difficult stage of neoliberal reform. By the 1990s, for example, larger shares of the public sector workforce were being pushed into early retirement. What effect these economic changes have had on Costa Rica's class structure is still difficult to say. Clark (2001:113–8) contends that by the mid-1990s, the economy had sufficiently recovered and Costa Rica had returned to being a regional leader in social welfare. Between 1980 and 1995, for example, life expectancy at birth rose from 70 to 77 years, and by the late 1990s, almost one-third of young adults were attending university (Clark 2001:32–4, 95). The current situation, however, is arguably more complicated. Part of Clark's argument is that the tourist and newer export sectors had soaked up unemployment by this time. Yet employment in these sectors is unstable, low paid, and poorly regulated (Molina and Palmer 2000:126). Even Clark admits to the rising social ills throughout the country, such as a rise in child prostitution, violent and property-based crime, and school dropout rates.

Thus, even if indicators suggest that Costa Rica stabilized economically in the 1990s, its society had changed enormously in response to structural adjustment. Those changes were not without consequence. During the 1990s, political mobilizations began to critique the neoliberal reforms of the previous decade. In 1995, when the leaders of Costa Rica's two main political parties—the Social Christian Unity Party (Partido Unidad Social Cristiana [PUSC]) and the National Liberation Party (Partido Liberación National [PLN])—signed a pact to accelerate structural adjustment reforms, protests erupted in San José.[18] Attempts to privatize the Costa Rican Institute for Electricity (Instituto Costarricense de Electricidad [ICE]) in 2000 ignited another round of mass protests—the so-called "Combo ICE protests"—which effectively shut down the country and the privatization effort. However gradual their implementation, neoliberal reforms have never been widely celebrated by those whose lives have been so wholeheartedly transformed by them.

An Ethnography Begins

In the midst of Costa Rica's late twentieth-century political, economic, and social upheaval, I traveled to Costa Rica for the first time. It was 1994, and I was then an undergraduate at the University of Michigan and eager to learn Spanish. The journey began on a disastrous note. The airline lost my luggage and, during my first night in the capital of San José, I threw up on the only shirt I had. On my second day in Costa Rica, wearing a cotton T-shirt now scrubbed raw but still stained down the front, I boarded a bus for Heredia, where I was to study. After a 20-minute drive, the bus came upon a working-class *barrio* (neighborhood) to the southeast of Heredia's city center. In Heredia's early years, the *barrio* was known as *La Puebla de los Pardos de Cubujuquí* and was home to the town's black and racially mixed population, then segregated from the rest of town by the river Pirro (Melendez 2001:15). Over time, the neighborhood became known simply as La Puebla and, although it would lose its distinction as a *barrio* for Heredia's racial "other," it remained a working-class section of town. I knew none of this in 1994, but the neighborhood stands out in my memory nevertheless. From La Puebla, I could see the city's historic church, *La Inmaculada Concepción*, poking up from the Central Plaza. It was late May and, it being the rainy season, the grass was so green it seemed to float. From my window seat, I observed the dark brown soil saturated beneath the greenery. Here was a small patch of coffee bushes, and there was a mangy stray dog sniffing an empty can of Coca-Cola.

The landscape that lay before me that day had changed drastically in the years that preceded my first visit. The earliest vista of the entrance into Heredia that I have seen is depicted in a sketch by Mario Ramirez Segura based on a 1926 engraving by the famous *Herediano* painter Fausto Pacheco. A quaint stone bridge straddles the Pirro River, beyond which small adobe houses dot the landscape. What the picture does not show, but older *Heredianos* recall, is a road just beyond these homes, which led to a number of coffee-processing plants and the city center. Over time, these plants would pollute the river to the extent that, today, a stream of sudsy

This was the road leading into Heredia in 2001. It looked very similar to what I saw in 1994 but completely different from earlier images of Heredia that depict this entrance as a quaint stone bridge straddling the Pirro River below. In an earlier era, adobe homes and coffee-processing plants could be found on the other side of the bridge. By the late twentieth century, these features had been replaced by a slew of fast-food restaurants and office buildings. The image suggests the profound transformation that had occurred in cities such as Heredia.

green water is all that is left of the river. Nothing is left of the early coffee plants either, which had already been replaced by McDonald's golden arches when I proceeded across the river in 1994. Indeed, the urban growth in Heredia is visibly arresting. Just one generation ago, writers described an Heredia of bucolic beauty and insulated social structure, a landscape defined by family coffee farms and a small town center. Today, new urban developments encroach on old coffee farms as buses and cars clog an inadequate infrastructure made for oxcarts and horses. That these urban developments should be filled with migrants and San José commuters suggests that what used to be an isolated provincial town is rapidly transforming into a diverse urban center.

My luggage finally showed up at Juan Santamaría International Airport on that afternoon of my second day in Costa Rica in 1994. By then, I had already attended a brief orientation at Universidad Nacional (UNA) on Heredia's east side, where I would study that summer. As the orientation came to a close, a middle-aged woman with short, curly black hair approached me, saying something quickly in Spanish. Completely clueless as to what she was saying, I looked around the room wildly for help. The director of my study abroad program quickly came over to translate. "This is Margarita, your host mother," he explained. I smiled nervously as he and Margarita spoke rapidly to one another in Spanish. Finally, he turned to me, cocked his head to the right, and quipped, "She says you look nothing like your picture." Margarita, a homemaker from Heredia, would turn out to be one of my closest confidantes. But that first day when she introduced me to her modest and tidy home in the quiet neighborhood of Pueblo Tico, all I could say was "*Su casa es bonita*" ("Your home is pretty"). Over the years, as I learned more Spanish, revisited Costa Rica, and shared her home for varying lengths of time, I eventually became a close friend of the family, which included Margarita's husband, Ricardo, and their two daughters, Violeta and Cecilia. In May of 2001, I settled into their front bedroom for a year of fieldwork. I would return, in 2003, 2006, and 2014 to conduct what Burawoy (2003) calls "ethnographic updates."[19]

As I mentioned in the introduction, Heredia is, in many ways, emblematic of the larger changes going on in Costa Rica. The town not only had an important role to play in coffee production, but it has been a key investment site for newer export industries. Four of Costa Rica's sixteen free-trade zones are located in the province of Heredia. Major multinational companies also have industrial campuses here, including Intel and British American Tobacco. In addition to global production, the town represents a key segment of the country's public sector workforce. Not only does the town host a public university and regional offices of public ministries, but a significant portion of public sector workers that commute to San José each day for work reside in the city. Heredia, then, holds three important threads to Costa Rica's economic restructuring: (1) agricultural restructuring, (2) nontraditional export development, and (3) public sector restructuring. But as I explained in the last chapter, we cannot hope to understand what this restructuring has meant for ordinary people unless we pan in more closely to the everyday lifeworlds associated with this city. It is, of course, nearly impossible to capture Heredia or *Herediano* life at any one moment in time. After all, my observations of the city spanned a twenty-year time period in which intense economic and social change was occurring. Each time I revisited Heredia, the landscape and lifeways I observed in an earlier period had already changed. It was like trying to photograph a speeding train and hoping for some semblance of focus. Therefore, my objective in the narrative that follows is not to paint any definitive account of *Herediano* society. It is merely to try and capture as best I can an emblematic Costa Rican city at an important moment in time. And I will do this by introducing you to some of the people who call this city home.

CHAPTER 3

Mobility in the New Millennium

A bar known as *Bulevar* sits one block west of Heredia's public university. It is a frenzied place frequented by university students and young *Heredianos*. With no walls closing off the bar from the outside, customers drink lazily atop tall stools while watching the late-night traffic outside. Large round tables and intimate wooden booths also offer seating, as does the main bar, where young men sit alone and in silence watching soccer games playing on television sets hung high. Female bartenders, wearing tube tops tight across their chests, cater to the men efficiently, offering up sweaty bottles of Costa Rican beer and small bowls of crisp popcorn. In 2012, Costa Rica would pass a law banning smoking in almost all public places. But on a Saturday night in July of 2001, clouds of cigarette smoke hang like chandeliers above crowded tables as salsa music pulsates from large black speakers. I peer into the haze in search of Luis, winding my way through a maze of tables to find him, grinning, with a finger pointing repeatedly to a watch on his right wrist. I am 20 minutes late.

"Only *gringas* are on time, right?" I laugh as I throw my purse on the table and lean over to peck his cheek in greeting. "You *are* a *gringa*," he responds with a smile. "Ah, but a *gringa* studying *Tico* (Costa Rican) culture. So more like a *gringa-Tica*," I throw back at him. We are playful, and Luis is neither annoyed nor angry at my tardiness. He is accustomed to being here at *Bulevar* alone, eating a small dinner in silence as he watches his beloved San José soccer team, Saprissa, on television. Indeed, this is how I first found him, months before as I was just starting my fieldwork. Sitting quietly at the main bar, he was observing the final seconds of a soccer game intently. Two empty stools sat next to him on which I and a friend took seats. The presence of two foreign women at night at a bar dominated by lone men was unusual, but not unheard of, in 2001. With the rise in drug-related and violent crime in Costa Rica, anyone would be well advised today to be much more cautious about socializing with random strangers and in public places.[1] But this was a time before drug trafficking, urban violence, and other crimes would become so widespread that late-night movement and sociability would be ill-advised. As such, as the soccer game came to a close, we struck up a conversation that led to enduring friendship.

Since that first encounter, Luis and I met often for dinner and a beer when he was in town, both of us young, single, and workaholics in need of a break. But Luis was more than a friend. He was also a window into a rapidly evolving professional class in Costa Rica's urban Central Valley. Students of Latin America typically hear very little about the region's varied middle classes, in part because scholars tend to focus on the working poor in urban Latin America. This scholarly fascination gives us a very partial picture of the larger class structures evolving in this part of the world. The upper and lower middle classes of Latin America should also command our attention, not only because they play an important role in the political and economic dynamics of the region, but because they, too, experience lives in transition. If we are to understand how individuals in countries such as Costa Rica experience and respond to economic change, we must take as our starting point the broader class spectrum of these individuals. Costa Rica's evolving professional class is as good a place to start as any.

Luis' Story

Age 30 when I met him, Luis was a topographer, or a land surveyor. During the week, while I was busy conducting interviews and typing up field notes, he traveled to different parts of the country surveying construction projects as a salaried employee for a private firm in San José. He returned to Heredia on weekends, to a small house he shared with two other single men in a middle-class housing division on Heredia's east side. If Luis' work life was one of constant movement and adaptation, so too was his work history. Born in the province of Limón, in the shadow of large banana plantations, Luis had made the leap from being part of the working poor to being part of a class of educated technical workers. His early work history, which began at age 15, was defined by seasonal employment on large banana plantations. During his youth, unskilled jobs on these plantations were plentiful, and he returned year after year to work alongside his siblings during his holidays from school.

While Luis and his siblings worked in the banana plantations, Luis' mother toiled around their perimeter, cooking and selling hot meals to banana workers. Luis' father was a truck driver, who came in and out of his family's life intermittently until he finally disappeared altogether sometime after Luis celebrated his seventh birthday. In this respect, Luis's family was a poor one that often struggled. His siblings ended their formal education after primary school to help out at home or work full-time. But like Luisa, whose biography introduced the previous chapter, Luis' educational trajectory was to be a unique one in his family. "I was special," he explained with a wide smile. More precisely, he was young, enjoying the advantage of having ten older siblings who helped out with domestic obligations and income generation. Luis was the only child in his family to finish secondary school. And after graduating, he took advantage of a scholarship program for youth in rural areas to study at Universidad Nacional (UNA), the public university in Heredia. Originally interested in pursuing a degree in agronomy, he chose, instead, to specialize in topography. His reasoning was quite simple: a technical degree in topography required two years less schooling than agronomy. With topography, he minimized his time in school and made rapid his leap into full-time employment.

Luis made his move to the busy streets of the urban Central Valley in 1990, a year in which Costa Rica was inching toward a more intense phase of neoliberal restructuring. In a previous generation, Luis might have completed a technical degree and found work in an expanding public sector. But this was not to be his fate, coming of age as he did at a very different moment in the country's economic history. When he completed his technical title in topography in 1993, Luis struggled to find work in a more daunting private sector. Having been born in the Atlantic lowlands to a working poor family, he had limited social connections in the Central Valley and certainly no connections to the professional sector. So he perused job boards at the university and called upon professors and classmates to inform him of employment opportunities. It was on a job board that he spotted an advertisement for a job in San José, a job for which he was subsequently hired.

Since that first employment experience out of school, Luis had taken a variety of jobs for firms in the metropolitan area. Some of these jobs were temporary in nature, offering him work for a year or two on a major development project. Other jobs were permanent but short-lived, as companies restructured, downsized, or otherwise went defunct. Always, he relied on newspaper advertisements and a growing network of professional contacts to help him find new employment opportunities. He had the advantage of having skills that were in high demand—surveying land for major construction projects throughout a rapidly developing country. As he worked, he continued his education at night, keeping his residential base in Heredia to connect him to the university there. When I met him, he had been at the same job for three years and was avidly pursuing his *licenciatura* (bachelor's degree) at the university at night. Although he had a mere technical degree, he was the most educated child among his siblings, whose own educational backgrounds limited them to such occupations as taxi drivers, construction workers, and banana packers. Luis visited them occasionally, traveling back to the Atlantic lowlands in his blue jeep.

Luis continued to live in Heredia. But his lifeworld and daily experience extended far beyond Heredia's borders. Not only was he born in the Atlantic lowlands, with family still living there, but the firm for which he worked was based in San José. In addition, his work-related projects took him throughout the country to distant provinces and towns. Friends from his childhood and his schooling were sprinkled throughout the metropolitan area, and I would accompany Luis often to hang out with them in bars and clubs dotting urban thoroughfares and neighborhoods. Luis was less attached to Heredia, then, than he was to his car. Indeed, given the congested streets of the urban Central Valley, he spent most of his time in traffic driving from one place to another. Had he a family life of his own, he might have found himself rooted more deeply to a specific place and people. But his 48-hour work week and ambivalence toward marriage and parenthood had not led him down this path. "Our generation is more individualistic. We're just different," he explained, using pieces of burnt popcorn at *Bulevar* to depict a life centered on school and work.

Luis described and shared his hectic urban life with me without much emotion. His life and his relationship with me was what it was. But there he was each Friday evening calling me from his cell phone as he made his way to Heredia: "Guess what, Susie? Your team is playing tonight! And we're going to destroy you! *Pobrecita, mi amiga Herediana*" (my poor Heredian friend). On these nights, I was not a *gringa*; I was Luis' connection to Heredia, rooting for Heredia's soccer team, but expecting defeat from Luis' beloved Saprissa. "OK, Luis. Pick me up at 9," I would say, preparing to contend with Margarita's badgering. It tortured her so that I would not define my relationship with Luis. "What a *Tica* wouldn't do for a hardworking man like that," she huffed one evening as I applied makeup before a night out with Luis. But by my own reckoning, my ill-defined relationship with Luis was no indication of a US–Costa Rican cultural divide. I had only to think of Margarita's niece, a professional engineer working in San José who had herself frustrated the family with her single, childless state. No, this issue signaled a class and generational divide. Like me, Luis was not looking for marriage or even a relationship. In his detached lifestyle, I had found my comfort zone.

In the years that followed, I would visit Luis and listen to his tales of occasional travel and job transition. Our relationship evolved into a comfortable friendship as I married and had children. By 2014, he was living alone in an urban subdivision in Heredia, continuing to commute to projects throughout the country as his job demanded. Now a manager, but still single and childless, he described himself as a "hermit" who had become comfortable with his freedom and mobility. Even so, his single status became something of a liability when the 2008 global financial crisis hit. The Costa Rican economy, which has always relied heavily on US investment and demand, experienced a dramatic downturn in the aftermath of the crisis. As a result, Luis' firm, like many firms, implemented layoffs, for which single, childless employees were targeted. The executives at his firm reasoned that employees with no dependents would be better able to withstand the layoffs and hunker down until the global economy recovered. Without a dependent wife and children to protect him, Luis lost his job. "What did you do?" I asked. "I took off for Spain," he laughed. "I thought I would take advantage of the free time."

After returning from Spain, Luis found temporary employment. And after a year and a half, he was able to secure full-time employment as a manager with his former company. What he did not find, however, was a family of intimates, friends, or even coworkers to anchor him in place. He was a free-floating figure who knew how to navigate highways and markets but not a home or a relationship. On our last night together in July of 2014, sitting on the balcony of a mountaintop restaurant overlooking the Central Valley, he pointed to the new highway that had been constructed since my last visit. The Central Valley was no longer contained by the potholed highways that slowed movement in and out of this populated urbanscape. "It's sad," I said, observing how the lights of the Central Valley encroached ever further up the mountains surrounding it. "Susie," Luis said smiling, "highways are good! People can move around more easily." But what is lost, I wondered. Luis had achieved social and geographic mobility but had lost his sense of belonging. Indeed, later in our conversation, he would admit that he yearned for a family of his own, but felt "too closed and detached" to make it happen. There we sat, on the perimeter of a city to which neither of us really belonged, sipping beer and watching distant lights flicker long into the night.

Heredia's New Professionals

Luis was a member of a rapidly growing technical-professional class in Costa Rica's Central Valley. His life story offers us some clues about the workers who make up this class, the features of their everyday life, and the nature of their future aspirations. I am loosely defining this group as middle- to upper middle-class and distinguishing it by higher education, employment in professional occupations, and experience with or expectation for upward social mobility.[2] Here, in this sliver of Heredia, a heterogeneous group of educated workers is situated—from lawyers-in-training to engineering consultants, from elementary school teachers to government economists, from corporate sales representatives to skilled executive secretaries (see Table 3.1). Portes and Hoffman (2003:52) estimate that in 2000, 6 percent of the Costa Rican workforce was made up of executive and professional workers. This number has likely risen over the past decade as educational levels have continued to increase in Costa Rica. Indeed, because I am distinguishing this group by their university training, statistics of university attainment may also give us some sense of the prominence of this group of workers. In 2011, 19 percent of the Costa Rican population age 15 and over boasted a university degree.[3] The kind of professional and technical workers who are the subject of this chapter, then, represent roughly 10 to 20 percent of the economically active population of Costa Rica.[4]

For the workers in this group, education is a passport to upward mobility. These workers invest in education strategically in order to carve a niche in the global economy for themselves. Between 1985 and 2004, enrollment at institutions of higher learning in Costa Rica increased threefold (Programa Estado de la Nación 2005:100). Indeed, a close look at Heredia's professionals reveals almost an obsession for technical titles, professional programs, and university degrees. Not only were the fourteen professionals I interviewed incredibly well educated, but four were attending night classes to obtain a further degree in their profession and three were planning to enroll in night school for this purpose. These educated individuals do not stop with university titles; they are also avid consumers of private language and computer schools, which dot highways

TABLE **3.1** The Professional Class

	YEAR OF BIRTH	PLACE OF BIRTH	CIVIL STATUS	NO. OF CHILDREN	LEVEL OF EDUCATION	OCCUPATION
Alberto	1952	Heredia	Married	3	University	Arts coordinator (government)
Ana Lucía	1975	Heredia	Single	0	University	Engineer (government)
Cristina	1976	San José	Single	0	University	Executive secretary (government)
Fabian	1980	San José	Single	0	Some university	Student/ Part-time internet café assist.
Gabriela	1968	San José	Married	0	University	Economist (government)
Laura	1971	Puntarenas	Single	0	University	Economist (government)
Luis	1970	Limón	Single	0	University	Topographer
Manuel	1959	Limón	Married	1	University	Agronomist
Mauricio	1955	Heredia	Married	2	University	Community organizer (government)
Mercedes	1984	Heredia	Single	0	Secondary	Student/ Part-time daycare worker
Miguel	1946	Heredia	Married	5	University	Topographer (self-employed)
Oscar	1976	Heredia	Single	0	University	Lawyer (self-employed)
Pilar	1975	Heredia	Married	1	University	Public school teacher
Teresa	1969	Heredia	Married	0	University	Public school teacher
Violeta	1982	Heredia	Single	0	Some university	Student/ part-time administrative assistant

Note: Unless otherwise noted, all occupations listed are held in the private sector.

and downtowns of the urban Central Valley. At least four of the individuals in my group of interviewees were learning English, either in private night schools or in evening classes sponsored by their employers. These skills and titles become vehicles for professional marketability, as well as symbols of their belonging in an emerging urban culture that is worldly, technological, and bilingual.

The quest for higher education by the individuals in this group is abetted by a well-established state university system in Costa Rica, as well as the proliferation of private universities under economic restructuring.[5] The 1949 constitution guarantees state funding to the Universidad de Costa Rica (UCR), Costa Rica's first public university, which was founded in 1940. This funding guarantee was later extended to three other public universities, all founded in the 1970s: the Institúto Tecnológico de Costa

Heredia's new professionals invest strategically in higher education to secure a position in the country's professional labor market. Their efforts are aided by a well-established public university system in Costa Rica. In this photograph, a college student walks alongside the campus of the Universidad Nacional (UNA), one of five public universities in Costa Rica. In addition to these public universities are a host of private universities and "para-universities," which have proliferated under neoliberal restructuring.

Rica (1973), the Universidad Nacional (1973), and the Universidad Estatal de Distancia (1977). (A fifth public university, Universidad Técnica Nacional, was created in 2008.) During the restructuring of the 1980s and 1990s, these universities were able to withstand budget shortfalls in education precisely because of this constitutional guarantee (Clark 2001:98).[6] The programs offered by these universities, especially those physically located in the Central Valley, have attracted students from around the country and around the Americas to such cities as San José and Heredia.

In addition to Costa Rica's public universities, private universities and "para-universities" have sprouted up in and around the Central Valley, offering a wide range of technical and professional degrees to meet the increasing demand for university credentials. Today, more than fifty private universities operate in Costa Rica, the bulk of these established in the 1990s (Programa Estado de la Nación 2013a:202). The percentage of university students in Costa Rica attending a private university jumped from 14 percent to 52 percent between 1985 and 2012 (Programa Estado de la Nación 2005:100, 2013a:209). Given the rising number of private universities, a larger share of university diplomas are now awarded by private universities in Costa Rica.[7] Twombly (1997) connects the rise in these private universities to the globalization of Costa Rica's economy and the privatization of its public sector. Rather than provide a liberal arts education for the purpose of cultivating a critically thinking citizenry, which was and is the thrust of Costa Rica's public university system, private universities are oriented more toward technical-professional training, understood by Twombly (1997) as a hallmark of a market-driven economy. As such, private universities do not require liberal arts courses and offer shorter educational programs (two to three years compared to four years at a public university). But private universities are also more expensive and have less scholarship money available. Of the two, the public university system tends to be the more selective and prestigious, with UCR in San José ranked highest. This characteristic creates something of a paradox. The public universities are less expensive, more prestigious, and dominated by students who attend academically rigorous and often private secondary schools. In contrast, the private universities are more expensive, less prestigious, and dominated by students who attend poor-quality public secondary schools.[8] Arguably, this has created a two-tier system of higher education that exacerbates income polarization in the country.

The rise in institutions of higher learning has occurred in step with an expanding technical-professional labor market in the urban Central Valley. Such expansion may be traced back to the 1960s and 1970s, when a growing government bureaucracy opened up opportunities for technical and professional workers. Despite the restructuring of the 1980s and 1990s, Costa Rica's unique experience with neoliberal reform has resulted in a still-substantial government sector, in which university graduates may find at least some prospects for professional employment. In addition, an expanding private sector has created a number of jobs in technical and professional services, especially in such areas as software design, medical tourism, and high-end manufacturing. Alternatively—this path seems an increasingly popular one for Heredia's young professional class—professionals may start consulting businesses of their own, negotiating contracts and projects with the government or private companies.

The occupational decisions and aspirations voiced by this group of workers differed to some extent for men and women in that women were more apt to work in the public sector. In that these workers were not randomly selected into my sample, I cannot say whether this is the case for all professional workers in Heredia. But among the men and women I interviewed, six women and only two men opted for work in the public sector.[9] In part, this reflects women's over-representation as public school teachers. But among the *Heredianas* I interviewed, only two of these six women were public school teachers. Of the four remaining women, their choice to look for work in the public sector reflected a conscious decision to avoid the demanding schedules and intense workloads associated with the private sector. Laura's first job as an economist, for example, was with a private bank. She left after only six months because of the 12-hour days and pressure. Days after quitting, she deposited her résumé at the Ministry of Economy and was offered a job. Ana Lucía also applied for and considered private sector jobs. She noted that her classmates who had taken jobs with multinational corporations were well paid but were forced to work longer hours and under much stress. So she opted for a position as civil engineer for the Costa Rican Institute for Electricity (Instituto Costarricense de Electricidad [ICE]). This is not to say that public sector jobs did not have drawbacks. All six of the female public professionals complained of the low pay and limited promotional opportunities. Perhaps as a result, three of these women planned to start their own companies later, either in conjunction with their public sector job or in place of it.[10]

The aspirations toward small consulting businesses were not unique to the professional women in this group. Once settled into salaried positions in either the public or private sector, many of the women *and* men in this group envisioned consulting companies of their own. Five of the fourteen individuals I interviewed spoke of future plans to start a consulting company in their area of expertise with friends, family, or colleagues. Two individuals had already made the transition from salaried employee to independent consultant. The entrepreneurialism demonstrated by this group may be interpreted as one way to command more money for their skills and training. Indeed, it was widely accepted that independent consulting was more lucrative than salaried employment. I would argue, however, that these ambitions may be interpreted another way. At the center of the neoliberal paradigm is the idea of a free market, where buyers and sellers interact freely. Independent consulting is the embodiment of the free market. As Barley and Kunda (2004) note in their study of skilled US technical contractors: "[Contractors viewed] themselves as independent owners of their own human capital, as entrepreneurs who relied on their own skills to navigate between success and failure" (p. 289). Rather than view themselves as employees, then, technical contractors envisioned themselves as entrepreneurs in a knowledge economy (Barley and Kunda 2004). This identity shift has come about at a particular historical moment in which the obligations of employers and employees has broken down and the free-market paradigm has surfaced anew. In a sense, the professional-cum entrepreneurs in this group are neoliberalism's poster children—mini-entrepreneurs who negotiate the global marketplace with the resources available to them, in this case their long list of educational credentials that reads like a grocery list on fancy résumé paper.

Although Molina and Palmer (2000) call them the "post-modern *Ticos*," this group of young, educated professionals could more aptly be described as the "neoliberal *Ticos*" because they thrive under conditions of competitiveness and individualism. As well, they embody the neoliberal ethos of entrepreneurialism. Although the public sector still figures prominently in the work lives of this group, especially the women, government employment is pursued strategically and perhaps even temporarily as people in this group build their professional networks and make plans to consult on their own. Not only are these people equipping themselves to succeed in a professional labor market, they are obtaining the tools and the knowledge to adapt to a global, cosmopolitan way of life. That is, these people help construct a cosmopolitan urban culture that is rooted in San José, with Heredia as one satellite. With ease, they move between these two cities—but also between the San José metropolitan area and urban centers in the United States. Indeed, stints in North America become a kind of rite of passage, a badge of global savvy, and a way to cement their place in this young, urban professional class. In the section that follows, I delve into the lifeways exhibited by this new professional class in order to explore how these economic changes translate into new forms of consciousness and identity for Heredia's new professionals.

The Making of a Gated Community

During my year in Heredia, I moved comfortably among this group of urban professionals. I was college-educated and working on my doctorate, I hailed from a middle-class background in the United States, and I transitioned easily between Spanish and English. In addition, I understood and indeed had lived the kind of work-dominated, consumer-oriented, urban life that this class was actively constructing. As if to solidify my place in this class in 2001, I secured employment as a part-time English instructor in San José. And, two days a week, I became part of the commuter flow from Heredia to San José. Waking up at 6:00 in the morning, I would stumble into the dining room where the morning news would already be playing on television and the smell of eggs, rice, and beans cooking on the stove would be filling the air. Margarita would enter the dining room and initiate the same conversation that we had every morning I embarked for San José to teach English. "Why so early, *chiquilla* (little girl)? You need your sleep!" she would say, always acting genuinely surprised. "I have to go into San José to work, Margarita. It's Monday," I would respond. The conversation happened with such regularity that I felt as if I were taking part in a play—a drama about a middle-aged *Herediana* who was taken aback by the time I spent in San José, far removed from Pueblo Tico where life moved at a snail's pace and Margarita and Cecilia shared gossip over bitter cups of coffee.

My commute to San José was far from unusual. Margarita's eldest daughter made it each morning during my field research, as well. For hundreds of *Heredianos*, the morning commute to San José was and is woven intricately into the routine of everyday life. Marching on foot toward buses or train stations, or in file behind gridlocked cars, these *Heredianos* constitute a particular weekday ritual in the fresh cool air of morning.[11] At this time of day, storefronts are not yet open, children have yet to make their appearance in crisp school uniforms, and stray dogs are still sleeping soundly. But in the town's Central Plaza, workers are already walking rapidly in all directions, some stopping in the church to pray before work, others pausing to buy a newspaper at the corner of the plaza, and still others running to get a decent place in line for the bus or train to San José. The men are dressed in ties, ironed slacks, and button-down shirts. The women wear sharp polyester suits, whose bright colors add life to the otherwise damp mornings filled with the sounds of high heels, honking, and birds.

During my year of fieldwork, I commuted to San José by bus in the morning, but I returned to Heredia at night by carpool, crowded into one of my student's jeeps with three of his coworkers. The four of them, all professional employees of a German-owned agrochemical company, commuted each day to San José, making their way back to Heredia once the sun had set and the cool night air of the Central Valley had taken over. Manuel, my student and our driver, hailed from a small village in the Caribbean coastal province of Limón. He had moved to San José to study agronomy at UCR in the late 1970s. For years, he had been in and out of corporate jobs, specializing in the sale of agrochemicals. Age 41 when I met him, he had settled into a well-paying job with the German agrochemical firm. He, his wife, and their 11-year-old son were living in a house in a new urban subdivision on Heredia's east side. Heredia was conveniently located between his office in San José and his sales districts outside San José. He felt strongly that the city would offer more educational opportunities for his son. As for Manuel, he and his coworkers stayed late two evenings a week to attend on-site English classes provided by their employer. I met them at their offices, hitching a ride back to Heredia once we had exhausted conversations in English. The minute we boarded Manuel's jeep, the group relaxed back into Spanish, teasing one another about their poor English accents and discussing work-related issues.

One night in late October of 2001, on our ride home, Manuel mentioned to the group that I was doing a study of Heredia. I was seated in the front passenger seat and noted murmurs of approval coming from the back seat. "Do you know that Heredia has the highest level of education in the country?" one woman pointed out. "And the most professionals," the other woman added. Antonio, a third coworker squished between the two women, winked at me and said, "No baker says his bread is bad, eh Susie?" Proud *Heredianos* they were, but I soon discovered that only one person in the car was actually born in Heredia. And as Manuel dropped off one coworker after another, it became clear that they inhabited a very different Heredia than those who had been born and raised in the shadow of *La Inmaculada*. Indeed, their Heredia extended far beyond the Central Plaza, engulfing a conglomeration of cities throughout the Central Valley that defined their work, family, and social life. That all four of these individuals worked for a German-owned company, had traveled at least once to the United States, and could speak at least conversational English suggested that their Heredia extended far beyond Costa Rica as well. Their Heredia, in short, was both metropolitan and cosmopolitan. How had this sliver of Heredia arisen? And how did it transform Heredia socially and economically?

The cosmopolitan culture that Heredia's professional class was helping to construct in early twenty-first century Costa Rica had its roots in the rapid urbanization that occurred in the country's Central Valley during the second half of the twentieth century. Urbanization took what were once four distinct provincial towns (San José, Cartago, Heredia, and Alajuela) and transformed them into one large metropolitan area centered in San José. Margarita and Ricardo, my host parents, watched this process unfold as they married and raised a small family. Ricardo had been born and raised in the northwest city of Liberia. He came to Heredia in the 1970s to study biology at UNA and, once he married Margarita, he made Heredia home. "Susie, before 20 years ago, Heredia was a very different place. Very closed. Very conservative. By 5:00 in the evening, everyone had gone home and shut their doors. But in the 1970s, more people began moving here, many of them for the university. So it's become a little more open and a little more progressive over time," he explained. Thinking for a moment, he added, "You know, when I first started dating Margarita, no one knew my last name. They thought I was Venezuelan because many Venezuelans had come to Heredia to go to the university. Even Margarita was suspicious of me, but she'd pass by my lab fifteen times in one day just to look at me!" Margarita, who herself studied for a secretarial certificate at UNA, protested, "I had to, Ricardo! My class was just past yours! You wooed me, remember?"

Heredia was described as once "closed" and "conservative" by many people whom I interviewed. I drew on my own memories of a town that completely closed down for an afternoon siesta when I first studied here in 1994—a town quiet after dark, the Central Plaza all but empty. This was a far cry from the Heredia I now knew, where life began just after sunset and stores stayed open late with flashy sale signs in the window. How did Heredia transform from a quaint provincial capital to a suburban satellite to San José? As Ricardo suggested, Heredia's growing metropolitan nature emerged long before neoliberal reforms and had much to do with the establishment of UNA in 1973. Students from around the country and, indeed, around Latin America infused this town with foreign-sounding last names and new perspectives. But Heredia's urbanity was also a product of the rise of a metropolitan labor market and substantial migration into the Central Valley from coastal areas. Both occurred in the 1960s and 1970s with the expansion of the public and private sectors. Coupled with the demographic explosion of the time, these trends created what is now known as the greater San José metropolitan area, or the *Gran Área Metropolitana* (GAM). As a result of these developments, urban planning became a national priority. In late 2000, the government initiated the *Plan Nacional de Desarrollo Urbano* (National Plan for Urban Development), its fourth attempt to grapple with the chaos associated with unplanned urban growth.[12] Transportation was a key concern, because data in 2000 suggested that if the number of cars continued to increase, the roads would be gridlocked within 15 years (Avalos 2001, 2002). Of perhaps greater concern was housing, most notably the explosion in one-story, single-family homes, which did not meet the needs of an area of skyrocketing population density (Avalos 2002). These concerns continued in the debates leading up to the passage of the most recent urban development plan—the *Plan Regional Urbano del Gran Área Metropolitana*, or Plan GAM—signed in early 2014.

The rapid and chaotic urbanization that has occurred in Costa Rica's Central Valley has created a long list of problems for metropolitan residents, including pollution, congestion, and crime. The rise of violent, drug-related, and property-based crime was particularly troublesome. Most of this began in San José, spreading outward in the 1980s and 1990s as new suburban communities grew around the city's perimeter. In response, many people began flocking to the outlying towns of Alajuela, Cartago, and Heredia, where defunct farms and open spaces were rapidly being converted into suburban developments. In 2001, a full 80 percent of all construction projects in the country took place in these three provinces alone (Leiton 2002). Cities such as Heredia became popular among Costa Rica's professional class because they offered the benefits of urban living, with the secure small-town feel lacking in San José (Boddiger 2002). The added incentive, of course, was proximity to jobs in San José.

Although population increase, in-migration and economic expansion in the Central Valley spurred the development of GAM, neoliberal policies arguably intensified the migration from coastal communities and neighboring countries. Such policies also constrained state resources to adequately address urbanization and structured a professional class with a taste for suburbia. The neighborhoods around which this professional class has coalesced are relatively new. For example, Heredia's middle class urbanizations of La Esperanza, Santa Elena, and María Auxiliadora were not even on the radar screen for young families in early Heredia, who instead settled in and helped develop *barrios* closer to the city center, such as Barrio Fatima. These newer urbanizations reflect the new professional class that inhabits them. Most have been built as separate subdivisions in the past two decades, and they are typically equipped with more modern amenities. Often, these subdivisions are built within existing neighborhoods, but they are enclosed in high cement walls and guarded gates. In many ways, they are communities within a community, separate from an older and often poorer Heredia by way of their urban, middle-class lifeways and their fortress-like dwellings (Starcevic 2002).

Here, private guards, garbage collection, and water services offer improved private services that duplicate the infamously deplorable public services offered through the municipality (Starcevic 2002). Gated communities offer their own parks and social networks, cars provide access to upscale shopping malls, and private bilingual schools reproduce the cosmopolitanism of this new urban class. Even such basic activities as shopping are bifurcated between a layer of native, nonprofessional Heredia, which shops at the traditional Central Market, and a nouveau professional class, which inhabits a North American–style consumption space that includes upscale malls (*Paseo de las Flores*), modern grocery stores (Walmart), and membership-based food warehouses (PriceSmart). Thus, to say that Heredia has become a "bedroom community" to San José's labor market is a misnomer of sorts. Mere pockets of the city's landscape have become San José's satellites, and they are typically not well integrated into other parts of the community. Neoliberalism has unleashed not simply a free-market ethos; it has unleashed a new way of living that emulates urban lifeways in countries such as the United States. Heredia's young professionals are at the forefront of both, at once shaping a particular response to economic restructuring and constructing a new Heredia in which community takes on new meaning.

An urban development known as La Esperanza and the life of one professional residing in it offer a glimpse into this new, upscale way of life. Neighborhood watch signs dot tidy sidewalks, a stark contrast to the cobblestone pavement of Heredia's city center and the deteriorating sidewalks around the center's perimeter. Middle-class houses line the street on both sides, with Land Rovers and Jettas parked neatly in newly paved driveways. Here, in La Esperanza, lies the house of Gabriela and her husband, two young, professional economists. Gabriela, age 33 when I interviewed her in 2002, grew up in San José, the daughter of a public school teacher from Guanacaste and a curtain-maker from San José. When she began studying economics at UNA, Gabriela did not move away from home. Rather, she commuted by bus to Heredia to attend class. It was not until after she graduated from college, at age 25, that she moved to Heredia to live with her older sister, then married and herself an economist working

The neighborhoods that Heredia's new professionals inhabit are distinctly different from other neighborhoods in the city. Most are separate subdivisions that have been built in the past two decades, and many are gated communities that are surrounded by cement walls. These subdivisions typically feature private garbage collection and water services in order to avoid the deplorable public services of the municipality. Here is a typical new urban development in Heredia. Note the car in the driveway.

for UNA. "Why did you move to Heredia?" I asked, a reasonable question, I presumed, because she had gotten a job by then at Banco Central in downtown San José. "Well, it is true that I was working in San José by this time," Gabriela began, "but I guess I felt comfortable in Heredia. It was my place (*mi dominio*). Plus, San José had become very populated by that point. Heredia was like a city, but still kept its small-town (*pueblo*) feel."

Gabriela would go on to live with her sister and brother-in-law in their home in La Esperanza for six years. All the time, she continued her job with Banco Central, moving up in the ranks from an entry-level position in their accounting department to a managerial position in their administrative department. At age 31, she married her college sweetheart, also an economist who worked for a private bank in San José. After marrying, they rented their own house in La Esperanza, just down the street from Gabriela's sister and family. Gabriela and her husband had not had any children at the time of our interview. When I asked whether she envisioned children in her future, Gabriela rested her elbows on the conference table in Banco Central where we were seated, propped her chin on her hand, and furrowed her brow. After a pause, she admitted, "I don't know." It was clear that this was not the first time she had thought about children. It was also clear that she had come up with no real decision. "We very much enjoy our lives. We have friends now in Heredia, and we enjoy going out with them. I make a very good salary, and so does my husband. Children would change our lives," she explained. Until she decided, Gabriela had plenty to keep her busy. Two days a week, after work, she took an English class provided by her employer. On another two evenings, she attended classes at UCR to get her *maestría* in economics. She and her husband were saving money to buy a house. And they had even begun talking about starting their own consulting business.

How significantly Gabriela departs from our common stereotypes of Latin American women—be they the dutiful housewife, low-wage factory worker, or impoverished street vendor. Here, we have an educated woman eager to construct a life and a community oriented not around family and children but around work and self-making. This is not to suggest that Gabriela had somehow become unbound to gender as a result of neoliberal opportunities.[13] One only had to envision the possibility of children in Gabriela's future to predict that she would be burdened by a "second shift" in a way that her husband would not (Hochschild 1989). But with a professional pedigree that matched her husband's and a home life free of children, Gabriela and other women like her had achieved at least the veneer of gender egalitarianism. They inhabited work and social spaces with men and were not at all relegated to the home and a social world dominated by housewives and children. Like men, they moved freely, ever vigilant of commitments like children, which might limit their mobility. Her decisions around work and family reflected her ideas of what it meant to be a professional Costa Rican woman—someone who was "modern" (read individualistic and egalitarian) in aspiration and outlook and not bound by commitments to family and home.

No doubt, this new egalitarian ethos is at least partially responsible for the shift to older ages for marriage and childbearing, which we see in Gabriela's case. Arguably, it has also contributed to the significant rise in cohabitation among highly educated women such as Gabriela (Esteve, García-Román, and Lesthaeghe 2012). In that cohabitation increases the probability of single motherhood, such egalitarianism might be related indirectly, too, to a rise in single motherhood among highly educated women.[14] Historically, cohabitation rates in Latin America have been highest among those with less education. For the more well educated, marriage has been viewed as an essential marker of middle- and upper-class status. Since the 1970s, however, there has been a rise in so-called "new cohabitation," wherein those with higher levels of education are catching up with the lower classes in cohabitation rates. Esteve et al. (2012) argue that the 1980s economic crisis probably facilitated these trends, although it did not cause them. Rather, they point to the liberalization in attitudes that led to a destigmatization of cohabitation and more egalitarian gender relations in Latin America during this time.

It was not simply gender egalitarianism that signaled Gabriela's membership in a modern global society—but class mobility and cultural tolerance. Embracing the idea that women can and should pursue careers alongside men, that professional ambition can and should take precedence over commitment to others, and that cosmopolitanism can and should be valued over provinciality suggests that the members of this group are in step with the "modern" world. Like shopping at upscale malls, these ideas set the Manuel's and Gabriela's of Heredia apart from an older, more "traditional" layer of *Herediano* society. But as the next section suggests, these ideas are not easy to reconcile in the larger social contexts in which these individuals are embedded. As the members of this group piece together professional careers, urban lifeways, and modern families, they must draw from an eclectic source of material—their cosmopolitan and modern ideologies, their economic and human resources, and their society's gendered expectations. Like the urban housing developments now dotting Heredia's landscape, their decisions often lack coherence and display marked contradictions because their fate is to be caught between the new and the old.

Violeta's Rebellion

As the discussion above suggests, economic change and the responses to such change have sparked transformation in the social fabric of Heredia. But they have also provoked tension in the daily lives of this professional class. As we step up for a closer look at Heredia's professional workers, we note that the transition toward a global economy, a metropolitan labor market, and a cosmopolitan Heredia has not been without conflict and contestation. As individuals work through these changes, they confront older gender regimes, established class hierarchies, and more "traditional" lifeways in their families, neighborhoods, and communities. During my own stay in Heredia, I confronted this each day as Margarita and I contested my relationship with Luis, my work in San José, and my free, uninhibited movement around the Central Valley. But I was not Margarita's daughter. As such, I confronted her disapproval, not her wrath. Violeta was an altogether different story.

Studying to become a customs agent at a private university in San José and working full-time as an assistant at a customs agency in San José, Violeta was well on her way to becoming the kind of young, urban professional that Heredia was increasingly accommodating. She envisioned a life for herself that included a career and perhaps even her own consulting business, a house with modern furniture, and a car of her own to make her way through the congested streets of the urban Central Valley. Although Margarita certainly supported Violeta's educational advancement, she was offended by what she considered to be Violeta's selfish and disrespectful ways. To Margarita, Violeta was a good student but a difficult daughter who put her own ambitions and desires before family. The conflict, dare I say the war, between Violeta and Margarita, was not an easy one to live with when I resided with this family in 2001 and 2002. Each day, I awoke to a new drama, which I watched with unease from the sidelines, often stepping in to soothe wounded feelings on both sides.

Just weeks after arriving in country for my fieldwork, I was finishing a breakfast of fresh fruit when Margarita sat down beside me at the dining room table and announced firmly, "Violeta and I are divorced." "Like a separated couple?" I asked quizzically. "Yes," Margarita replied. She recounted an argument between her and Violeta, which had started when Violeta failed to get up early on a Saturday morning to attend a computer class she had been taking. When Margarita tried to get her up and out of bed, Violeta, hungover and impatient, screamed at Margarita, calling her a *metiche* (meddlesome and snoopy woman). Violeta declared that although she lived in Margarita's house, she wanted nothing to do with Margarita. "'Don't cook for me' she said," Margarita remembered. "'And don't tell me when to come home. And don't ask me how my day was.'" Tears of outrage were falling swiftly down Margarita's cheeks as she finished recounting their argument. Rebuffed, Margarita declared that she would do nothing more for Violeta.

The tension between Margarita and Violeta went from a boil to a slow simmer by June. But it was always just below the surface of their daily interactions. Ricardo, Cecilia, and I tiptoed around the house, hoping to make it through each day without a major fight between the two of them. In early July, the underlying tension boiled over anew. Violeta announced that she was going to the beach with classmates for a weekend vacation. Her boyfriend was among her classmates. Margarita flew into a rage that echoed throughout the neighborhood. When I caught Margarita alone in the kitchen later on that afternoon, I asked what had happened. "*Mal-creada*," Margarita declared in reference to Violeta—ill-bred, spoiled, rude. According to Margarita, Violeta lacked respect for her parents, had no sense of obligation toward her family, and ignored basic norms of decency. "I respect every culture, Susie. But here, in Costa Rica, it doesn't matter if Violeta and Mauricio do anything physical while they're at the beach. Her reputation will be ruined. What will my family think? What will this neighborhood think? Violeta, she doesn't understand or respect this. Now, this whole neighborhood will know I cannot control my own children. They'll know Violeta has no respect for what is decent."

Violeta's rebelliousness reached an unprecedented level in late July. She had called the house from work and told Margarita and Ricardo that she had something she needed to talk to them about. Upon her arrival home, the three of them filed into Margarita and Ricardo's bedroom where they spoke in hushed, tense tones, while Cecilia and I struggled to eavesdrop from the outside. After two hours, they emerged. Ricardo looked exhausted. Margarita was hard to read. Violeta was ecstatic. She skipped over to Cecilia and me and announced that she was moving to the United States. She had contacted a US woman she had met in Heredia who owned an interior decorating company in the States, asking if she might live with and work for her for a year to learn English and earn money. The woman had agreed. Violeta was just 19 years of age. She had never been on an airplane before. She had been fighting with her mother for more than a year just to work and socialize in San José. And here she was, bound for New Orleans, a North American city known for debauchery and sin. We were awestruck and stupefied to the point of silence.

Violeta's rebellion encapsulates three stories in one. First, it is a story of a young Costa Rican woman who was able to capitalize on her middle-class resources to take advantage of some of the opportunities that economic restructuring offers—educational advancement, professional training, and international travel. Hers is also a story of a community in the throes of rapid social change, with professional men and women taking on new life-ways that challenge the existing middle-class culture of Heredia. Although expected to stay close to home, remain a virgin, and get good grades, Violeta had ambitions and a style of her own. She drank beer with friends at bars, traveled to the beach with her boyfriend, and migrated (alone) to the United States. This was not simply a case of Violeta's "stubborn" ways, as Margarita contended. This was an emerging way of life that extended far beyond the confines of Margarita's hearth, Heredia's city center, and Costa Rica's national borders.

Finally, Violeta's rebellion is a story of how families contest power during times of economic change. What is fascinating is that Ricardo was more or less a troubled bystander in this struggle. It was Margarita who battled with Violeta over what it meant to be a proper woman, what it meant to "get ahead" in Costa Rican society, and what it meant to be part of a community. Perhaps this issue was Margarita's domain because it centered on the family, in particular the eldest daughter of the family. Perhaps Margarita was more attuned to and bothered by Violeta's rebelliousness because the household was embedded in a tight-knit neighborhood that consisted of Margarita's extended family. Perhaps Margarita simply played a more central role in reproducing established gender norms and social mores. Whatever the case, this was understood as *their* battle—a contest of power between mother and daughter that sharpened over time. Even so, this battle was and is emblematic of a larger struggle between an older and a newer generation.

I certainly did not have the opportunity to peer inside the households of every family in Heredia to observe and document this gendered generational conflict. What I did have were subtle hints and more obvious suggestions that this was a defining feature of *Herediano* life at the turn of the twenty-first century. During an interview, Fabian, a 22-year-old medical student living with his parents, switched effortlessly into English each time we discussed his romances with blue-eyed *gringas* and his entrepreneurial plans to open an Internet café. His mother, cooking chicken in the background, eyed us carefully, but, lacking knowledge of English, could not comprehend when Fabian described their bitter fights over his penchant for foreign beauties and risky investments. On another occasion, while seated in the cramped quarters of Vicky's Hair Salon watching Vicky carefully paint the toenails of an older *Herediana*, I listened as the older woman lectured me about the "ways of young women" today. Gesturing with gnarled hands whose fingers were tipped in bright-red paint, she bemoaned what young women lost with their sexual freedom. "'Friends with privileges' (*amigos con derechos*)? Please! Tell me, *hija*, what do women get out of this kind of relationship?" she demanded. "Sex?" I offered. "No," she replied, "sex without power. And a man with no sense of responsibility or obligation toward her."

Indeed, it was not the materialism or the entrepreneurialism that older *Heredianos* found so distasteful about this emerging class of young professionals. It was their individualism, their lack of decency, their departure from established social codes and obligations. Independence, to them, was selfishness, and a dangerous path down which younger generations were traveling. No longer was there respect for elders, no longer was the relationship between man and woman sacred, and no longer was the family central. Instead, money-making, pleasure-making, and self-making had become the central preoccupations of this professional class, which found a kind of liberation in neoliberalism's ethos. Ethnographically responsible for capturing these two worlds, I sympathized with Violeta's rebellion while I struggled to appreciate what older women in Heredia tried to tell me: freedom came with a steep price.

The Pitfalls of Progress

In the short story "The Targuá Tree," esteemed Costa Rican novelist Fabián Dobles explores an earlier Central Valley and its march toward modernity through the relationship between two brothers—Chayo and Lolo. Having inherited the family farm from their father, Chayo works diligently to profit off agriculture while Lolo wiles the day away in the shade of the targuá tree. The tree sits atop a hill behind the farm house, with the Central Valley stretched out below. From its shadow, Lolo had watched with his father when electricity came to the valley for the first time, with lights "like frogs croaking in a huge pond" (Dobles 1994:40). After his father's death, Lolo watched as "the frogs continued extending their domain over the valley" (Dobles 1994:40). The targuá tree was both silent witness and protective shelter as Lolo's father and then Lolo himself tracked the rapid pace of change in the valley below. As Dobles' story goes, Lolo returned home one day to find the targuá tree gone, axed by his brother Chayo and turned into a neat stack of firewood. After the incident, the brothers remain estranged until they reconciled in old age when both were nearing death. Dobles' story compels its reader to feel first for Lolo, whose lack of ambition represents a kind of innocence lost in Costa Rica's modern growth and then for both brothers, whose competing world views tear them apart.

Dobles came of age intellectually in the 1940s, a markedly distinct period of social change in Costa Rican history. Nonetheless, he captures the ambivalence associated with the country's modern growth. I reflected on this story often as I watched Luis make plans to replace old wattle-and-daub houses with cramped parking lots, and each time Margarita and Violeta battled over the meaning of "decency." Luis, Gabriela, and Violeta were, no doubt, the modern-day versions of Chayo. Able to harness various resources to ensure their movement upward in society and eager to don the lifestyles of a jet-setting professional class, they, along with other new professionals, were the vanguard of many of the transformations overtaking Heredia and Costa Rica's urban Central Valley. For better or for worse, and probably a mixture of both, they were a social and an economic force with which to contend. They constituted an enormous part of Costa Rica's human capital, they propelled economic expansion through their growing consumer power, and they contributed to the country's economic vitality through small business development. But if they were Costa Rica's greatest strength, they were also Costa Rica's greatest weakness—as their urban developments enveloped open spaces and older homes, their cars clogged highways and airways, and their supermarkets outcompeted small vendors and vibrant older markets. As Birdsall, Lustig, and Meyer (2014:141) have argued, the private services, exclusive schools, and gated communities around which this group has revolved may also contribute to the decline in public services "by reducing accountability of the state to improve the quality of these services." In short, there are consequences associated with the ascendancy of this professional class whose consumer tastes and career ambitions fuel so much of the unchecked growth and private development in this country.

And what of the political implications of the rise of this new professional class? With some exceptions (e.g., Shakow 2014), research on Latin American politics has not given much attention to the region's middle classes, much less its new professionals, who have benefited from neoliberalism's growth-equity tradeoff.[15] There has been some social movement research on middle-class, professional women in Latin America, who were the primary constituents of the region's elite-based feminist movements.[16] From this research, we might deduce that the women featured in this chapter would be sympathetic to mainstream feminist demands such as abortion rights, especially because their educational and career success depend so largely on controlling their fertility.[17] But among the professional women I interviewed, the most pronounced characteristic of their political perspective was their almost complete lack of political interest. Disgruntled by the corruption scandals characteristic of early twenty-first century Costa Rica and preoccupied with their social mobility, they were disengaged from political matters and seemed to presume that any limits to their mobility (e.g., gender-based wage discrimination) could be surmounted by economic rather than political strategizing. Birdsall (2012) opines that in general, Latin America's growing middle class will tend toward a moderate politics that favors sound macroeconomic policy and effective social welfare programs. Although this may be true, the group of professionals I interviewed was not particularly politically motivated and, if anything, articulated contradictory viewpoints on issues such as abortion, free trade, and public sector reform.[18] Economically and politically, then, Heredia's new professionals were decidedly individualistic and arguably short-sighted in their drive to move up their country's social hierarchy and into a world of middle-class consumption and complacency.

True to her word, Violeta left for New Orleans in late 2001. Her letters and calls home suggested that she was extremely homesick. She said she found it difficult to adapt to a new language and culture. Rather than stay a year, she decided to stay for just six months. In a letter written a month into her stay, she reported that prices were so expensive in the United States that she had to "adjust [her] dreams" of buying herself a new car. Margarita, in turn, wrote long letters to her daughter in the United States, praying each day that God would return her to Heredia safely and quickly. Violeta did return home safely and, within three years of her return, married her boyfriend Mauricio and started a family. By 2014, they had two young daughters and a newly built house in a gated subdivision on the outskirts of town. Mauricio had ascended the ranks of a global shipping company, first as a customs agent and then as a manager. For her part, Violeta left the customs industry. Overwhelmed by the stress, long hours, and competing demands of motherhood, she opened a small restaurant in the center of Heredia. When the restaurant failed to turn a profit, she left the labor market altogether to focus her energies at home.

In addition to becoming a stay-at-home mother, Violeta used the comfortable earnings of her husband to transform their house into a suburban oasis. Replete with granite counter tops, five flat-screen televisions, and two brand-new Toyotas in the driveway, the house identified Violeta and Mauricio as members of an elite professional class. As if to solidify that membership, Violeta went to school part-time to learn English. It came in handy when they traveled yearly to vacation in the United States. I kept a picture of her, baby in arm, posing in the French Quarter of New Orleans alongside photographs sent from Luis from his adventures in Venezuela, Spain, and Argentina. However problematic their materialistic ambitions and political complacency, how could I not but respect and love them? In their efforts to embody an elite consumer culture, Luis became his family's shining star and Violeta a fiercely independent woman whose daring made me smile.

CHAPTER 4

Love and Money
in the Middle Class

O n a Sunday in late May of 2001, Margarita's family organizes a meeting at the farm of Armando, Margarita's older brother. The purpose of the family meeting is to plan a surprise birthday party for Margarita's mother, who will be turning 80. After a breakfast of *gallo pinto* (black beans and rice), stale bread, and runny eggs, Margarita, Ricardo, Cecilia, and I pile into the car. Slowly, we make our way past the small town of Barva, up the dormant volcano on whose slopes Heredia sits, and toward Armando's *finca* (farm). The day is hot, but as we ascend the mountain on narrow, winding roads and into the dense forest of pines, the air becomes cool and the fog thick. We pass large farms of ornamental plants, their industrial greenhouses protecting high-value plants bound for suburban homes in the United States, as well as monstrous buses burping heavy clouds of exhaust into the crisp mountain air. Peering past Cecilia's nest of cascading black curls and out the back window, I watch the Central Valley spread out below us like a cluttered diorama.

At a nondescript fence post, Ricardo slows the car and turns onto a steep gravel driveway, taking us into a clearing where three panting mutts run to greet us. Armando stands beneath a small shelter, wearing khaki work pants and carrying a machete in his right hand. Most of the family has already arrived, and we hug one another tightly and pull on sweaters for warmth. The older women confer and decide to take a walk through Armando's orchard to collect fruit to take back home. They descend into the tall grass with large sacks, the rest of us following not far behind. After stuffing her sack full of apples, Margarita scurries behind a tree. Within seconds, she comes out from behind the tree with her hands on her hips and two apples stuffed under her shirt and atop her chest. "Hey, *guapo* (handsome)" she says with a wink to Armando. The men giggle uncomfortably and turn to make their way back. But the older women cackle loudly, slapping their thighs with delight as Margarita struts up and down the aisle of the orchard with the apples poking out of her chest. Margarita's older sister, Rosalina, laughs so hard that she loses her balance, falling over into the tall grass until all we can see are her brown shoes sticking up and into the air.

I delight in the camaraderie shared by this tightknit group of women, whom I have known since my first visit to Heredia. In kitchens scrubbed clean after lunch, I have sat often with them as they offer marital advice, tidbits of neighborhood gossip, and packets of saltine crackers. Rosalina is a favorite among the women in this group, known for her forthrightness and her keen sense of humor. And in the contours of her life, we find another story of Heredia at this moment in history—one that was born in the midst of Costa Rica's celebrated social democratic experiment but now watches as the state is restructured alongside the economy. The Rosalinas of Heredia are members of a lower middle class whose modest but comfortable lifestyles were made possible by the expanding public sector of post-1948 Costa Rica. As their lives become more insecure with periodic economic crises, selective government downsizing, and stagnant real wages, this group has had to find new ways to strategize economically. Similar in entrepreneurial fervor to the professional class we just examined, but rooted in older lifeways that center on families and neighborhoods, this class embodies a particular response to economic restructuring that is at once conservative and enterprising. Nowhere is this more evident than in the life story of Rosalina.

Rosalina's Story

Born in Heredia in 1942, Rosalina self-identified as a homemaker. Indeed, *ama de casa* (homemaker) was listed as her occupation on her Costa Rican identification card. But everyone on Heredia's west side knew her as a businesswoman, baking and selling cakes out of her home kitchen. Her cakes were exquisite centerpieces for birthday parties, weddings, and holiday parties. She was in high demand throughout the year, having built a remarkably successful business with relatively little education. As the oldest of twelve children, she was forced to drop out of primary school to help her mother with domestic work. If she was bitter about this, one would never know. She lamented simply, "We were many and we were poor." When asked why she never worked for pay, because technically this would have helped her family out as well, Rosalina giggled uncontrollably. Wiping tears of laughter from her eyes with the frayed edge of her cotton apron, she explained, "Eh, Susie, my father forbade his daughters from working outside the home."

Incredibly strict and very *"macho"* (masculine), Rosalina's father was a craftsman, and he made his living making shoes. "He had an artistic side," Rosalina remembered. "And he was a communist. Always reading about the French Revolution, *mi papa* (my father)." According to Rosalina, he regulated his daughters' every movement in and out of the home. As such, Rosalina was rarely permitted to go to the municipal market, even though it was just across the street from her childhood home. It was only because Julio spied on her from his market stall that Rosalina came to have a boyfriend and later a husband. They dated for five years before marrying when Rosalina was 25, their love *"un amor profundo"* (a deep love). Julio was also a native *Herediano,* who inherited his father's fruit stand in Heredia's municipal market. He continued working as a market vendor long after he and Rosalina married. So, too, did Rosalina continue to spend her days cooking and cleaning after moving out of her father's house and into a home that Julio inherited just blocks from Heredia's city center.

Soon after marrying, Rosalina gave birth to two sons—Marcelino and Oscar.[1] When her youngest, Oscar, entered kindergarten, Rosalina considered ways that she might bring money into the household. Even in Rosalina's childhood, it was not uncommon for married women to undertake some income-generating activity. But they typically did so within the confines of their home, sewing clothes for sale or baking goods to sell in the market. Rosalina explained that home-based work was considered "respectable." Thus, there was nothing unusual about Rosalina taking on a sideline economic activity in the home. What was unusual was the sense of urgency with which she pursued this livelihood strategy. Rosalina started her business in 1981. It was no coincidence that this was the same year that Costa Rica defaulted on its debt and that inflation skyrocketed. When a friend told her about a course on cakemaking, Rosalina decided to attend, thinking it might provide her the means to earn money at a time of financial insecurity. After completing the course, she started an informal cakemaking business from her home.

Rosalina's first client was her brother. From there, she began accumulating clients through familial, friendship, and neighborhood networks.

She was eventually able to complete around 25 cakes per week. As she had envisioned, the business was centered in her modest home, which was tucked behind a tidy wrought-iron fence and carefully placed potted ferns. By noontime, her kitchen was invariably stacked with dirty spoons, dusty mixing bowls, and pieces of paper scribbled with orders. At the center of this chaotic mix was Rosalina, rushing between hot oven and ringing telephone, perspiration trickling down her plump cheeks and clouds of cake mix rising off her apron. Between curse words and loud sighs, she managed to keep her orders over the years and build a loyal clientele. Her monthly income was no small matter. When I interviewed her in 2001, she was pulling in almost just as much as her husband, the market vendor and official family breadwinner.

With a second income, Rosalina and Julio were able to put Marcelino, their first born, in college. During his third year at Universidad Nacional, he started complaining of headaches. A trip to the doctor revealed that Marcelino had a malignant brain tumor. He entered the hospital in March and died three weeks later. He was just 19 years old. The night he died, Rosalina had decided to stay overnight in the hospital. This was unusual, and she could only credit God for putting her there that night. "I held his hand," she explained, "and I told him that it was alright to let go. 'Go to God,' I said to him. 'Go to his loving embrace.'" As she recounted the night, she and I sat in her living room on a soft blue sofa, a dust-free statue of the Virgin Mary peering at us from a corner. Rosalina shed no tears, but a deep reservoir of pain was everywhere evident on her face—the slight crinkle of her forehead, the downward turn of her mouth, and the vacant eyes that looked out the window at nothing in particular.

Left with an empty bedroom where her eldest son once slept, Rosalina mourned for a year before deciding to rent the room out to students attending the public university nearby. It was the late 1980s, and cake orders were low as Costa Rica's economic crisis worsened. Her grief notwithstanding, Rosalina had stumbled upon another income-generating activity centered on her home. Rosalina had been raised to care for others, and this she continued to do—sometimes cleaning rooms and baking cakes free of charge for her living son and husband, sometimes cleaning rooms and baking cakes in exchange for money. At once a homemaker and a home-based worker, she provided a second income that was crucial to the reproduction of her family's middle-class standing. With her and Julio's financial support, Oscar completed an accounting degree at a private university. The year before my fieldwork, he established his own bookkeeping business in an office attached to their home. Because Oscar had yet to marry, he continued to live with Rosalina and Julio, each day at noon making his way through a door that connected his business to Rosalina's kitchen. There, she had his lunch carefully laid out between cooling cakes. Julio, too, arrived daily for lunch. After a warm embrace with his wife, he sat with Oscar to eat while Rosalina mixed frosting and washed dirty dishes. For all three, but especially for Rosalina, the fine line between work and family life was a blurry one that disappeared often over the course of the work day.

When time permitted, her cake orders filled early, Rosalina hung up her apron and walked the four blocks between her house and that of her mother's. There, she invariably ran into sisters and sisters-in-law, neighbors and family friends, and distant cousins and aunts. It was this world of family, of neighbors, and of women that was the centerpiece of her life, just as her cakes were the centerpiece of her clients' celebrations. Rosalina had tried to share her knowledge of cakemaking with a couple of her sisters who were also looking for home-based work. But as her sisters themselves admitted, they did not have the patience or the talent for cakemaking. They did share, however, other income-generating activities. Indeed, it was one of her sisters that suggested Rosalina convert Marcelino's old bedroom into a room rental, as the sister herself had done in a spare bedroom the year prior. These women counseled and encouraged one another over telephone conversations and late-afternoon coffee, commiserating over the hard economic times and constructing strategies to keep one another's families afloat.

So, too, did these women hold one another accountable to the norms they had inherited from a previous generation of women—staying within the respectable bounds of the home, doting with motherly care on men and children, and comporting to the standards of "decent" behavior. In the same breath, they lamented the laziness of their husbands and advised me that marrying was the only respectable path for a "pretty woman like [me]." Their daring and bravado limited to their clandestine business pursuits and their sisterly gatherings, the women in Rosalina's circle would no more think of challenging their husbands than they would accede to their daughters that sexual freedom was a birthright. Thus was the nature of womanhood for this generation, pushing the boundaries of the female-homemaker–male-breadwinner household only so far and strategizing within the confines of the "patriarchal bargain" each had struck with their respective spouse. Kandiyoti (1988) uses the term "patriarchal bargain" when referring to the traditional gender norms that women and men generally follow once they marry. However enterprising and lucrative their businesses, women such as Rosalina ensure that their activities and orientation remained strictly centered on home and hearth.

This patriarchal bargain, and the contradictory ways in which these women adhered to it and tested it, became crystal clear on a hot December afternoon in the cool sanctuary of Rosalina's mother's living room. Rosalina had fetched a handful of ice-cold popsicles from the neighborhood *pulpería* (corner store) for the women who had gathered on this day. We each pulled back the sticky paper wrapping to find relief from the heat in the cold sting of the popsicle on our tongues. For once there was silence in this circle, the six of us lost in the sweet taste of Rosalina's treat. Margarita broke the silence. "I need to go get dinner started for Ricardo," she began. "Susie, I don't care how modern you are; the way to a man's heart is and always will be through his stomach." I looked up from my lap to find Rosalina staring at me with a wide grin, her cherry Popsicle having stained her lips a bright red. "Or through his trousers," she said with a wink. Margarita clapped her hands with a hearty laugh as their mother smiled surreptitiously, her shoulders shaking through a spasm of stifled giggles.

Heredia's Storied Middle Class

Rosalina's story embodies another critical layer in *Herediano* society—one that I am loosely identifying as lower middle class and made up of vocationally trained white-collar workers and small-business persons.[2] Again, because I am delineating the groups in each chapter in terms of class location, this group consists of people that share a similar class position but who occupy very different positions in the labor market. For example, it includes people such as Rosalina who are technically not economically active but who secured this class position through marriage or pension. The group also consists of people in very different occupations—everything from clerical work to retail sales to food preparation (see Table 4.1). Given the sheer variety of people within this group, it is important to remember how the group coheres. In this case, the group has in common a modest middle-class location without the anchor of the kind of professional degrees explored in the previous chapter.

In part, the group depicted in this chapter is defined by the generation in which they came of age—a period of time that many consider to be Costa Rica's golden era. Indeed, all but two individuals in this group were between the ages of 45 and 65. These were the major beneficiaries of the country's post-1948 social democratic reforms. They took advantage of a protected national economy, growing public sector opportunities, and a sturdy social welfare system to piece together a modest middle-class lifestyle for themselves and their children. As they married and started families, the women

TABLE **4.1** The Middle Class

	YEAR OF BIRTH	PLACE OF BIRTH	CIVIL STATUS	NO. OF CHILDREN	LEVEL OF EDUCATION	OCCUPATION
Claudia	1941	San José	Married	4	Secondary school	Housewife
Eduardo	1958	Heredia	Married	1	Secondary	Store owner (self-employed)
Emilia	1939	Heredia	Single	1	Secondary and technical	Nurse's aide (government)
Eugenia	1943	Heredia	Single	0	University	Librarian (government)
Fatima	1955	Heredia	Married	2	Secondary	Disabled
Fernando	1965	Heredia	Married	2	Some university	Restaurant owner (self-employed)
Juan Pablo	1955	Heredia	Married	4	Some secondary	Police officer (government)
Julio	1943	Heredia	Married	2	Some university	Market vendor (self-employed)
Marcela	1949	Heredia	Single	0	Some secondary	Housewife
Margarita	1954	Heredia	Married	2	Some university	Housewife
Patricia	1955	Heredia	Married	4	Some university	Housewife
Ramon	1953	Heredia	Single	0	Some university	Inventory clerk (government)
Ricardo	1947	Puntarenas	Married	2	Some university	Inventory clerk (government)
Rosalina	1942	Heredia	Married	2	Primary	Housewife

Note: Unless otherwise noted, all occupations listed are held in the private sector.

in this group receded into the home as a sign of middle-class status, their husbands enjoying entry-level jobs in the public sector or small-business opportunities. The age specificity of this group is due primarily to the fact that younger age cohorts who would have otherwise found their way into this lower middle class (i.e., those aged 15 to 25 during the 1980s), were likely to experience *downward* class mobility in the 1980s.[3] As public sector training and employment contracted and unemployment rose, it made little sense for individuals just coming of age to remain in school in the hopes that they would land a well-paying job. Therefore, many simply dropped out and worked—formally or informally—at whatever job they could find. This had serious ramifications for their mobility. Hence, this younger age cohort was more likely to find itself in the formal or informal working class by the time of my research.[4] Heredia's lower middle class was populated by those who had *already* come of age and been able to take advantage of the opportunities in entry-level white-collar work.

Portes and Hoffman (2003) identify two classes of workers that have relevance to the present group of workers: small-business persons and white-collar workers. The former corresponds to the classic Marxist category of the "petty bourgeoisie," which Marx understood to be in a contradictory class location between the upper and lower strata of society. Portes and Hoffman (2003:52) estimate this group of workers to be around 11 percent of Costa Rica's workforce in 2000. Portes and Hoffman also identify a vocationally trained class of white-collar workers, which they estimate to be 14 percent of the economically active population in Costa Rica in 2000 (2003:52). Using the white-collar estimate as the lower-end estimate, and combining the figures for small-business persons and white-collar workers for the higher-end estimate, we may estimate the present group of white-collar workers and small-business persons to be somewhere between 15 and 25 percent of the Costa Rican workforce.[5] Again, in addition to economically active individuals, I am including many economically inactive women in this chapter.[6] Such women are connected to the small-business sector and public sector by virtue of their marriage to men employed in these sectors.[7] As well, many of these women dabbled in microenterprises themselves as a form of supplemental income generation.

More than any other group of Costa Rican workers, this group is tied to the restructuring of the state under neoliberalism. To begin, these individuals came of age during a period of marked public sector expansion. Between 1950 and 1980, the public sector workforce grew from 6 percent to 20 percent of the labor force (Itzigsohn 2000:67). Given the relative stability and decent pay associated with government jobs in Costa Rica, scholars have tied this expansion to the growth and stability of the country's middle class (Gindling 1991; Itzigsohn 2000; Molina and Palmer 2000; Tardanico 1996). The expansive public sector also helped support almost full employment (Clark 2001:34; Itzigsohn 2000:68). Costa Rica's public sector was important to the present category of workers in at least one other respect: it provided a set of public benefits that enabled households to flourish on one source of income. Since the early 1940s, the Costa Rican Social

Security Fund has provided sickness and maternity health insurance as well as a pension program. These programs were universalized in the 1970s.[8] Thus, by the early 1990s, health insurance coverage in Costa Rica was nearly 90 percent (Clark 2001:33).[9] These social welfare programs and the expansion of the public sector not only helped constitute a solid middle class but also a particular form of household organization, one that revolved around a male breadwinner and a female homemaker.

Given Costa Rica's more gradual approach to liberalization, the public sector remains a major fixture as employment generator and welfare provider. Even so, neoliberal restructuring has constrained the public sector and employment within it (Tardanico 1996). The first government workforce reduction program, known as *movilidad laboral*, or labor mobility, occurred in 1991.[10] By most accounts, this and other reduction programs were small-scale and unsuccessful in putting a serious dent in public sector employment (Clark 2001; Tardanico 1996). Indeed, public sector employment actually grew in the 1980s and 1990s, although the rate of growth was much slower than in previous decades. An in-depth analysis of government employment data suggests that government employment expanded primarily for highly educated workers (Tardanico 1996). Among less skilled workers, government jobs declined. Thus, the workers described in the previous chapter were more likely to find a place in Costa Rica's public sector at the turn of the century. In turn, the individuals described in this chapter were more likely to be displaced by state restructuring. Of the thirteen men and women I interviewed, eight had worked for the public service for the better part of their career. Only four of these individuals had managed to keep their government job at the time of our interview, one of whom was facing another round of workforce reduction.

Displaced public workers have generally been hard-pressed to find decent opportunities for work. Not only did formal employment grow at a very slow pace in the 1980s and 1990s, but less-skilled, middle-age displaced workers have found themselves ill-equipped to meet the requirements of a more demanding job market. Those private sector jobs that are available have typically been of a low-paid and unstable nature. The few "good" jobs that have come out of private sector expansion have tended to go to the university-educated professional workers described in the previous chapter (Tardanico 1996). Thus, for many former public servants, entrepreneurial activity has become a kind of "safety valve" (Portes and Hoffman 2003).[11] Itzigsohn (2000) found that the proportion of the Costa Rican workforce that was self-employed grew from 12 to 19 percent between 1980 and 1991. More recent research indicates that self-employment in Costa Rica continued to capture a sizable segment of the labor force thereafter (Gindling and Oviedo 2008). In this chapter, we will consider small-business persons who either work for themselves or employ fewer than five people in their business. Seven of the thirteen individuals featured in this chapter are small-business persons, four of whom had been displaced from the public sector.

Another factor fueling the rise in microentrepreneurial activity in Costa Rica over the past few decades has been the degradation in wages and social security coverage, which has pushed an increasing number of economically inactive women into the labor force in search of supplemental income for households (Itzigsohn 2000; Tardanico 1996). Studying San José's labor market in the 1980s, Tardanico (1996) found that labor force participation rates increased for almost every age group of women. But the increase was most pronounced for 40- to 69-year olds. These women did not have the credentials or work experience to vie for jobs in the formal sector. They were also bound to older social norms that frown on work outside the home. As a result, they, too, turned to self-employment, constructing "economic solutions through petty enterprise" (Portes and Hoffman 2003:48). Note that although these women could be considered economically active, all four of the self-employed women featured in this chapter considered themselves economically *in*active because their income generation was constructed as something done "on the side." Rosalina, of course, had her cakemaking business. Fatima sewed clothes for sale to local clothing stores, which she had done since taking an early retirement from the government. Margarita and Patricia, who were also former government workers, rented rooms to local university students. None of these women paid into the state insurance or pension plan and none of them self-identified as workers. Rather, they were considered "housewives."

According to many scholars, the rise in self-employment is a critical piece of the neoliberal project (Itzigsohn 2000; Portes and Hoffman 2003). Not only does it offer a kind of "refuge" to workers ejected from state and state-protected jobs (Portes and Hoffman 2003), but self-employment reflects the kind of work promoted under neoliberalism: entrepreneurial and market-driven. Because self-employment rises as the state recedes, and because it has become a major economic alternative for those displaced from the public sector, the story of the small entrepreneurs and struggling bureaucrats who are the subject of this chapter is wrapped up in the story of the Costa Rican state. It is a story of how a country made famous by its state programs chipped away at the very thing that made it so exceptional. The irony of this group of workers is that they have played

Due to government downsizing and the decline in wages that began to occur in Costa Rica in the 1980s, many economically inactive women went to work to supplement household income. Other women, especially those with family responsibilities in the middle class, pursued sideline economic activities out of their homes. Here are signs in front of a middle-class home advertising tamales and popsicles (*helados*) for sale. Other examples of women's microentrepreneurialism include renting a room to university students, taking in sewing, and running a home-based gift shop (*bazar*).

a role in this process. Although they do not embrace the neoliberal agenda, having been born and bred on the idea of a strong development state, their entrepreneurial spirit provides a kind of lifeblood to the neoliberal project. This class is certainly getting by in the new economy, but the transition into the new economy has not come easy or without a price.

Our Lady of Neighborly Love

The lower middle-class *Heredianos* featured in this chapter were well represented in my neighborhood of Pueblo Tico. Here, weekday afternoons were relaxed but bustling. After the lunch dishes had been washed, the afternoon *siesta* had occurred, and the hottest part of the day had passed, neighborhoods came alive with the footsteps and greetings of older, married women. They used the afternoon hours to visit neighbors, friends, and family, socializing regularly and comfortably in the confines of one another's living rooms. Front doors were left open to let in the afternoon breeze and to spy on the late-afternoon pedestrian traffic. Often, Ricardo and I arrived home from work before Margarita's return from her afternoon visits. When she would walk into the house screaming *"Buenas tardes* (Good afternoon)!" he and I would scream back *"Callejera!"* (woman who walks the streets). It was of course a joke, because Margarita's time outside of her home was brief, limited to the few moments she passed outdoors on her way to another woman's living room. With quick steps, she would run to the kitchen to put on a pot of coffee. The three of us would perch on wooden stools at the kitchen counter, reviewing together the news of the day. At this hour, women's time gave way to women's work, with family conversations competing with the sound of plantains sizzling on the frying pan.

Life in Pueblo Tico had a comfortable routine to it, even during the rainy season when afternoon showers broke up otherwise predictable patterns of everyday life. Much of what gave the neighborhood its character was a sense of history, which stretched back some twenty-five years when a growing middle class claimed farm land around Heredia's city center to build modest single-family homes. From the neighborhood, it was just a short walk to the bus stop to travel to San José or any number of outlying towns in the Central Valley. It was also just a short walk to Avenida Central, Heredia's major thoroughfare leading to its commercial district. Somewhere in between this commercial and residential space sat Eduardo's auto parts store. The store was easy to miss, situated as it was in a residential neighborhood and located in the front room of Eduardo's home. The only real sign that business took place here was a tiny metal sign announcing in simple yellow letters that auto parts were sold there. Eduardo's store had the advantage of being located on a corner lot. Cars were able to park in a semicircle around the store, as if they were props to attract passersby who might be interested in all things automotive. Some of the cars were for sale, with handwritten "For Sale" signs perched on windshields. Other cars were owned by customers who had arrived in desperate need of an auto part.

Eduardo's store was not so much a store as a counter behind which were heavy metal shelves holding auto parts in simple clear plastic bags. In front of the counter was a small reception area where three people could stand comfortably. Because the space did not afford much room for interaction, the social life of this store spilled out onto the sidewalk outside. On a Wednesday afternoon in early December, the rains having died down and given way to heat, Eduardo and an assistant were working behind the counter. Three customers were lined up in the space in front of the counter. Two men gathered outside to lean against the store's outer wall and talk about the day. I had passed Eduardo's store often on my way to Heredia's city center, the men greeting me with whistles or wide grins. This was clearly a male-dominated space in which I was not expected to pass the time. But on this day, I had been invited to interview Eduardo and I was received with polite accommodation.

Short in stature with a head of thick, dark graying hair, Eduardo offered me a warm smile and an easy laugh at my bad jokes. Eduardo was a native *Herediano*, having been raised by a dairy farmer and a housewife in the nearby town of Barva, which shares the name of an inactive volcano on whose outer edge it sits. Like many people of his generation, Eduardo grew up around the coffee harvest, collecting coffee during the annual harvest starting at the age of 12. The harvest occurred from November to January, during the vacation from school. For many families, it represented an annual income-earning project in which the entire family partook. After completing secondary school, Eduardo secured a job at a state-owned bank in Heredia as a janitor. He worked there for two years, after which he took a civil service course that qualified him to take an administrative position at the bank. Eventually, he would become an assistant manager for the bank, a position at which he worked for 20 years. With little more than a high school education, he had done quite well for himself. But the 1990s had not been kind to public sector workers, especially middle-age workers with little education—workers such as Eduardo. Recognizing that his time in the public service was limited, he took an early retirement and invested in a small business.

In so many ways, Eduardo embodied the group of workers that are the subject of this chapter. He was the twelfth of eighteen children but the father of an only child. He was raised by a poor farmer but became an assistant manager of a bank. He was fast-tracked into a well-paid government job but fast-tracked out of the job after many years of service. Put simply, he had traversed a traditional, modern, and post-modern Costa Rica in his forty-three years. In spite of these changes, Eduardo remained remarkably rooted in place. He put in some fifty-four hours a week at his store. But at 6:00 o'clock each night, he hung up his apron on the south wall of the store, pulled the metal door of the store shut, and passed through a door in the back to make his way into his adjoining house.

His small business, his extended family, and his personal history were concentrated in five city blocks. Whereas the professional workers of the previous chapter are transforming parts of Heredia into a suburb of San José, Eduardo and his counterparts had turned parts of Heredia into a suburb of Heredia's city center. Their Heredia was more provincial, more neighborly, more *Herediano*.

The differences between the individuals in this chapter and the individuals from the previous chapter are subtle and complex. In part, it is a generational difference. Eduardo and his counterparts were quite simply older, many of them parents to the kind of professionals described in the previous chapter. During the economic crisis of the 1980s, when the "new professionals" were mere teenagers, this group was struggling to make household budgets stretch so that food could be purchased and bills could be paid. In addition, these were men and women who had been born in Heredia and/or who had married native *Heredianos*. They were not transplants who decided to make Heredia home on account of its proximity to San José. As such, they had a deeper connection to the city's history. They could take me to houses where they had been born and churches in which they had been married, as Margarita did on Costa Rica's Mother's Day in 2001.[12] Pointing to a loading dock across the street from a store selling cheap women's underwear, she declared: "That's where our house once stood. I lived there until Ricardo married me. There were fewer cars and more houses here back then."

In terms of life stage, *Heredianos* such as Eduardo, Margarita, and Rosalina were also at an age in which they were more rooted in place. Many began their careers commuting to San José like the professional workers in the previous chapter. Indeed, they had helped construct the *Gran Área Metropolitana* through their residential and commuting patterns. But as they formed families, the women in this group became more homebound, tied as they were to particular notions of "proper" mothering. Their tug of home was not the same as their mothers, who contended with such large families that working outside the home was virtually impossible. Their tug was more ideological, tied to a middle-class understanding of privatized motherhood. This middle-class ideology was supported by a robust public sector that enabled men to financially support a homemaker and dependent children on his earnings alone. Indeed, many of the men in this group would have continued commuting to San José to work their state jobs had neoliberal restructuring not coaxed them into early retirement. Once retired from the civil service, they retreated to Heredia, where they could put their severance packages and dense neighborhood networks to use for the purpose of small-business development. Many, if not most of these men could not pursue the kind of professional consulting that the workers in the previous chapter envisioned. They simply did not have the professional skills. As such, they were more likely to invest in retail operations, which tied them, like their wives, to the rhythms and rituals of neighborhood life in Heredia. In doing so, they helped transform what would otherwise have been sleepy neighborhoods into spaces where family and work life intermingled.

The secure and well-paid jobs in the civil service initially afforded individuals in this group the ability to construct modest single-family homes on Heredia's outskirts. But their middle-class resources were not so abundant as to give them the ability to own a car or otherwise pursue a more lavish lifestyle. Thus, they could not establish the kind of gated communities we see among Heredia's contemporary professional class—communities that were predicated on car ownership and thus less connected to Heredia's city center. Instead, we see this group push out from the city center, helping to create neighborhoods on the city's perimeter where they could get to the center of town by bus or on foot. As such, the neighborhoods inhabited by this group still felt very much a part of Heredia proper, although they were distinct in outward appearance and class structure. Moving from the historic city center into these outlying neighborhoods, wattle-and-daub houses give way to brightly painted cement structures encased in heavy metal bars. Like the gates surrounding Heredia's newer residential communities, the bars provided Heredia's earlier middle-class protection against the real and imagined crime associated with rapid urban development. Cubujuquí is a typical neighborhood in this respect. Built in the second half of the twentieth century on Heredia's west side, it was one of the earlier signs of the town's urban development. The houses here, all of them one-story, share walls and crumbling sidewalks, as if one floor of an apartment building had been carved out and laid down to cover a city block. Unlike the city center, which is laid out in grid-like fashion, the streets here curve and meander. Sprinkled throughout are a video store, a corner store, and small fields of coffee, which crop up stubborn and rebellious against Heredia's suburban development.

Tucked quietly behind a now polluted stream that runs through Cubujuquí, which coffee pickers once used for refreshment, was the home of Fatima, a middle-aged *Herediana* housewife. Inside Fatima's home, watercolor paintings dotted the walls and an entertainment center featuring a television and video recorder sat prominently in the living room. As she prepared lunch for her husband, 19-year-old son, and 9-year-old daughter, she

The stable, well-paid jobs associated with the public sector allowed many middle class families in Heredia to construct single-family homes around the city's perimeter in the 1970s and 1980s. These homes were accessible to the city center on foot or by bus, but the neighborhoods in which they were located had a more suburban feel. This photograph of a set of homes in a neighborhood known as Cubujuquí is illustrative of this era of urban development. The heavy metal bars in front are typical of these earlier suburban homes and the growing middle-class anxiety about urban growth and crime.

recounted a childhood that revolved around her grandfather's coffee farm and an annual coffee harvest in which the entire family participated. Fatima would go on to graduate from one of Heredia's vocational schools with a certificate in secretarial skills, eventually securing a position at the Ministry of Public Education. After 22 years of public service, she took an early retirement. "Why did you take it?" I asked. "I was exhausted," she explained. The Ministry had already undergone extensive restructuring. Between the staff reductions, the new technology, and the constant insecurity, she was unhappy, even depressed, about her future prospects in the government.

Although Fatima received a severance package from the government, she described her need to bring money into the household as urgent. Her husband still had his job with the government. But he, too, was feeling pressure to retire early. And there was her son to consider. He was on the verge of graduating from secondary school and eager to attend a university.

So Fatima decided to go back to something she had done since a teenager—sewing clothes for sale. "I had to brush up on my skills," she giggled. She took a free class on sewing at the National Training Institute (*Instituto Nacional de Aprendizaje* [INA]) and went to work sewing dresses and blouses for neighbors and family members. Like Rosalina, she also rented out one of her rooms to college students attending the university. "Thanks to God, I have this house," she confided. She and her husband had saved dutifully in the early years of their marriage to build the home. When her son turned 8, they had pieced together enough money to start construction. The year was 1988, a time when the neighborhood was little more than a tiny stretch of houses and empty plots of land.

Although Fatima left her government job only after restructuring pushed her out, four of the six remaining women in this group left the workforce to devote more time to family.[13] The workforce departure of these women hinged on their husbands' ability to provide financially for their households. Indeed, a homemaker-breadwinner household was something of a status symbol among this group of *Heredianos*—a sign to family, friends, and neighbors that a man had secured a good job and commanded a respectable salary. Although their jobs entailed little more than filing papers, the office setting, the job security, and the respectable wages were signs of achievement for the men in this group, whose own parents had been manual laborers. As state jobs disappeared under neoliberal restructuring, however, these middle-class foundations threatened to crumble. Husbands, and in some cases wives, returned home with paltry severance packages that did little to protect households against rising food costs and school fees. Thus, bureaucrats became entrepreneurs and homemakers became breadwinners. And just as they tested the boundaries of Heredia's city center with their neighborhoods, so they tested the boundaries of their household gender order with their livelihood strategies. At times, even often, their strategies upended and unnerved the patriarchal bargain and marital peace in the lower middle-class households of Heredia. Stepping into the household, then, we see household conflict for this group. Nowhere was this conflict more evident than in the relationship between Margarita and Ricardo.

Margarita's Problem

At first glance, Margarita was a quintessential middle-class housewife. On any given day, she could be found in her orange cotton tank top and lime-green shorts, a broom in hand or perhaps a bundle of dirty laundry in her arms. For Margarita, the connection between womanhood and home-making was common sense and crucial to her understanding of middle-class respectability. But Margarita had not always been a housewife. Indeed, in the early years of her family's formation, she was a working mother. In 2001, she showed me photographs of her years working as a secretary for the government in downtown San José. In the pictures, a young Margarita dressed in tight beige pants smiled flirtatiously at the camera. As she explained, she enjoyed her life then: "Look, it wasn't that I liked the job. I was in charge of logging receipts for employees needing reimbursements for transportation. It was boring! But I loved the people I worked with. We had fun, me and the other women there."

Margarita did not work for just any government agency. She worked for one of the most notorious government agencies, one that came to embody the state's "inefficiencies." The *Corporación Costarricense de Desarrollo Sociedad Anónima* (CODESA) was founded in 1972 as a public corporation that would invest in enterprises deemed too expensive or risky for the private sector. The idea was that the state would assume the initial risks and hand over the enterprise, once established, to the private sector. Although the public corporation invested in countless enterprises, it never quite managed to sell them off, and the public corporation became massive and unwieldy (Vega 1989).[14] Thus, when the Costa Rican government made its neoliberal turn in the 1980s, CODESA was among the first to be privatized. Margarita left CODESA at precisely the same moment it was auctioned off to the private sector. But in her telling, she left for an entirely different reason. Three years after giving birth to Violeta, Margarita gave birth to Cecilia. Now the mother of two young daughters, Margarita felt like she was not a "good" mother if she did not stay at home to raise them. In defining what a "good" mother was, Margarita drew upon norms that placed her in the home with the task of caregiving.

Without question, Margarita left the workforce for a complex set of reasons, including public sector restructuring, domestic work obligations, and middle-class expectations. Historically, the ideal household in Costa Rica has been nuclear in structure and headed by men, with men associated with breadwinning and women with caregiving. So it is no surprise that Margarita retreated into the household sometime after having children. What makes her story historically unique was that Margarita left the workforce just six years after Costa Rica defaulted on its debt. Her own state position had been eliminated, and her husband's was increasingly insecure. Indeed, Ricardo, a college dropout with basic administrative skills, had just the kind of public sector job considered worth cutting: an inventory position at the Ministry of Health. In this context, Margarita was compelled to find some income-generating activity. Convinced that to be a good mother, she had to remain in the home, Margarita turned to God to find some way of earning money at home: "I said, 'God, send me something, a message or an opportunity, so that I can work out of the home but also bring in money'." According to Margarita, she ran into a friend shortly thereafter who suggested she rent rooms to foreign exchange students attending the university nearby. Ricardo converted the dining room into a spare bedroom, and they began accepting students one year later. In 1994, I became the second student to live in her home while I attended Universidad Nacional as an exchange student. As a host mother, Margarita cleaned the rooms of her exchange students, provided them laundry service, and offered them prepared meals.

It should not surprise that Margarita's income-generating activity, like that of Rosalina and Fatima, was focused on the home and her role as homemaker. But her informal activity of boarding students took on increased financial importance over time. Indeed, within just eight years, Margarita had gone from supplementing Ricardo's primary wages to being a co-breadwinner for this household. As such, the boundaries between nurturing and breadwinning became blurred, complicating the line demarcating "proper" gender roles. With this blurring came conflict over the division of labor. By the time I arrived in 2001, Margarita was huffing and puffing her way through household chores, doling out heavy sighs and off-hand remarks about Ricardo's laziness. One weekend, Ricardo suggested we take a day trip to the mountains. "A trip to the mountains?" Margarita screamed. "Exactly when do you think I'm going to get this house cleaned? In my sleep?" "I'll sweep the floor," Ricardo offered. "Ha!" Margarita spat, ending the discussion. Days later, I found her sitting alone in the dining room. "Susie," she confided, "I want to run away for a week. See how they survive without me."

To some extent, Margarita was simply feeling overburdened by her domestic duties. The onerous nature of these duties, however, was due in part to the fact that Margarita had commercialized domestic work, increasing her workload and her workday. Thus, it is certainly possible that she was expressing a deeper frustration, one that had to do with Ricardo's failure to live up to his role as family breadwinner.[15] In this instance, household chores became a backdrop against which Margarita contested her newfound responsibility as coprovider and, by association, Ricardo's failure in this role. For Margarita, a clean home was a sign of middle-class status. But it was also a signal to others that Ricardo could provide for his family. As she struggled to keep up the appearance of a "respectable" middle-class home, Margarita was more frustrated that she had to do it all than she was angered that Ricardo did not clean house. Indeed, although she criticized his unwillingness to "help out" around the house, what Margarita had in mind for Ricardo were not household chores at all. Instead, she imagined entrepreneurial ventures for him that might provide for the family financially. In early 2002, she came up with a business plan in which she would make *tamales* and Ricardo would market the food to nearby restaurants and stores. Months later, when I asked what had happened to the idea, Margarita threw her dish towel over her right shoulder and sighed. The idea had fallen on deaf ears when she mentioned it to Ricardo, she explained. "You know in the past, I was so much more aggressive about this stuff," she explained. "But you know Ricardo, so laid back. After so many years together, you start mirroring your spouse. Eh, Susie, find yourself a man that's a doer."

It is difficult to say how Ricardo felt about Margarita's frustration. This was never something he was able to express to me despite the enormous level of trust that existed between us. One evening, I asked how things were going at work, and Ricardo replied that it looked very bleak. At a meeting, officials at the Ministry of Health had informed Ricardo and other low-level administrative employees that their jobs would soon be phased out. They had the option to retire early with a cut in their pension and a small sum of money. Ricardo was hesitant to take it. "It's a bad deal, Susie," he explained. Ricardo talked about one coworker's efforts to get a lawyer through one of the public sector unions to help protect their jobs. But the majority of his coworkers seemed too discouraged to fight: "They just sat there and accepted it! I said, 'Let's *do* something! Let's protect our jobs!'"[16] In addition to fighting the cutbacks, of course, Ricardo could have been devising a sideline business as many people in Costa Rica were doing. He did in fact speak of starting a paint distribution service but had worked out few details or plans. Alternatively, he could have been contributing more to the upkeep of the house. In a few instances, I observed him ironing and once sweeping the dining room floor. But for the most part, he was not particularly helpful around the house, holding onto the title of breadwinner through a set of patriarchal norms that were slower to change than the economic realities of this family.

As González de la Rocha (2001:91) suggests, "The role of women as breadwinners rather than generators of 'additional' incomes is increasing [in Latin America]." She goes on to explain that "this place[s] an increased burden on women, since the transformation of households [does] not include a gendered redistribution of tasks within the household division of labor" (González de la Rocha 2001:84). In Margarita's case, her role as coprovider *and* homemaker led to major conflict in this household, but it did not lead to a real shift in gender roles and it did not lead to divorce.[17] Rather, Margarita accepted the terms of the unspoken and unwritten contract she established upon marrying. Her aim was not to change the contract but to compel Ricardo to hold up his end of the bargain. As Kandiyoti (1988:282–3) argues, "when classic patriarchy enters a crisis, many women may continue to use all the pressure they can muster to make men live up to their obligations and will not, except under the most extreme pressure, compromise the basis for their claims by stepping out of line and losing their respectability." Although Margarita's sideline work had taken on financial importance and new meaning, the informal and home-based nature of this work tended to maintain the façade of a breadwinner-homemaker household. And as Margarita's story makes all too clear, this façade was just fine with Margarita, who clung to older ways of "doing gender" that placed middle-class women in the home and their husbands in the world of work.

Lessons from the Corner Store

Writing "in defense of the corner store" in an article by the same title, Spanish philosopher and Costa Rican transplant Constantino Láscaris waxed nostalgic about a traditional neighborhood institution known as the *pulpería*. The *pulpería* is a small neighborhood store that provides families with basic necessities, such as tortillas and eggs, which can be bought on credit from the *pulpero*, or store owner. *Pulperías* also serve as neighborhood gathering places, wherein neighbors can socialize, gossip, and discuss current affairs. Láscaris thus described them as "the nerve center of a group of houses" (2004:194). With the rise in supermarkets and more dispersed neighborhoods, *pulperías* have had to compete with large retail outlets for middle-class customers. But they remain in many neighborhoods as a place where "news of the neighborhood can be gotten" and "a good woman's hardships are listened to" (Lascaris 2004:197).[18] The *pulpería* captures the heart and soul of an older Heredia wherein basic needs and neighborhood sociability come before profits and progress. Here, in this dusty cement box of a store, we find the same charming inefficiencies associated with the development state and the contours of a Costa Rican lifeway in major transition.

Like the *pulpería*, Costa Rica's development state met the basic needs of workers, although it has been maligned as inefficient and much too generous. On a hot summer night in 2001, I listened as a US expatriate in San José decried how "bloated" Costa Rica's government sector was. In my opinion, she did not grasp the paradox of the Costa Rican state. Government expansion may have produced an inefficient state bureaucracy, but it also produced a solid middle class that helped stabilize the country and embodied its exceptionalism. Thus, to applaud Costa Rica's high standard of living and to criticize its unwieldy public sector is to miss the connection between the two. Costa Rica earned its reputation as a peaceful, stable, and prosperous country precisely because of the state's social welfare investments and infrastructure. In its efforts to reduce the state's role in this area, then, the neoliberal project poses a fundamental challenge to the post-1948 contract that the state established with the citizens of this country. That contract guaranteed a modicum of social security and human investment in exchange for peace and stability among the working population.

To be sure, the Costa Rican development state was not perfect. It gave rise to an older middle-class lifeway that relied on a particular gender script, one that limited women's achievements and status to mothering and household caregiving. Under neoliberal restructuring, such women confronted the fragility of their middle-class existence but also took their first tentative steps out of the home and into the world of work. For her part, Margarita both pushed the envelope of existing gender norms and pulled back into the confines of her home. Her oscillation was evident not simply in her household battles with Ricardo but in her political work during Costa Rica's 2002 presidential election. During this historic election, Costa Rica's two-party system was challenged by a third-party contender. Ottón Solís of the Citizen Action Party (*Partido Acción Ciudadana* [PAC]) effectively won over much of the country's disenchanted middle class, especially its vulnerable public sector workers, by his critique of government corruption and downsizing. Margarita and family were avid PAC supporters, attending rallies and organizing meetings, although Margarita's activism proved short-lived. As PAC's campaign gained momentum, Costa Rica's traditional two parties, the National Liberation Party (PLN) and the Social Christian Unity Party (PUSC), scrambled to discipline wayward party members.[19] So, too, did Ricardo reign in Margarita from her political participation. He chided her for wearing a PAC T-shirt when she walked about town, hissed at her at rallies when she chanted with organizers, and complained when her attendance at meetings took her out of the home at night. By the time the February 3 election rolled around, Margarita had backed out of most PAC activities, claiming a series of mysterious headaches. Instead, she cooked food for the volunteers working the polls on election day.

How do I make sense of Margarita's marriage and her stalled revolution during this moment of social change in Heredia? When I entered the field in 2001, I was single and a Marxist-feminist. As such, I was somewhat naive and entirely dogmatic about marriage and the market. In my mind, they were both exploitative and would never offer real freedom for Margarita— or any *Herediano* for that matter. Thus, I wrote confidently that Margarita was stifled both in marriage and in the free-market reforms taking over her country. It was also evident to me that her sideline economic activities helped fuel the neoliberal project while keeping Margarita within the proper bounds of her patriarchal marriage. Thus, it appeared that she accommodated both an older household division of labor and a newer neoliberal model that offered her little in return. But an observation two years later gave me pause. I had returned to Costa Rica for Violeta's wedding and, after the wedding, had stayed to conduct an ethnographic revisit. One night, while watching television, I spied Ricardo leaning over to plant tiny kisses on Margarita's neck. Margarita giggled like a school girl. I was stunned. Was this the same couple who two years before had battled over dishes and dollars, their affection hung out to dry like pieces of wet laundry? The next day, I said to Margarita, "I've never seen you and Ricardo so affectionate." "Really?" she asked genuinely surprised.

Had I been blind to the affection in this marriage during my year of fieldwork? Had I found conflict only because I had been looking for it? Or was this conflict a fleeting manifestation of the tensions that existed at that moment in time? My guess is that this household was particularly conflict-ridden during the year in which I observed it. That year, Margarita had an established sideline business as a "host mother" and was reaping the rewards and problems associated with this role. Ricardo had entered a more intense phase of state restructuring and was worried about his future job prospects. Cecilia and Violeta had entered young adulthood and were pushing for more freedom in an increasingly cosmopolitan Heredia. The result was a rather volatile family dynamic. Even so, this family dynamic was illustrative of the tensions and contradictions that arose for this middle-aged and middle-class group of *Heredianos* at the turn of the twenty-first century. In effect, this group had come of age under two social contracts—one pertaining to gender norms in marriage, another pertaining to state obligations to citizens. These contracts spelled out what men and women might expect from marriage and the state and what was expected of them in return. Neoliberal economic reforms eroded both contracts, causing confusion and consternation for this group. In the end, the patriarchal bargain was slower to change than the social contract established with the state, leaving women such as Margarita to shoulder older and newer responsibilities.

In the decade that followed my fieldwork, Margarita would continue with her sideline business of hosting students, continuing to identify primarily as a family caregiver. Although her daughters grew older and left home, Margarita's caregiving responsibilities continued unabated. Margarita's mother, who suffered from advanced diabetes and lived just around the block, required round-the-clock care and Margarita provided it, running between her house and her mother's with syringes, laundry, and food. As for Ricardo, he withstood the threats to his public sector job and was able to retire with a full pension. But as Costa Rica entered the second decade of the twenty-first century with the highest accumulated inflation rate in the region, his pension was hardly sufficient. A former colleague who had left the public sector many years earlier to start a medical supply company offered him a job in sales, and Ricardo took it. Now in the private sector, he was required to work 48 hours a week. Like Margarita, he was working more in retirement than he had been at middle age. The two of them spent evenings soothing aching legs and their own diabetes with herbal remedies and variety shows on television.

In my follow-up research in 2014, I learned that Rosalina had abandoned her cake business after WalMart opened a store in Heredia and lured away many of her clients with low-priced baked goods.[20] Not so for Eduardo, who actually expanded his business in the years following my initial interview with him. By 2014, he was living in a newly built house on the outskirts of town, having established multiple successful auto parts stores in the surrounding area. Although anecdotal, these cases suggest that women might have been less successful in their entrepreneurial endeavors than the men in this group, leading them to fall back into their role as primary caregivers. But I suspect that the real reason for the enduring association between womanhood and caregiving for this group was more complex. Women such as Rosalina and Margarita had entered into a contract with their husband and their country. In exchange for their labor and love, they had the right to lay claim to their resources, services, and allegiance. However unstable those claims were, they had neither incentive nor inclination to break these contracts. Indeed, the contracts and the feelings that bound them were *meaningful* to them. "Put this in your book," Margarita directed me as she cooked pot after pot of macaroni for poll workers on election day in 2002. "Write down that I am doing this because

I love my country. And this is how I serve it." To be sure, Margarita's husband and country fell short on their end of the bargain. But Margarita still looked to them to uphold their obligations, she still had faith in them, and she still loved them. I did not understand this in 2002, when I watched, frustrated, as Margarita remained "just a housewife." I wanted her to threaten divorce, start a legitimate business, and claim her newfound political voice. I never quite understood that to do so would threaten her fragile claims on and abiding love for Ricardo and her country.

For her part, Margarita never asked that I understand her plight or make sense of her experience. She just asked me to be a friend, to listen to her as she herself tried to make sense of the contradictions that defined her experience. During my year of fieldwork, I would come home often to find her reading the Bible in silence. At times, she would ask me to sit and listen as she read passages out loud. "Sometimes when I'm so angry at Ricardo that I cannot breathe," she said during one of these moments, "I read this part from the Bible. Listen, as I read it to you. Listen, so that you, too, will understand: 'Love is patient; love is kind . . . It bears all things, believes all things, hopes all things, endures all things . . . '" Margarita taught me a valuable lesson about marriage that afternoon, a lesson that I would reencounter later both as a sociologist and as a wife. Marriage is a contract underwritten by duty and bound by love. And although love in the time of neoliberalism may be difficult, even disappointing, it endures.

CHAPTER 5

....

Fragile Families
and Feminized Work

Opened in 1904 as the city's first secondary school and declared a national monument in 1977, the *Liceo de Heredia* is both a functioning school and an historic fixture. On a Tuesday evening in late October of 2001, the school is bursting at its seams, its hallways and classrooms cluttered with students and teachers. Having just shut its doors after the regular day schedule, the school has reopened for the evening session. Those who flock to night classes in Heredia include women who had dropped out of school years earlier to give birth and raise children, men whose poverty had pushed them out and into the world of work in their youth, and teenagers who were compelled to work full-time during the day. Their reasons for going to night school are as diverse as their histories. For some, it is to be a proper role model to their children. For others, it is to improve their chances of finding a job. Whatever the reason, their evening shift starts as the sun sets and the nighttime shadows fall upon Heredia's cracked city sidewalks.

I am ushered into the school on this particular evening past a sleepy doorman, who greets me with a relaxed smile. He directs me to the office of the school's director, who is off attending to a "problem student." In the office, I perch on a sticky vinyl blue sofa and wait in silence, my limp, wet umbrella dripping between my legs. The air is damp and musty, thick with the heat of student bodies coming in from the pouring rain. Anita, a plump middle-aged woman, sweeps into the office with a pronounced sigh. As the director of the night school, this is her busiest hour. Even so, she carves out five minutes for me, enough to describe the particular challenges facing night students and to approve my presence in the school. The working class and poor students in Anita's charge are her primary concern, and she turns to them immediately after accommodating me. "They come here straight from work," she explains as she hurries out and into the damp hallway. "They're exhausted."

A young man named Mario had once studied under Anita's worried and watchful eye. Like the students limping through the *Liceo*'s hallways that night, he had arrived nightly to work toward a much coveted secondary school degree. Like many night students, he had failed. With few educational credentials, he was left afloat in a competitive labor market where jobs were scarce and good jobs scarcer. In addition, he must compete in this labor market with a growing number of women, who outcompete him with their acceptance of lower wages and the promise of their more docile and disciplined ways. Although the women in this group alternate between caring for families and enabling Costa Rica's economic expansion, the men in this group alternate between being powerless at home and powerless at work. Together, they have elaborated their own responses to neoliberalism that reinforce and challenge the class and gender divides historically defining this country.

Mario's Story

Mario was born in 1980, on the eve of his country's debt default. In this sense, he was born and came of age under the shadow of the neoliberal project. Had he been born in an earlier era, he might have learned a trade to become a tailor, a shoemaker, or perhaps a butcher. But this was not to be his fate, having been born at a time when free trade and export-led development began squeezing out the small tradesman and craftsman. Instead, he found himself working in a most uncraftsman-like job: a pizza delivery man for the North American–based pizza chain Papa John's. Mario's father, a bus driver, and his mother, a domestic worker, expected their three sons to begin work early to contribute to household income. They expected Mario's two sisters to do most of the domestic work. The family of seven lived in a small house in a working-class neighborhood just off the highway between Heredia and Barva. Thus, Mario's work history began early, when he was 12.

Mario's first position was as a door-to-door salesman. In this position, he sold various products on credit to working-class households throughout Heredia. The pay was low and the position physically taxing. "I hated the collections aspect," remembered Mario. "Selling was no problem. It's when I had to return to collect payment. And there were the dogs. They barked; they tried to bite. I *hate* dogs." Mario was paid in cash and on a commission basis. He could not recall the name of the company—only the supervisor who supplied him products, forms, and instructions. By age 15, Mario could legally work. And his older brother helped him find and apply for a job at Papa John's. At the time, his brother held a job at the Burger King next door to the pizza chain. Together with a Kentucky Fried Chicken, a McDonald's, and a Taco Bell, the chains helped form a constellation of fast-food restaurants at the southeast corner of Heredia. In his new job at Papa John's, Mario delivered pizzas, using a small moped to zip through Heredia's crowded and narrow streets at evening time.

Before getting the job at Papa John's, Mario had managed to remain in school, attending the *Liceo* at night while he worked during the day. His transition to Papa John's, however, cut his secondary education short. "You don't deliver pizzas in the morning. You deliver them at night," Mario reasoned. His shift ran from 11 o'clock in the morning to 10 o'clock at night, making it impossible for him to attend day or evening classes. So after just two years in secondary school, Mario dropped out. He had put in enough time at the *Liceo*, however, to meet and begin dating Lucy. Like Mario's sisters, Lucy spent her days cleaning and cooking while her mother worked outside the home; her nights were devoted to studying at the *Liceo*. Described by Mario as a good student, Lucy was determined to get her secondary school education. She never quite made it. At age 18, she became pregnant with Mario's baby and dropped out of school herself. Mario did the "respectable" thing and married her, although he knew full well that a job as a pizza delivery man could not fully support himself, his wife, and child.

After some brainstorming, made urgent by the impending birth of his daughter, Mario and his cousin decided to go into business together. Their plan was to buy household items and resell them door-to-door in Heredia for a mark-up. Unlike his previous stint as a door-to-door salesman, Mario and his cousin sold the goods for cash, eliminating the miserable task of collections. Moreover, they would be working for themselves, splitting the profits fifty-fifty. For a time, they managed to do reasonably well. Mario left his position at Papa John's and threw himself into the business. But after just nine months, Mario's cousin disappeared with the profits, which he used to migrate to the United States to find work. "This was not a good time," sighed Mario. We were seated at a booth in Papa John's. Outside, night had descended and the windows mirrored back our tired reflections.

Outfitted in a shiny red Papa John's jacket and a mesh Papa John's baseball cap, Mario looked incredibly young. It was hard to imagine him with a wife and child at home. "What else do you want to know?" Mario asked with a tired smile. "Well, what happened? How did you end up back here?" I asked. "I came back on hands and knees!" he exclaimed. With no money and no job prospects, Mario returned to his manager at Papa John's and asked for his job back. The manager knew him well and welcomed him back as a delivery man. At the time of our interview, he had been working the 11 am to 10 pm shift again for just less than a year. Although Mario was able to secure work, a familiar problem had reappeared: money. He quite simply did not earn enough at Papa John's to support his wife and child, now age 2. Compounding the problem was the fact that Mario's wife was expecting a second child, due to arrive within months of our interview. Mario was seriously looking for another job, and of this he was quite open. "Look, Susie, if I found a better job, I would leave," Mario explained. "I appreciate that my manager gave me a job when I was in a bad situation, but I don't feel any loyalty or need to stay if I find something better." Ideally, Mario wanted to drive a delivery truck, which would pay better. In the meantime, he was putting pressure on his aunt, the mother of his former business partner, to pay up for her son's theft. "One thing I have learned," Mario cautioned, "is never to go into business with family."

Indeed, entrepreneurship would probably never resurface in Mario's work future, which would likely be characterized by low-wage jobs well into his late adulthood. Lacking the financial capital and middle-class networks that individuals such as Rosalina and Eduardo enjoyed, Mario was not well-positioned to become self-employed. Another option, one taken by the very cousin who allegedly robbed Mario of his share of business profits, was to migrate north to the United States or Canada in search of work. International migration, however, was expensive and risky. Given that the outmigration from Costa Rica is concentrated in particular communities and smaller in scale compared to other migrant-sending countries, the social networks that facilitate the flow of young *Heredianos* northward are less robust. Mario did not mention seeking employment in one of the free-trade zones sprinkled around Heredia's perimeter. This is perhaps unsurprising. Although many of the working class men I interviewed had worked in these zones, their employment stints were typically short. The pace of work was so intense and the pay so low that these jobs were undesirable, even to men such as Mario. Instead, these jobs went to Mario's female counterparts—women such as Lucy who might venture out into the world of work after children have been weaned in order to supplement the paltry wages of their husbands. Instead, Mario focused on the few remaining occupations in Costa Rica's urban labor markets that were semiskilled and male-dominated, occupations such as mechanics and transportation. Indeed, Mario's options and choices were as much about gender as they were about skills matching and income potential.

Historically, Costa Rica's working class has been constructed in masculine terms. Wage-earning men supported large families even on limited means, marking their transition into adulthood through marriage, childbearing, and some skilled or semiskilled craft. Today's working class is explicitly constructed in feminine terms, incorporating a larger pool of women workers and relegating working class men to low-wage, "women's work." Thus, economic restructuring, for Mario, is an experience of marked emasculation. At once stripped of his ability to financially provide for his family and forced to contend with the growing presence of women in the labor market, Mario finds little basis to construct a masculine sense of self. His wife is unlikely to fair much better. Were I to have followed them over a period of time, I would expect Lucy to have gone to work—probably in one of Heredia's manufacturing plants—sometime after their second child was born.[1] And I would not be surprised if she were a single working mother at this point, abandoned by Mario after his failure to live up to the expectation of being a family provider. Just contemplating their future exhausted me, and I concluded my interview with Mario deflated. With some abruptness, I left Papa John's and this world of fast food and flexible work behind.

Heredia's Changing Working Class

Studies of Latin America's contemporary working classes typically focus on low-wage female workers, who fast became the backbone of the region's industrial expansion after the 1970s. Certainly, this focus is warranted. For one, women are a relatively new segment of the industrial workforce. Although Latin American women have always helped generate income for the household, their participation has been concentrated in the informal sector of the economy. Public sector expansion throughout the 1960s and 1970s brought at least some of these women into the formal working class as "pink-collar" workers, as we saw in the case of Margarita. More recently, however, multinational investment and nontraditional export production have brought many more women into the fold of the blue-collar industrial class. Indeed, under neoliberal restructuring, women have been constructed as an ideal labor source in that their wages are comparatively low, they are seen as more obedient and disciplined, and they are the most easily hired and fired (Lee 1998; Ngai 2005; Salzinger 2003). As a result, the study of low-wage women workers has more or less defined the study of work in Latin America in recent years.

Given the literature's attention to women, I could have opened this chapter with the story of a young woman working in an export factory in Costa Rica. Were I to have done so, I would have fallen in step with a genre of research that has permitted these women to stand in for an entire working class. Instead, I headlined this chapter with the story of Mario because I want to suggest that his story is part of the larger puzzle that is gendered class restructuring in Costa Rica. As I mentioned in Chapter 1, the pronounced attention to low-wage women workers in Latin America has resulted in something of a disappearing act. Namely, it has rendered invisible the other workers who help populate Latin America's diverse working class, including men who must now compete with low-wage women workers in rapidly changing labor markets. Later in this chapter, I will highlight one woman who does work in an export-processing zone, but I want to emphasize that such work is one of many formal working-class jobs in countries such as Costa Rica. From delivering pizzas to driving taxis, from door-to-door sales to packaging fruit, from caring for children to ringing up groceries, the workers highlighted in this chapter constitute a diverse group of unskilled and semiskilled workers (see Table 5.1). What unites them is that they have managed to find formal work in the service or manufacturing sectors of the economy—but at a time in which formal labor markets are eroding.

Studies of work in Latin America typically distinguish between a formal and an informal working class. The reason turns out to be quite important. Informal work takes place outside the regulatory framework of the state, meaning that it offers no labor protections and few state benefits. Unsurprisingly, wages and working conditions in the informal sector are among the worst in Latin America (Portes 1994; Portes, Castells, and Benton 1989). I will delve into the lives of informal workers in the next chapter. Suffice it to say here, work in the informal sector is arguably less desirable because it is less secure, less protected, and lower paid. Thus, I am distinguishing the present group of workers by virtue of their privileged labor market position vis-à-vis informal workers.[2] Although the workers described in this chapter may have some past or present experience working in the informal sector, they have spent the better part of their working years in the formal sector.

TABLE 5.1 The Working Class

	YEAR OF BIRTH	PLACE OF BIRTH	CIVIL STATUS	NO. OF CHILDREN	LEVEL OF EDUCATION	OCCUPATION
Alejandro	1952	Colombia	Married	2	Secondary	Store owner (self-employed)
Alma	1957	Guanacaste	Single	0	University	Domestic worker (with benefits)
Alvaro	1967	San José	Divorced	2	Secondary	Woodworker (self-employed)
Andrea	1967	Heredia	Single	2	Some university	Receptionist
Bernardo	1970	Heredia	Single	0	Some secondary	Taxi driver (self-employed)
Carlos	1971	Heredia	Married	1	Some secondary	Transportation driver (government)
Carolina	1980	Heredia	Single	0	Some secondary	Student
David	1976	Heredia	Single	1	Secondary	Car salesperson (self-employed)
Emilio	1982	Heredia	Single	0	Some secondary	Fumigator assistant
Ernesto	1956	Puntarenas	Remarried	6	Some primary	Taxi driver (self-employed)
Gerardo	1965	Heredia	Married	3	Some secondary	Disabled
Iliana	1966	Nicaragua	Divorced	1	Some primary	Factory worker
Isabela	1983	Alajuela	Single	0	Some secondary	Student
Joaquin	1981	Heredia	Single	0	Some secondary	Factory worker
Jose Luis	1972	San José	Divorced	1	Some secondary	Sales representative

(*Continued*)

TABLE **5.1** *(Continued)*

	YEAR OF BIRTH	PLACE OF BIRTH	CIVIL STATUS	NO. OF CHILDREN	LEVEL OF EDUCATION	OCCUPATION
Karla	1973	Heredia	Married	1	Some secondary	Market vendor (self-employed)
Lourdes	1972	Heredia	Remarried	3	Some primary	Housewife
Luisa	1948	Heredia	Separated	4	Secondary	Cleaning person
Maria Jose	1986	San José	Single	1	Some primary	Student
Mariano	1965	Heredia	Divorced	0	Some secondary	Maintenance person
Mario	1980	Heredia	Married	1	Some secondary	Delivery person
Marta	1949	Heredia	Married	3	Secondary school	Housewife
Natalia	1981	Heredia	Single	0	Some secondary	Student
Pamela	1980	Limón	Single	0	Some secondary	Student
Paola	1953	Heredia	Remarried	4	Some secondary	Daycare assistant (government)
Rafael	1973	Alajuela	Divorced	0	Secondary	Internet café owner
Sandra	1973	Heredia	Single	1	Some primary	Factory worker
Susana	1973	Heredia	Married	2	Some primary	Housewife
Sylvia	1982	San José	Single	0	Some secondary	Factory worker
Vanessa	1979	Guanacaste	Single	1	Some primary	Factory worker
Vicente	1945	Heredia	Married	3	Secondary	Disabled
Vicky	1955	Heredia	Married	2	Some secondary	Hair stylist (self-employed)
Victor	1980	Guanacaste	Single	0	Some secondary	Store assistant

Note: Unless otherwise noted, all occupations listed are held in the private sector.

Portes and Hoffman (2003:53) distinguish between a nonmanual formal working class, comprised mainly of low-level white-collar workers, and a manual formal working class, comprised mainly of unskilled and semiskilled workers in industry, services, and agriculture. Those *Heredianos* who were the subject of the previous chapter would have been considered part of the nonmanual formal working class. Although workers such as Ricardo were essentially working class, their concentration in white-collar work, their employment in the public sector, and their civil service and technical training put them a step above manual, or blue-collar workers. The *Heredianos* that are the subject of this chapter are primarily blue-collar, although many are what some would call pink-collar, which refers to unskilled or semiskilled work in the service sector. Portes and Hoffman (2003) estimate that somewhere between 28 and 33 percent of the Costa Rican workforce in 2000 was in this manual formal working class.[3] In addition to these workers, I am including economically inactive students, disabled workers, and unemployed workers in this chapter. Although they were not economically active at the time of my interview with them, these workers were once a part of the formal working class before going to school, becoming disabled, or being laid off.[4]

In comparison to other Latin American countries, the formal sector is larger in Costa Rica, which has translated into a better standard of living for a larger portion of workers (Itzigsohn 2000; Portes and Hoffman 2003).[5] The growth of the country's formal economy was especially pronounced after 1948. Between 1950 and 1980, for example, formal employment as a percentage of the urban economically active population grew from 71 to 81 percent in Costa Rica (Itzigsohn 2000:69). The expansion of the formal sector, however, stalled with neoliberal restructuring. Thus, after reaching a high of 80 percent in 1980, the percentage of Costa Rica's urban economically active population employed in the formal sector declined to 50 percent by 1998 (Portes and Hoffman 2003:57, 69). Again, Clark (2001) argues that the formal sector largely rebounded as jobs were created in newer export industries and in the tourism sector. Indeed, of the thirty-five individuals featured in this chapter, seventeen had spent some time, past or present, as export factory workers. Another four were employed in the tourist industry at the time of my interview with them. But the nature of these new jobs and the profile of the workers flocking to them have changed quite dramatically. These are not the well-remunerated and unionized jobs associated with the public sector; these are jobs that are typically low-wage and highly sensitive to fluctuations in market demand. In addition, these are jobs that tend to be dominated by women. Four of the five *Heredianos*

The formal sector contracted in Costa Rica following the country's 1980s debt crisis. But it began to rebound as new jobs were created in the nontraditional export and tourism sectors. Almost 50 percent of the formal wage workers I interviewed had been employed at some time as an export factory worker. But as their job histories indicate, and as research suggests, these jobs tend to be low paid and very unstable. These are also jobs that tend to be dominated by young women. Featured here is the entrance of one of Heredia's free-trade zones in 2002.

working in a factory at the time of my interview with them were women. In addition, of the twelve workers who had worked in a factory in the past, six had worked there for less than two years before being laid off or forced to quit due to pregnancy. To many scholars, these trends signal a feminization of labor markets in Costa Rica that hurt women and men alike (Hite and Viterna 2005; Standing 1999).

The contraction and feminization of formal labor markets in Costa Rica has meant fierce competition for low-wage jobs. To sift through the competition, employers often screen out workers with less than a secondary school education, a screening device that is highly problematic for workers who have dropped out of school due to family poverty or adolescent childbearing. Among the only possibilities for educational advancement for these workers are night schools. Sixteen of the thirty-five *Heredianos* featured in this chapter were attending night school, and another two planned on enrolling in night school. But evidence in 2002 suggested that a full four in ten night students dropped out due to the demanding schedules of work, school, and family (Cantero 2002). Perhaps for these reasons, a recent report indicated that the country was producing far fewer skilled workers than needed to support a high-tech economy (Programa Estado de la Nación 2013a).

At a time of contracting job opportunities and deteriorating job conditions, Heredia's working class was looking at other ways to secure a livelihood. Like the workers featured in the previous chapters, small businesses were a popular option for at least some of these *Heredianos*. Because they lacked the professional skills that would allow them to become independent contractors, the inheritances of established businesses that would allow them some economic stability, or the government severance monies that would allow them to create small business establishments, they had to make do with more informal business ventures. Vicky cut hair out of her living room; David and Alvaro bought and sold cars on a quiet city corner; and Alvaro crafted leather products out of his workshop from home. Only Rafael, who we met in Chapter 1, and Karla, who ran a small photography studio in the municipal market, ran formal business establishments. But neither Rafael nor Karla employed staff and, like the other four, both had spent most of their careers working as low-wage factory and service workers. In addition to these individuals, five workers in this chapter maintained informal sideline businesses to earn extra income. Carlos and José Luis, for example, worked on the side as *piratas*, or unlicensed taxi drivers.

Another livelihood strategy that was either pursued or imagined by this group was migrating and working abroad in either the United States or Canada. Costa Rican migration to the United States was and is not as robust as other Latin American migration streams. Indeed, the country receives more migrants than it sends.[6] But for those able to secure a visa, traveling and working in the United States can provide a lucrative source of income to send back to or reinvest in Costa Rica. According to the 2000 census, 87,000 Costa Ricans were living abroad, most of them (around 75 percent) in the United States (Organisation for Economic Co-operation and Development [OECD] 2009).[7] This amounts to a little more than 2 percent of the population. This figure, however, includes only documented immigrants. According to estimates that include the undocumented population, as many as 220,000 Costa Ricans, almost 6 percent of the population, were living in the United States in 2005 (Feigenblatt 2005).[8] Many of these emigrants are people such as Violeta, who use their middle-class status to secure tourist visas and connections in the United States.[9] But many more of these emigrants are people such as Rafael and David, who travel to the United States to live and work as undocumented laborers. Like Rafael,

David had family connections in the United States, which he used to secure a visa and, then, work without papers in the construction industry.

Apart from these microenterprises and livelihood strategies, the bulk of the *Heredianos* in this chapter earned their living solely from the jobs they were able to secure in the formal labor market. Although privileged in comparison to the informal workers described in the next chapter, these workers were hardly secure and certainly not well-off. Especially for the women in this group, but also for the men, unplanned pregnancies or declines in market demand could signal job loss and the loss of a major household income earner. Moreover, the influx of women into the labor market had the effect of destabilizing the balance of power in many working-class households. Although the women in this group had a newfound source of income and arguably a growing basis for independence, there was a growing sense of crisis surrounding manhood that was deeply connected to the feminization of work under neoliberalism. As the next section shows, it was in the home that frustration over a restructured economy was vented and couched in terms of what made a "real" man and a "good" wife.

The Ties That Break and Bind

Within a short walk of my home in Pueblo Tico sat a working-class *barrio* that skirted the northern edge of Heredia Central. Here, early evenings carried a mixture of exhaustion and exhaust as rusting commuter buses dropped off bleary-eyed workers amid suffocating clouds of smoke. As the sun slowly set, workers summoned their last bit of energy to make their way home, the smell of warming tortillas beckoning them. Taxis swerved in and out of traffic, honking feverishly and impatiently. And the mountains, once cut in sharp relief, disappeared in a layer of smog. Not everyone in this busy working-class neighborhood made their way home immediately after work. Many took a moment to buy groceries, socialize with neighbors, or run errands that they could not otherwise do during the day. For this reason, 5 o'clock was always the busiest hour at Vicky's hair salon, which sat at the heart of the neighborhood.

Vicky ran the salon out of the living room of her home, and she was well known in the neighborhood for her skilled haircuts and reasonable prices. Often, Vicky's clients knew one another. More often, they did not. But this did not stop them from sharing polite opinions about national politics and global events. On the evening of September 12, 2001, talk turned quickly to the terrorist attacks that had occurred in the United States the day before. And I became a celebrity of sorts, the token *gringa* to whom questions were thrown about the Twin Towers and US foreign policy. "Tell us, *muchacha* (young woman)," a middle-aged man in jeans asked me, "what does this terrorist attack say about the world?" "What do you think?" I responded. "Well, *muchacha*, I like to blame everything on globalization," he replied laughing. "Where you have people with resources and people without, you have conflict. Now, *muchacha*, I ask you this: what is globalization?" All heads in the room turned to look at me. I remained silent, and the man paused for dramatic effect. "Economic colonialism," he declared. For the first time that evening, the room was quiet.

Clearly, these *Heredianos* understood inequality in the world system. In Central America, their country was a shining star. But pan out to the Americas as a whole, and their economic vulnerability and dependency became all too clear. In this larger picture, the United States was seen as a partner in modernity—but also a behemoth that bullied its less powerful neighbors and abused its economic power. Relatedly, Costa Rica was seen as an underdog that struggled to find a foothold in a global economy over which it had little control. The weeks following 9/11 brought these issues into sharp focus. As international travel all but halted, $140,000 worth of fresh-produce exports rotted at Juan Santamaría International Airport (Barquero and Delgado 2001). And despite a post-9/11 emergency tourism plan, which marketed Costa Rica as a safe haven in a violent world, 19 percent of the country's hotel labor force was laid off (Boddiger 2001; Leiton 2001; Pratt 2001). Of course, 9/11 alone was not to blame for the dismal economic picture. Poor economic performance in the United States had already translated into decreased demand for Costa Rica's exports, forcing six export-manufacturing plants to close in the first few months of 2001 alone (Murillo 2001). Mere hiccups in the US economy sent shock waves through countries such as Costa Rica, which pegged its economic prospects on exports. And major economic shocks, such as the global recession of 2008, threatened to bring the country's economy to a standstill. Within one year of the recession, urban unemployment jumped from 5 to 8 percent (Economic Commission for Latin America and the Caribbean [ECLAC] 2010).[10] The manufacturing and tourist sectors were particularly hard hit.

For workers such as Vanessa, a working-class *Herediana* who lived not far from Vicky's salon, the vulnerability of Costa Rica's economy to external shocks was not a matter of intellectual interest or polite debate. It was a matter of household survival. A young woman from Costa Rica's northwestern province of Guanacaste, Vanessa helped to support a 4-year-old son and an extended family as a *maquiladora* (export factory) worker in 2002. Her family migrated to Heredia after her father abandoned the family. They settled in Heredia, where Vanessa's mother found work as a restaurant cook and Vanessa's older sister secured a job stitching together leather purses for Coach. Age 12 at the time, Vanessa dropped out of school to care for her two younger brothers. Within two years, she would also take a factory job, cleaning and packaging fish for export. After three years at the factory, Vanessa became pregnant by a worker in the same industrial park where she worked. As her pregnancy progressed, she was forced to leave her job.[11] As it was, Vanessa would have been laid off anyway. The factory closed down just three months after she left.

Vanessa's relationship with the father of her child would prove shorter-lived than her factory job. He disappeared from Vanessa's life when their son was just 6 months old. With her sister's help, Vanessa got a job at the Coach factory, where she had been working for three years when I interviewed her in 2002. Along with her sister and brother, Vanessa provided financially for her natal family while her mother cared for Vanessa's baby and her sister's two children. This multigenerational arrangement was typical of many *Heredianos* in this group, who lacked the financial means and/or a stable partner to establish a household of their own.[12] Also typical was her strategy of returning to night school to finish her primary school education. What was less typical of the women in this group was Vanessa's desire to migrate to the United States to work, a desire that was expressed primarily by working-class men. Perhaps it was her migrant status and her employment in a *maquiladora* that made her less traditional in this sense (see Sassen 1998 for a longer version of this argument). In the end, Vanessa's priority was providing for her son and finding some semblance of stability. To these ends, she placed little faith in marriage. Having already been abandoned by two men in her life, she looked instead to migration, manufacturing work, and income pooling to ensure a livelihood and what little social mobility was available to her.

The province of Guanacaste, from which Vanessa migrated, is popularly known for its indigenous past and rural poverty. As such, it has been defined by high rates of outmigration over the past two decades, with a number of darker-skinned migrants from the area moving into cities such as Heredia in search of work. These migrants are joined by migrants from two other culturally distinct coastal provinces: Puntarenas and Limón. In 2000, more than 33,000 migrants from these three provinces were living in Heredia, representing more than 10 percent of the total *Herediano* population.[13] Another 24 percent of Heredia's population that year traced its roots to the remaining Central Valley provinces of Alajuela, Cartago, and San José. But in contrast to migrants from other parts of the Central Valley, coastal migrants were seen as racially and culturally distinct from native *Heredianos.* Whether they were English-speaking migrants from Limón, who descended from Afro-Caribbean migrants, or racially mixed migrants from Guanacaste and Puntarenas, who descended from indigenous groups and/or African slaves, coastal migrants were defined by distinct sociocultural traditions and a racial status below that of the *mestizo* population of the Central Valley. Such migrants also came from regions characterized by higher rates of poverty and female household headship (Chant 2000, 2002). Given their migrant status, Vanessa and her counterparts seemed to view Heredia as a temporary home. On holidays, they boarded buses to make their way back to the coastal lowlands to visit extended families. It was here, in the lowlands, where they dreamt of buying land and building houses. But the underemployment that has defined these coastal regions made it unlikely that these migrants would ever return on a permanent basis. Thus, this group of internal migrants became accidental *Heredianos* who shared their fate and day-to-day life with the city's native population.

Although many *Heredianos* in this group dreamed of migrating to the United States—and a few succeeded—their Heredia was hardly cosmopolitan. Their stints abroad were not viewed as a kind of status that afforded them membership in a jet-setting professional class. Rather, their time abroad was viewed as a means to save money for small-business development or the purchase of land and home. Neither was this group defined by dense and supportive neighborhood networks that afforded them a sense of rootedness and secure livelihood. Although this group typically knew their neighbors and, in some cases, relied on them, it appeared that their neighborhood relationships were less close knit. At the very least, they were less well established because more than half of the individuals in this group had lived in their current neighborhood for five years or less. Perhaps for these reasons, it appeared that many *Heredianos* in this group turned inward, relying on kith and kin to find work and make do. Certainly, families were crucial to the upward mobility of the groups described in the previous two chapters. But these groups also had other social resources to draw upon—professional networks, workplace connections, and neighborhood ties. For the *Heredianos* in this chapter, there were no stable occupational identities to provide a basis for occupational networks, no lengthy job tenure to provide for workplace connections, and no lifelong neighbors to strengthen neighborhood ties. Instead, there was the natal family, which provided the only real thread of continuity and stability for a group that did not have the luxury to stay for long in any one school, job, or house.

Many of the families formed by the individuals in this chapter proved incredibly unstable, in part due to the instability of their work lives. Men especially have experienced declining wages and increased job competition as jobs in Costa Rica have become feminized. As a result of this and women's increased financial independence, many romantic relationships and marriages fall apart for this group. An increasing number of women, such as the one shown here, are heading households of their own or are becoming part of multigenerational households with their natal family.

To be clear, it was not the nuclear, conjugal family—that badge of lower middle-class status—on which this group of *Heredianos* relied. Indeed, the conjugal family proved as unstable as the low-wage jobs that defined this group. It was the extended family, formed by birth rather than marriage, which bolstered the livelihood strategies of this group. Family members provided valuable connections for migration to the United States, they offered space in houses to sleep and share resources,[14] and they pooled income and investments to survive the low-wages and occasional layoffs associated with industrial and service work. Of course, as the situation between Mario and his cousin–cum–business partner suggests, even family ties could sour. But this did not change the fact that, for this group, extended-family networks were crucial. It could be that this group relied on extended family because their ties to romantic partners and neighbors were so tenuous.

In a context in which labor markets and workplaces are becoming feminized (i.e., dominated by women and degraded in working condi-tion), the ties that once bound together neighborhoods and nuclear households are arguably less robust. This was not a feature of Heredia's early working-class *barrios* (neighborhoods), which developed around a masculinized working-class culture centered on the skilled craft shop and neighborhood soccer field. The historic Barrio Los Angeles, which sits just to the south of Heredia's city center, is typical in this regard. At the turn of the twentieth century, when land from an old coffee farm was sold to the town municipality, a soccer field appeared around which the *barrio* first began to emerge (Elizondo 1997:241–2). In the 1930s, a Catholic church was established on the southern side of the plaza, and the *barrio* took its name after the church (Martínez and Ducca 2001:34). The church remains there today, a towering structure painted mint green in 2002.[15] As households moved outward from the city center to make way for urban development, the *barrio* lost much of its original character and certainly its dense neighborhood networks. The soccer plaza is now just a public plaza around which buses destined for export-processing factories wait impatiently. And grocery and clothing stores compete for space with rental houses long vacated by owners. In 2001, one of these houses was the temporary residence of José Luis, a 29-year old auto parts salesman.

José Luis' 29 years had taken him on a circuitous route to Barrio Los Angeles. He was originally from San José, where he began work at age 13 in his father's butcher shop. Halfway through secondary school, José Luis dropped out to work at a textile factory in an industrial park in San José. These actions should be put in their proper context. Recall from Chapter 4 that those *Heredianos* in the lower middle class were mostly of an older age cohort who had come of age before the debt crisis of the 1980s. Not so for José Luis, who entered secondary school in the 1980s when unemployment and inflation were rampant. His was a generation lost to the crisis. Lacking much incentive to stay in school, because good jobs in the public sector were disappearing, and in need of income to help his family, José Luis left school and found whatever job he could, in this case loading cloth onto the assembly line for the female assembly workers. The job was boring, and the pay was low. So when José Luis started his own family, he took a job at an auto parts store, driving a taxi at night to bring in a second income.

Upon taking the job at the auto parts store, he moved them all to Heredia where he thought life would be safer and where his wife could find work at a nearby *zona franca* (free-trade zone). But if Heredia featured less crime, it did not ease the tensions brewing between José Luis and his wife, who successfully secured a job in an export-processing plant. No more than a year after moving to Heredia, José Luis returned home from work to find his belongings thrown out of their apartment window onto the street below. José Luis did not go into detail about why his wife kicked him out, mentioning only personality conflicts and financial problems. Whatever the case, José Luis was ashamed to return to his parents' house, because he was "now a man that should be able to take care of [him]self." So he moved in with a friend in Barrio Los Angeles.[16] Still trying to rebuild his life, he was looking for an apartment of his own and hoping to register for night classes so that he might finally complete secondary school.

For men such as José Luis, finding stable, decently paid employment was a critical fulfilment of their masculine sense of self. But the downsizing associated with older economic sectors and the feminized nature of jobs in manufacturing and service left little basis for household headship, and hence, masculinity. In addition, José Luis came of age right in the middle of this economic transition, which meant he suffered the labor market consequences of dropping out of secondary school long into adulthood. His circumstances were not unusual. In his analysis of Costa Rica's restructured economy, Arias (2001) found that young, less educated men suffered the most in the 1980s and 1990s. Although overall unemployment remained comparatively low in Costa Rica during these two decades, the unemployment rate for men ages 15 to 25 increased from 9 percent in 1980 to 12 percent in 1995 (Arias 2001:12). They also experienced unemployment for increasingly greater lengths of time (Arias 2001:23). More recent data indicates that these trends have continued and even worsened. In 2011, for example, the unemployment rate for men aged 15 to 24 stood at 13.5 percent.[17] For men such as José Luis, a basic education provided some access to work. But such jobs offered little in the way of financial stability or upward mobility. This, combined with women's growing labor force participation, meant that men in this group found their traditional source of household authority eroding. Indeed, the act of throwing José Luis out of the apartment sent a not-so-subtle message that his wife no longer needed him financially, no longer saw him as the head of her household, and no longer considered herself under his control.

Carlos' Mistake

As the story of José Luis suggests, nuclear family life was indescribably fragile for this group of workers. In stripping working-class men of the ability to fulfill their role as breadwinners and in burdening working-class women with the responsibility of paid and unpaid work, the feminization of labor had the effect of destabilizing gender norms and expectations in working-class households. On the whole, this group remained fairly committed to traditional gender scripts, especially as they related to marriage and child-bearing. Where this group stumbled was in enacting these scripts. This situation was not altogether different than that of the lower middle-class men and women described in the previous chapter, whose traditional division of labor was tested by men's declining wages and women's income-generating activities. But lower middle-class men had more stable employment and their wives had the option to earn money while remaining in the home, both of which gave these partnerships at least the appearance of a traditional division of labor. Not so for Heredia's lower working class, for whom unstable wage work was a necessity for both men and women. This situation arguably had more destabilizing effects on working class marriages.

Increasingly unable to attain critical markers of manhood, including the ability to secure stable employment, and increasingly resentful of women's growing financial independence, men in this group were bewildered and disgruntled by the changes wrought by economic restructuring (see also Chant 2000, 2002). In response, some men raged against their partner's newfound economic power through verbal or physical reprisal. Others left their wives and children through abandonment or separation, typically retreating back to their natal families. The nuclear family, in this context, became not a foundation for adult life, but a real or potential failure. For women, the ramifications of all this were mixed. On the one hand, restructuring increased their responsibilities; they became de facto breadwinners and, in many cases, sole caregivers. On the other hand, restructuring gave them access to an independent income; they became financially capable of leaving unequal, loveless, and often abusive marriages. To some extent, then, working-class women enjoyed some opportunities as a result of the global feminization of labor, although this was often hard to detect beneath the workplace and household drudgery that defined their everyday life. But whether men or women were outraged or outspent by economic change, the result was the same: a growing number of children born out-of-wedlock, a considerable rise in female-headed households, and a steady retreat of men and women back into the fold of their natal families. The family life of Carlos and Monica provides one portrait of these trends.

A trim man with curly hair and a wide, seductive grin, Carlos was well known in his extended family as an able mechanic and an overprotective brother. At age 15, his father became permanently disabled after a workplace accident left him without the use of his legs, forcing Carlos to drop out of school and take a job at a shoe store to help support his mother and four siblings. As he did so, he continued to date his high school sweetheart, Monica, who managed to finish secondary school and get a secretarial job through the government. At age 19, Carlos completed a course in mechanics at the National Learning Institute (*Nacional de Aprendizaje* [INA]), which he used to obtain a more skilled position at a factory in Heredia. In both respects, Monica and Carlos were lucky to have secured a modicum of human capital and relatively stable work. So it was perhaps no surprise that when Monica found herself pregnant at age 24, both Monica and Carlos welcomed the surprise and planned a hasty wedding. Having already helped to support a mother and four siblings, Carlos was confident in his ability to provide for a family. He had the added benefit of inheriting a small plot of land from a deceased and childless aunt that was just around the corner from his parents' house.

This, then, is the story of how Carlos and Monica's household began—how the small house a stone's throw from his parents' house came to be built, how Carlos and Monica became husband and wife, and how Carlito was born. It is a story that was typical of many native-born, working-class *Heredianos*. It was often the case that weddings followed accidental pregnancies, because it was expected that able-bodied men would take responsibility for the woman and child. Like Mario, Carlos never questioned marrying Monica. It is what any respectable man in his position would do. Likewise, it was never a question that he would become the household breadwinner, leaving Monica to devote her time and energy to raising Carlito. But as it turns out, this household arrangement never quite came to pass. After taking off a couple months to give birth and tend to her newborn, Monica returned to work. Her government position was a coveted one in a time of public sector downsizing. And it was hard to imagine a stable financial future in which Carlos, a secondary school dropout, provided the only family income. Upon her return to work, Monica promptly placed Carlito in the care of Carlos' mother around the block.

For his part, Carlos tried his best to fulfill his role as household head and breadwinner. Almost immediately after marrying, he began looking for a job outside the factory with health and retirement benefits. He, too, managed to find a government job driving a commuter van for public sector workers. Although the benefits were better, the public sector wages in the late 1990s lagged far behind inflation and the expenses of a new household. Thus, Carlos also began working nights as an unlicensed taxi driver, again, known in Costa Rica as a *pirata*.[18] Using his skills as a mechanic, he bought an inexpensive car on which he worked, giving him the means, if not the license, to prowl the streets at night offering rides for a fee. He had even produced business cards, which he handed out in clandestine fashion to those who might use his services discreetly.[19] Carlos' *pirata* work was not just a way to earn extra money; it was arguably an attempt to save face and maintain some modicum of power in his dual income-earning household. With both Carlos and Monica working, the domestic work in the household piled up. In hushed tones one afternoon, Carlos' mother revealed, "Monica doesn't even bother to cook for him, Susie." Monica was, according to Carlos' family, a pretty woman but a lazy wife. In response, Carlos had begun bringing his dirty laundry to his mother's house for her to do, and she in turn had begun letting herself into Carlos and Monica's house to clean during the day while they were both at work. Monica's commute to San José was a substantial one. She left around 6:30 in the morning and did not get home until around 6:30 in the evening. That the laundry should go undone and the dirty dishes should pile up in the sink was not a surprise. But to Carlos' family, Monica's obligations as a mother and wife were paramount. Although at this early stage of a family's formation, grandmothers often offered to *help out*, they did not expect to *take over* a wife's role in the home. Periodic unemployment and downward pressure on wages had pushed many households into a dual-income earning structure. But it was working women, not working men, who officially transgressed the existing household arrangements by going out to work and "neglecting" their families. Indeed, although their incomes were critical for household survival and their earnings provided resources for children, working women had become the target of much social anxiety in Costa Rica. Newspaper articles discussed what did and did not constitute *una mala madre* (a bad mother) (Arroyo 2001; Cantero 2001b), a telling sign that women were often seen as to blame for the "breakdown" of the family.

What is clear in the case of Monica and Carlos' family is that old and new pressures came to bear on working families in Costa Rica's Central Valley. Such families had to cope with the expenses and management of new households and young children, just as their parents had a generation before. But in an era of declining incomes, mounting inflation, and dwindling public assistance, such pressures were all the more intense. It is within this tension—between social expectations and economic realities—that working-class men and women struggled for family livelihood. Natal families helped ease this tension (e.g., providing child care), but they also exacerbated it (e.g., expressing disapproval). It was not unthinkable that these tensions might lead to divorce in the case of Monica and Carlos. Indeed, of the 17 *Heredianos* in this group who had married, six had already divorced by the time of our interview. And between my first visit to Costa Rica in 1994 and my last revisit in 2014, the country's crude divorce rate had risen from 1.5 to 2.5, not a small figure for a conservatively Catholic country.[20]

It may be that younger age cohorts of Heredia's working class will simply avoid marriage altogether, as the rising rates of cohabitation suggest (Esteve, Lesthaeghe, and López-Gay 2012). Larger demographic studies suggest that economic conditions alone do not explain these trends, but they do contribute to them (e.g., Esteve, Lesthaeghe, and López-Gay 2012).

Downward Mobility in the New Economy

Rarely does one think "working class" when one thinks of Costa Rica. The popular imagination, instead, turns to farmers and reformers, who have dominated scholarly and literary narratives about this country. Similarly, artistic renditions of Costa Rican life from the first half of the twentieth century depicted the country as a quaint rural paradise. In 1937, Costa Rican artist Claudia María Jiménez painted the country in altogether different terms. Her oil on canvas *Alleyway of Open Wounds* features an urban alleyway stretching beneath the shadow of a row of humble houses. The shadows and the title hint at a society much more urban and much less prosperous. Jiménez was part of a generation of artists and activists that came to articulate deep class antagonisms in Costa Rica. Before José Figueres' army of "national liberation" would overtake the country and institutionalize the Second Republic, political activist Carmen Lyra would translate the *Communist Manifesto* into Spanish (1920), Manuel Mora would found the Communist Party (1931), and Carlos Fallas would lead a successful strike against the United Fruit Company (1934). In short, a radical labor movement would call into question Costa Rica's ethos of agrarian egalitarianism (Molina and Palmer 2000).

Today, memories of this labor movement lay buried far beneath the rhetoric of Costa Rican exceptionalism and the virulent anticommunism that followed the 1948 civil war. Indeed, few Costa Ricans talk of the civil war, and even fewer discuss the time in which communists and reformers banded together to question whether the country's workers were enjoying the fruits of Costa Rica's early twentieth-century prosperity. It is not simply that these more radical impulses were repressed, even crushed, in the aftermath of the 1948 war, although this did happen. It is also that a reformist state emerged in the second half of the twentieth century that did a fairly good job of extending the benefits of economic growth to the country's workers. Through a grand expansion of primary education and formal work, a larger portion of the country's population came to enjoy economic prosperity, neutralizing and containing any radical impulses that remained.[21] Since the 1980s, however, economic reforms have altered this trend. Jobs in the formal sector have stagnated, been degraded, and/or gone to women and migrants. In a word, they have been feminized. Echoing early twentieth-century trends, Costa Rican workers are enjoying a far smaller share of the benefits of economic expansion. But this time, there is no labor movement to question these inequities and no Figueres poised to accommodate workers' demands. There are only "alleyways of open wounds."

These open wounds are fundamentally gendered. The feminization of labor has burdened women workers with a double shift and the responsibility for family survival, and it has stripped men of stable work and the ability to support a family. On a more intimate level, it has framed women as "bad mothers" and men as "useless husbands." Unlike Margarita, Ricardo, and the group of *Heredianos* they represent, the women and men in this group were rejecting the terms of their marital contract—and often the institution of marriage itself—as they came to terms with their new positions in the economy. This is not to say that this group had no faith in marriage and no appreciation for traditional markers of femininity and masculinity. As the stories in this chapter suggest, the women and men in this group tried their best to live up to existing gender norms. But the wholesale upending of the traditional division of labor left this group largely incapable of succeeding in this regard.

Why do we not see a renegotiation of the household division of labor for this group? Indeed, why did these *Heredianos* cling to established markers of womanhood (e.g., motherhood) and manhood (e.g., breadwinning)? It may be that women such as Vanessa continued to identify with motherhood and marriage precisely because their work life offered so little. Although it afforded them some power and income, it did not afford them any real status or possibility for upward mobility. These women might not even have ventured into the world of work had poverty and necessity not pushed them out the front door. Thus, these women expected, or at least hoped, that marriage and childbearing would solidify their status as respectable, adult women. As for the men, it may be that they embraced more established masculine ideals precisely because they were emasculated at work. Thrown into changing labor markets where they had to compete with women for low-wage jobs, rooted in households wherein women used their growing financial independence to contest patriarchal power, and faced daily with the possibility that they could not provide for their family on low wages, these men clung to an increasingly outdated masculine script that offered some degree of masculine privilege and status. In a sense, they struggled to be "manly" at a moment in which neo-liberalism rendered them "womanly."

Although the women and men in Heredia's working class remained faithful to existing gender scripts by forming families, establishing households, and, in some cases, marrying partners, their gender transgressions destabilized the families that they tried so hard to nurture. Women became formal workers, men became failed breadwinners, and families became fragile entities. Indeed, economic change rendered the nuclear household almost unviable for this group of *Heredianos*, who, after divorce or separation, retreated back to their natal family. It was here, in the natal household, where men tended to bruised masculine identities. Even for individuals such as Carlos, whose marriage and household, for a time, remained intact, natal families crept in quietly through back doors to help maintain the façade of a "proper" household. In this respect, Carlos' perspective was a torn one. On one level, he allowed his mother to clean his home and do his laundry. On another level, he argued bitterly with her over his wife's failure to meet her domestic obligations. He was embarrassed by Monica's inattention to their home, because it suggested that he could not control her and make her into a proper wife.

What was at stake in Carlos' case was not simply the stability of his household but his identity as a man and Monica's reputation as a woman. The breakdown of their family wounded Carlos' sense of self respect. How it affected Monica was more difficult to tell, because I never gained her confidence. But certainly among the working class women that I interviewed, family disintegration was more of a mixed bag. Vanessa, for example, was proud to earn her own income and thankful that a job provided her the means to support her child. But her independent wages also brought into sharp focus the ways in which men could not and were not providing for her and her family. As it was, Vanessa was neither alone nor destitute. She had her child, her siblings, and her mother. And with this, she crafted a multigenerational household that might withstand the wounds that economic restructuring and male abandonment inflicted. This and other households helped constitute an Heredia that was not so much rooted in place or in gender conventions, but in blood relations—the deep ties that bind. Turning inward to withstand personal and economic dislocation, this was a group of survivors.

The women in this group always impressed me. They were headstrong, deliberate, and savvy. They had weathered betrayal and layoffs, abandonment and harassment, as well as ill repute and humiliation. The men struck an altogether different cord in me. They were bewildered, exasperated, and ashamed. They struggled to find a foothold in the economy and in the household but never seemed to find their place in either. On a Sunday afternoon in early September of 2001, I sat opposite Carlos on a dusty patio overlooking Heredia and discussed his future. Among his goals were to finish secondary school and to migrate to the United States for work. But when I asked about his marriage, he paused to stare off into the distance. His eyes were bloodshot, the smell of marijuana clinging to his clothes. Finally, he looked at me, smiled blandly, and with resignation said, "Some things we can't change in life. They just happen and we have to accept them." "Do you want more children?" I asked, trying to think of something over which he did have some degree of control. Carlos shook his head decidedly. "I love Carlito and I love being a father. But I do not want more children," he answered. Two weeks later, Monica announced that she was pregnant.

How did the following decade play out for Carlos and Monica? True to my prediction, they separated, although their separation was a peculiar one. Indeed, their case was the one that surprised me most. Days into my 2014 trip, Carlos stopped by to see me, having heard I was in town. I had already learned that his father had passed away a month before my arrival, and I offered my condolences alongside a few select memories of his father, whom I had known for as long as I had known Carlos. "How long has it been, Susie, since we first met?" Carlos asked pensively. "Twenty years. Can you believe it?" I smiled. "The years have been good to you," he remarked kindly. "As they have to you," I replied. And they had. Although years of smoking had etched more than a few wrinkles across his face, it was as if not a day had passed since Carlos, then in his early twenties, had taken me to buy freshly baked bread in the early morning hours after a night of partying. "My life has changed a lot since I last saw you," he continued. "I got very serious after Paula was born. I started thinking, 'I drive a van. How is this going to look to my children when they get older and realize what I do?' So I finally finished secondary school. And I then I kept on going and I got my law degree," he said with pride.

Now working for Costa Rica's *Ministerio de Justicia y Paz*, Carlos had catapulted himself from the working to the middle class after nights of hard work and a heavy dose of maturity. As for his relationship with Monica, it never quite turned around. Five years after their daughter Paula was born, they separated and Carlos moved back in with his parents. Monica and the children remained in the same house, and the children moved back and forth between houses with ease so that Monica, Carlos, and Carlos' mother could care for them together. Monica and Carlos would occasionally date other people, but they would also periodically reunite. Given the episodic rekindling of their relationship, they never divorced. It was an arrangement that neighbors and even Carlos described as *"raro"* (strange). But Carlos insisted that it suited them well.

CHAPTER 6

Shadow Workers
and Social Exclusion

Heredia's municipal market takes up an entire block in the southern half of the city. It is positioned slightly below ground, with stairs on each side leading down into a chaotic grid of market stalls. Inside the market, the lighting is dim and the smell of raw meat overpowering. Emaciated dogs race between *carnicerías* (butcher shops) and *sodas* (lunch counters) hoping to catch fallen scraps on the dirty tile floor. Mothers, children, and workers walk quickly throughout the long corridors, while vendors lean casually against cluttered counter tops. Here, in these stained market walls, there is something for everybody: fruit stands, fabric stores, pastry shops, jewelry booths, and lunch counters. In addition to this potpourri of goods, the market offers respite from the blinding glare of the sun and the thick summer heat of the Central Valley. It is a world cut off from sunlight and traffic, a space where darkness and pedestrian prevail. Gripping a worn piece of notebook paper with directions scribbled in blue ink, I tiptoe into the bowels of the market in search of Fernando's *soda* on a hot summer day in 2002.

When I arrive, Fernando's large frame is perched on a stool at the lunch counter. He is in conversation with a vendor of large metal cooking pots. From behind glasses, Fernando studies three large pots that the vendor has laid out on the market floor in front of him. The vendor squats by his wares, looking up at Fernando with anxious coal-black eyes.

Fernando wants to see more pots. The vendor disappears for some sixty seconds, walking back quickly with three large mixing bowls. The muscles of his arms bulge and he leans back under the weight of the bowls. When he lays them down in front of Fernando, they fall with a thud. Fernando remains relaxed, leaning back against the wall with his chin resting on his hand. Calmly, he inquires about the price. The vendor replies, Fernando counters, and the vendor offers a price somewhere in the middle. Fernando nods his head slowly, eying the bowls carefully. Turning to one of his employees, he says: "Esperanza, come over here. See if you can lift this pot." Esperanza, tall and big-boned, immediately wipes her hands on her apron and makes her way from behind the counter. "It's heavy," Fernando warns. She grabs the mixing bowl, lifts it easily and high into the air. With a smile, she declares: "No problem."

Licensed as businesses but heavily dependent on the un(der)paid labor of wives, children, and workers, *sodas* are places where the informal sector bleeds into the formal. In technical terms, these are "very small establishments," which are small formal businesses that otherwise use informal labor practices (Castells and Portes 1989). Informal workers are paid off the books and often far below the minimum wage. Like the work at *sodas*, almost all of the economic activities in and around Heredia's municipal market are defined by degrees of informality. The lottery vendors who line the perimeter of the market, the itinerant traders who sell market goods door-to-door, the casual laborers who eat lunch in the market, and the informal workers that serve them—all of these workers are embedded in a vibrant informal economy that undergirds the city's economy. Heredia's informal class is no artifact of an older economy. This class is integral to neoliberalism because it captures the growing number of workers expelled from the formal economy and enables businesses to remain competitive in the market. Peel back the outer layer of neoliberalism and there are Esperanza and her counterparts, eking out an existence while ensuring neoliberalism's survival.

Esperanza's Story

Esperanza was born into a poor family in 1956 in Matagalpa, Nicaragua. One of seven children, she received just a few years of primary education before dropping out to become a domestic worker. By the time she was 17, Esperanza's mother had already died, her father had long disappeared, and Esperanza herself had been working as a servant for ten years. Aside from mentioning that they were both from Matagalpa, Esperanza said little about her parents. She had no idea what took her mother's life at the age of 49. And she had few ideas as to what her father did after disappearing, although he did send money to Esperanza's grandmother, who cared for Esperanza after her mother's death. From the time she could remember, Esperanza's life had been centered on work, not on family. Indeed, poverty and the struggle to survive left little room for sentimentality where family was concerned.

Esperanza found some respite from the world of paid work when, at age 20, she married and gave birth to the first of five children. For a little more than five years, she devoted herself to caring for her children while her husband took a position in the socialist Sandanista government.[1] Their marriage—and his life—would prove short-lived. In 1981, Ronald Reagan took office in the United States, and began financing, arming, and training counterrevolutionaries (Contras) to overthrow the Sandanista government. The violence that ensued claimed many lives, including the life of Esperanza's husband. A widow at age 25, Esperanza received a small pension from the Nicaraguan government for her husband's death. But it was not enough to support her and her children. And because jobs in Matagalpa were scarce, she decided to follow the steady stream of migrants leaving Nicaragua for Costa Rica in the 1980s.

Leaving her children behind with her mother-in-law in Matagalpa, Esperanza set out by bus to the southern border of Nicaragua. There, she crossed without documentation into Costa Rica, caught another bus to San José, and began looking for work. Esperanza disliked San José, but she found a small city, not unlike Matagalpa, in Heredia. So it was in Heredia that she secured a room for rent and a job cooking at a popular bar in town. Working the night shift Monday through Saturday, she was paid in cash and off the books because she did not have the legal right to work in Costa Rica. Her pay was steady, and she dutifully sent her earnings to Matagalpa each month to support her mother-in-law and children. It was difficult, painful even, to live and work so far from her children. So after some two years, Esperanza quit her job and returned to Matagalpa to visit her family. Although she had planned to return to Heredia after a short visit, Esperanza began a relationship with a man in Matagalpa, a former friend of her husband's, who proposed marriage. So she married a second time, had another child, and resettled into life in Nicaragua.

Esperanza's second marriage bore a striking resemblance to her first. Like her first husband, her second husband was a Sandanista. He was also heavily involved in fighting the Contras, who continued to try and destabilize the Sandanista regime. Eventually, the fighting took the life of

Esperanza's second husband, just as it had her first. Again a widow some five years into her second marriage, Esperanza packed her bags a second time to make her way south. Now with five mouths to feed, Esperanza headed straight to Heredia, where she found another room to rent. Her job cooking at the bar had long gone to someone else. But a friend told her about a man named Fernando who was looking to employ another cook at his *soda*. Esperanza made her way to Heredia's market, where she introduced herself to Fernando. She was working within a day. This initial meeting between Esperanza and Fernando was some ten years before I interviewed her in 2002. But Esperanza had not worked for Fernando during that entire ten-year stretch. At one point, he let her go because business was slow, and she found work at a restaurant in town. After a year, she returned to work at Fernando's *soda* but left again when she did not get along with the head cook. That time, she found work at a confectionery, also located in the market. The confectionery was owned by three sisters who fought bitterly with one another. So Esperanza again returned to work at Fernando's *soda*, where the head cook had since left. Esperanza and Fernando ended and restarted their working relationship with ease because they got along quite well and because Esperanza was paid in cash. Their relationship was, in a word, flexible, although it was Esperanza's livelihood that was always at stake. When I interviewed her, Esperanza had been working at Fernando's *soda* continuously for about a year, working six days a week from sun up to sun down.

During her second journey to Heredia, Esperanza decided that her move to Costa Rica would be permanent. To the extent that she could avoid deportation, she would remain in Heredia and save money to send for her children one by one. Nicaragua offered nothing but violence, unemployment, and heartbreak, and Esperanza was uninterested in returning. Beginning with her eldest daughter, Esperanza wired her children money for bus fare to the Nicaragua–Costa Rica border. There, she met them and brought them by bus to her small rented home in Heredia. By the time I met Esperanza, only three of her children remained living with her in a small, two-room house. Her eldest daughter had long since run away from home after a bitter falling out with Esperanza. Her next eldest child, a son, had since married and established a household of his own.

In 1999, the Costa Rican government offered amnesty to all undocumented Central American immigrants living in the country. The measure was adopted in the aftermath of Hurricane Mitch, which had devastated much of Central America. The amnesty granted permanent residency to some 150,000 Nicaraguans, one of whom was Esperanza. Although she was now permitted to work legally in Costa Rica, her labor status was still informal. She was not covered by labor laws or the social security system. But the amnesty did provide protection from deportation for Esperanza and the children she had managed to bring to Costa Rica by the time of the amnesty. Her eldest son was the only child who lacked permanent residency during the time of our interview. As such, he worked without papers in the informal sector. Enjoying the advantage of permanent residency, her 17-year-old son worked in the formal sector as a maintenance person, and her 13-year-old son studied in primary school.

Esperanza told me the details of her life as we sat at Fernando's lunch counter. Fernando had long disappeared down a dark market corridor. Esperanza's coworkers, all Nicaraguan women, busied themselves washing dishes and cleaning up after the day's lunch. The market was unusually quiet, save for the dogs barking over a piece of meat at the butcher shop next door. As Esperanza shared her life story, it became clear that her coworkers were listening with interest. Although they shared similar life circumstances, these women had never shared their histories with one another. During particularly poignant moments in Esperanza's story, her coworkers would stop what they were doing, turning off faucets or putting down wooden spoons to concentrate on her words. And when Esperanza recounted the violent death of her second husband, they gasped in unison, their brows furrowed with sympathy and indignation. Even to these women, who had themselves survived poverty, violence, and migration, Esperanza's life was tragic.

Her sorrows notwithstanding, it was difficult to see Esperanza as a victim. She was tall and imposing, a big woman with large bones and heavy muscles. The white chef cap she wore on her head appeared tiny, like a child's hat, against her large head of rich black curls. "When was the last time you were in Nicaragua?" I asked. "Three years ago," she replied. "I really have no reason to go back. My children are here." Indeed, she had lost contact with most of her siblings and her in-laws. Life in Matagalpa had receded like a distant memory. "What about marriage? Do you think you'll ever remarry?" I did not think this too unreasonable to ask. After all, Esperanza was just 46 years old. But her eyes grew wide with surprise at my question. "Tell me, *muchacha*, why would I?" she asked with some scorn. I paused and thought for a moment. "I don't know," I replied honestly. "Love?" I offered. Esperanza threw back her head in a howl of laughter, clutching my left arm as she did so. "Eh, *muchacha* (young woman), you are funny." I laughed with her, knowing full well that love had little chance of growing in the darkness of these tired market walls.

Heredia's New Urban Marginals

Esperanza and her coworkers were part of a substantial, though largely hidden, informal sector.[2] The informal sector is a sector of the economy that is neither taxed nor regulated by the government. It typically involves work that is "under the table" or "off the books." Informal workers tend to be the least educated and the most vulnerable members of society—single mothers, undocumented workers, unskilled laborers, and poor children. Twelve of the 22 individuals featured in this chapter, for example, were women, six of them single mothers with young children (see Table 6.1). Seven of the individuals were immigrants, and fifteen had a primary school education or less. Their lack of human and social capital threw them literally onto the streets, where they got by selling goods on street corners, soliciting day work in agriculture and construction, and seeking houses to clean and odd jobs to fill. Informal workers need not be self-employed. Many are employed by small businesses, whose own lack of resources compels them to hire off the books. Indeed, as the case of Esperanza suggests, informal workers may look like normal wage laborers in almost every respect. What sets these workers apart from formal workers is not the nature of their work, but their lack of state benefits and legal protection (Portes, Castells, and Benton 1989). As such, employers can demand that they work overtime, fire them on a whim and even underpay them.

Given the unregulated and underground nature of their work, it is difficult to arrive at accurate estimates of the informal workers in countries such as Costa Rica. Using two rough approximations, Portes and Hoffman (2003:52) estimate that informal workers make up some 34 to 39 percent of Costa Rica's economically active population.[3] Although Costa Rica has a small informal sector relative to other Latin American countries, the country's informal workforce rivals the formal workforce in size, a characteristic similar to other Latin American economies. Birdsall, Lustig, and Meyer (2014) arrive at a similar estimate to that of Portes and Hoffman (2003), although they conceptualize this group in slightly different terms. They refer to this group as the "strugglers," who are individuals living in households where daily per capita income is between $4 and $10.[4] Strugglers are more likely to be part of households where

TABLE **6.1 The Informal Class**

	YEAR OF BIRTH	PLACE OF BIRTH	CIVIL STATUS	NO. OF CHILDREN	LEVEL OF EDUCATION	OCCUPATION
Alejandra	1956	Alajuela	Divorced	3	Some primary	Domestic worker
Andrés	1979	Heredia	Single	0	Some secondary	Mechanics assistant
Angelica	1985	Heredia	Single	0	Some primary	Seasonal agricultural laborer
Carmen	1941	Heredia	Married	4	Some primary	Housewife
Edwin	1943	Heredia	Single	0	Some secondary	Security guard
Esperanza	1956	Nicaragua	Widowed	5	Some primary	Cook
Gabriel	1980	Cartago	Single	0	Some secondary	Hair salon assistant
Hugo	1948	Guanacaste	Married	4	Primary	Lottery vendor
Javier	1984	Heredia	Single	0	Some primary	Construction worker
Jesús	1971	Nicaragua	Married	6	Some primary	Construction worker
Jonathan	1984	Heredia	Single	0	Some secondary	Restaurant worker
Jorge	1978	Nicaragua	Single	0	Some primary	Cash washer
José	1980	San José	Single	0	Some primary	Door-to-door salesperson
Josefa	1942	Heredia	Single	1	Some primary	Lottery vendor
Luz	1982	Heredia	Married	1	Some primary	Housewife
Marco	1981	Heredia	Single	0	Some secondary	Unemployed
María Fernanda	1985	Heredia	Single	0	Some primary	Restaurant worker
Melissa	1981	Heredia	Single	1	Primary	Cook
Pedro	1980	Nicaragua	Single	1	Primary	Construction worker

(Continued)

TABLE 6.1   (Continued)

	YEAR OF BIRTH	PLACE OF BIRTH	CIVIL STATUS	NO. OF CHILDREN	LEVEL OF EDUCATION	OCCUPATION
Rebeca	1980	Heredia	Single	0	Some secondary	Unemployed
Roberto	1978	Colombia	Single	0	Secondary	Internet café assistant
Rocio	1953	Nicaragua	Married	4	Some secondary	Domestic worker
Yolanda	1944	Nicaragua	Widowed	10	Some primary	Cook

wage-earners are employed in the informal sector and where at least some household members, especially young household members, are un(der) employed.[5] In both respects, these are households that are at risk for falling into poverty.

One of the distinguishing characteristics of individuals in this group is their lack of a secondary school education (Programa Estado de la Nación 2013a:108).[6] In fact, finishing secondary school appears to be a key predictor of whether an individual will escape poverty, which is why the high rates of high school desertion in Costa Rica have been so troubling.[7] In 2006, Costa Rica introduced a poverty-reduction program called *Avancemos*, which sought to reduce high school desertion rates by paying individuals between the ages of 15 and 25 to remain in school.[8] The cash transfer is meant to replace what they would otherwise earn in the labor market if they dropped out. Meza-Cordero (2011) reports that high school attendance increased from 78 to 83 percent in the three years after the program was implemented. But there is no evidence that this increase actually reduced poverty. As Martínez and Voorend (2012) note, conditional cash transfer programs such as *Avancemos* focus exclusively on supply-side factors that inhibit a youngster's education in school, not on demand-side factors that limit the jobs available. In short, these programs have no job creation component, such that young workers, although better educated, may be no more likely to find formal jobs after graduating.

The number of formal jobs in Costa Rica has tended to vary over time. During the 1960s and 1970s, the formal sector expanded to envelop a larger share of the wage labor force, providing opportunities for workers outside of the informal sector (Portes and Hoffman 2003). Neoliberal reforms reversed this trend. In a study of Costa Rica's urban labor markets before and during neoliberal restructuring, Tardanico and Lungo (1995) found that employment in microenterprises, or companies employing less than five workers, rose from a little under 30 percent of total employment in San José in 1980 to 36 percent in 1991. They also found an increase in nonwage, part-time, and subminimum wage employment. On the demand side, increased market competition compelled many businesses to find ways to decrease the costs of production. For many firms, this meant finding ways to circumvent high wages and state regulations (Castells and Portes 1989). In maneuvering around the reach of the state, businesses either hired off the books or contracted out production to subcontractors, home-based workers, and casual laborers (Standing 1999).

On the supply side, privatization and trade liberalization have increased economic hardship for workers and their households (Benería and Feldman 1993; Safa 1995). Given the paucity of formal jobs, laid-off workers and workers entering the labor market to help make ends meet have

Historically, countries in Latin America have had large informal sectors, because the formal sector has never been large enough to absorb all workers. But the size of the informal and formal sector has varied over time. During the 1960s and 1970s, the formal sector expanded in Costa Rica as the economy and public sector grew. Neoliberal restructuring reversed this trend. Research indicates an increase in un(der)employment and subminimum wage employment in the informal sector. Women, immigrants, and child laborers are disproportionately represented in the informal sector.

found their way into the informal economy, where they either create work through self-employment or find unprotected jobs in microenterprises (Portes and Hoffman 2003; Standing 1999; Tardanico 1996). As a result, the data suggest expansion in the informal proletariat over the past few decades (Hite and Viterna 2005; Portes and Hoffman 2003). Indeed, Portes, Castells, and Benton (1989) caution against viewing the informal sector as a leftover of a premodern economy. Instead, they contend, the informal sector grows *alongside* the liberalized economy and is a defining feature of contemporary economic restructuring in Latin America.

Self-employment in the informal sector has been a historic livelihood strategy for the poor and unskilled in Costa Rica. And it remained a popular strategy for many of the *Heredianos* I interviewed between 2001 and 2002. Eight of the 22 individuals featured in this chapter were working as "own-account" workers at the time of my interview with them, and many more had done so at some point in their work history. Jesús, for example, worked in construction, hiring himself out casually to construction companies or households that needed extra labor for small-scale or large-scale construction projects. At least five other men in this group had done likewise in the not-too-distant past. The women in this group were more likely to be self-employed as street vendors.[9] Carmen, for example, worked for 15 years selling clothes door to door. Four other women in this group had also spent some time as street vendors. Selling food and clothes was also a popular livelihood strategy for the middle-class women featured in earlier chapters. But the informal working women described in previous chapters were more likely to take work *inside* the household than go *outside* on the street to work. The women featured in this chapter have little choice but to leave the home in search of a livelihood.

In addition to street vending, domestic work was a familiar form of informal work among the women in this group. Two of the women in this chapter were working as live-in domestic workers at the time of my interview with them. Five other women had worked as domestics at some point in the past. In all five cases, the women had started their stints as domestic workers when they were children. Josefa, for example, went to work as a live-in domestic worker for a household in Central Heredia when she was just age 13 years. She would go on to work for another family as a live-in domestic until she was 28, at which point an unplanned pregnancy forced her to quit. In three other cases, marriage or childbearing put an end to women's domestic work, reinforcing the ways that women's work was and is circumscribed by their role as mothers. As is often the case in domestic work (Hondagneu-Sotelo 2001; Nakano Glenn

1992), some of the women in this group were considered racially subordinate. One woman was a Nicaraguan immigrant; two other women were from Costa Rica's northwestern province of Guanacaste. In both cases, darker skin, higher levels of poverty, and unique cultural attributes marked these migrants as racially and ethnically distinct.

Because Costa Rica receives a number of immigrants from Central and South America, immigrants are especially well represented in the country's informal sector. In 2011, around 9 percent of the Costa Rican population was foreign-born.[10] The vast majority of this foreign-born population (about 75 percent) was Nicaraguan.[11] The growth in Costa Rica's foreign-born population has been nothing short of dramatic. In 1973, for example, only one percent of the country's population was foreign-born (Instituto Naciónal de Estadística y Censos [INEC] 2001:4). Thus, neoliberal restructuring has occurred alongside increased migration from nearby countries (e.g., Nicaragua, El Salvador, and Colombia). Indeed, the same year that Costa Rica's debt crisis occurred, US funding for Contras in Nicaragua commenced, unleashing major political upheavals that sent hundreds of thousands of Nicaraguans south into Costa Rica. The arrival of low-skilled Nicaraguan immigrants could not have been better timed, because the dictates of neoliberal restructuring (i.e., global competitiveness) pushed businesses to look for cheap, flexible sources of labor. Immigrant workers, especially undocumented immigrants, have been a popular labor source because they are willing to accept low wages, subpar working conditions, and insecure forms of work.[12] Taken as a whole, Nicaraguan immigrants dominate the most precarious and lowest paid jobs in Costa Rica—men in construction, women in domestic service, and both men and women in agriculture. Their overrepresentation in low-wage, informal work helps explain why some 80 percent of Nicaraguan immigrants live below the poverty line (Sandoval-García 2004a:435).

Because the migration of Nicaraguans into Costa Rica has occurred alongside neoliberal restructuring, Nicaraguan immigrants have been popular scapegoats for the economic dislocations wrought by free-market reforms (Sandoval-García 2004a, 2004b). Many Costa Ricans do not connect rising un(der)employment, downward mobility, and the deterioration in state services to the effects of economic restructuring. Rather, these are seen as symptoms of an immigration "problem"—an influx of "inferior" neighbors that have undermined Costa Rica's exceptionalism. There is little empirical support for this belief. Gindling (2009), for example, finds no relationship between Nicaraguan migration and the decline in earnings and rise in inequality in Costa Rica. Even so, Nicaraguan

immigrants are seen by Costa Ricans as darker-skinned, culturally inferior criminals who are robbing Costa Ricans of their jobs, gobbling up
state services, and turning a once exceptional nation into just another
Central American country (Sandoval-García 2004a, 2004b). Thus, for the
foreign-born, neoliberalism brings not simply marginalization from
formal labor markets but exclusion from the *Herediano* social fabric.
Along with the city's poor and informal workforce, immigrant workers
are relegated to both the dirty work of the economy and the slums at the
city's periphery.

Precarious Living and Livelihoods

Having restricted my research to small farmers and having lived with a
middle-class family, I had remained unaware of the slums that existed on
Heredia's perimeter in the years leading up to my fieldwork. The tourist
bureaus, the development agencies, the national media, and the *Herediano* people themselves excelled at keeping poor communities hidden and
Costa Rica's exceptionalism at the forefront. At the beginning of my research, as I was first starting to map out the different neighborhoods of
the city and its varied social and demographic groups, I asked Margarita
and Ricardo if they might show me some of the more impoverished parts
of the city. They exchanged nervous glances until Margarita finally declared, "OK, we'll show you Guayabal this weekend." That Saturday
morning, Margarita, Ricardo, Cecilia, and I filed into the car and made
our way to the southeastern corner of the city. Just beyond the city center,
the car dipped down a steep hill until it came to a small row of wooden
shacks where children with ill-fitting clothes lingered on sagging porches,
their feet bare and dusty. "It's all Nicaraguan now," Ricardo declared.
"But when I was young, this is where the poor *Heredianos* lived," Margarita
quipped, implying that Heredia's less fortunate had since been lifted out
of poverty.

Intrigued by Guayabal, I began to wonder what other pockets of poverty the city kept hidden. And that's when I learned about Guararí. I was
interviewing a 20-year old, native-born *Herediano* named Marco as he
waited to enroll in night school. "Where do you live?" I asked, jotting
down basic demographic information. "Guararí," he replied. I had detailed maps of Heredia and a fairly good handle on its various neighborhoods and districts. But I had never heard of Guararí. "Where exactly is
that?" I asked. Marco responded with a mumble, pointing vaguely with a
scabbed finger toward the south. Later, I would find a more detailed map

and locate Guararí on it. Marco had been born to this neighborhood in the year that Costa Rica defaulted on its debt. His later employment and educational experiences would become marked by short stints of work and shorter stints of school. His first job was at age 10, when he went to work as a casual laborer on a dairy farm. For a time, he also worked with a neighbor in construction, building modern houses throughout the San José metropolitan area. His last job was working for a vendor in Heredia's municipal market, selling fruits and vegetables for just under $5 a day. During his many periods of unemployment, he staggered through school, although he had barely an eighth-grade education.

Marco had no evidence of the entrepreneurial spirit characterizing Heredia's middle classes. Indeed, he appeared to be completely lacking in motivation. Often during our interview, he would stare indifferently at the space between us, allowing silence to settle uncomfortably on the graffiti-ridden table. Struggling to take command of the interview, I asked delicately, "So when you weren't working or going to school, what were you doing?" He looked up, surprised by my question. "Nothing!" he replied. "Don't you know what a *vagabundo* is?" I was, of course, familiar with the word *vagabundo*. Cecilia and Violeta used it often when they teased each other for being lazy. In Costa Rican slang, *vagabundo* was a do-nothing, a person who did not work, study, or contribute to society.[13] In that the word was used often when referring to drug-addicted, unemployed, male youth in Costa Rica, the word had dark connotations. And I was surprised that Marco would self-identify with the term. To be sure, he did not embrace the title of *vagabundo*; he was merely aware that others labeled him as such. He was quick to point out that he was ashamed that he did nothing to help his single, working mother. Marco's mother had herself spent most of her life in and out of domestic work, sometimes relying on the financial support of a boyfriend or an older brother. Marco had never known his father.

Aware that he needed to contribute to household expenses, Marco had gone looking for work just a week before our interview. He applied at a store selling perfume in a shopping plaza on the east side of the city. The manager told him that he needed at least three years of high school education. At this point in the interview, Marco rolled his eyes and asked me, "Why would I need three years of education to sell perfume?" Even so, he made his way to the *Liceo Nocturno* to sign up for night classes. With the staggering dropout rates associated with Heredia's night schools, it was hard to believe that Marco would succeed in completing his secondary school education. When I asked what his future plans were, Marco simply shrugged and said: "I don't have future plans because I don't have money." The one thing Marco did want to do was to settle somewhere in the countryside—to leave the city and everyone in it far behind him. In the meantime, he would hang out in Guararí, living with his mother and younger half-brother, among *gente mala* ("bad people").

As I began to meet more and more *Heredianos* from Guararí, my interest in the area grew. Behind Margarita's back, I beseeched Ricardo to show me Guararí. I was nervous Margarita would declare the area off limits due to its association with crime and violence. And I figured Ricardo would agree, at least on principle, that I needed to become familiar with the area if I wanted to write a book about Heredia. He agreed and one Saturday, while Margarita and Cecilia were sleeping soundly during the afternoon *siesta* (nap), we tiptoed out of the house and into the car. Again, we headed toward the southeastern corner of the city, this time winding our way through a new, middle-class subdivision. Eventually, we left the

Since the onset of neoliberal restructuring, income inequality has grown in Costa Rica and the poverty rate has not budged. One manifestation of these trends is a growing number of urban slums that have developed throughout the San José metropolitan area. These slums began as land invasions in the 1980s and 1990s, when the government failed to provide affordable housing to a growing population in the urban Central Valley. One of the largest slums in Heredia is Guararí, pictured here.

subdivision behind and found ourselves on a road twisting and turning through lush fields of coffee. Trees lined the streets, offering a bucolic view of Heredia's rural past and a stark contrast to the congestion and concrete of downtown Heredia. I was sure that Ricardo had no idea where he was going. But within minutes, the outskirts of Guararí come into view, shrouded by the smoke of fires burning along the road. Crowded dirt streets jutted out on both sides of the paved road, showcasing dilapidated one-room and two-room shacks (*precarios*) made of sheet metal, cardboard, and pieces of wood. Stray dogs slept in shaded corners or sniffed pieces of trash littered on the ground, while lines of drying laundry crisscrossed the dirt streets like dingy banners.

There were no cars in sight, just throngs of people everywhere. Two young women in tight jeans and tank tops emerged from the door of a small shack carrying babies on their hips. They made their way to the gravel shoulder of the paved road on which Ricardo and I were traveling, where they walked effortlessly between throngs of playing children. Young men lounged on worn chairs strewn about the streets, leaned on the rusted metal walls of houses, and stood with shoulders slumped in circles of other men. Most of the people were dark-skinned and more than a handful were severely disabled, a visual reminder of their lack of medical care and their war-torn histories. Guararí covers an area far greater than the stretch of impoverished houses that is Guayabal. If Guayabal was a small, unfortunate slice of a larger Heredia that was thriving, Guararí was a sign of concentrated poverty that was growing alongside the modern city.

How do we place this hidden, but significant, impoverished sector in the story of Costa Rica's exceptionalism, especially when the country has been defined by a lack of poverty and branded as a middle-class nation? A headline in *The Tico Times* in November of 2001 announced that the end to poverty in Costa Rica was in sight (Rogers 2001). But 20 percent of the country's households were in poverty throughout the late 1990s. And that percentage has not budged (Morales 2013). Meanwhile, the Gini Coefficient, a measure of income inequality, was 0.518 in 2012, the second highest in the period from 1987 to 2012.[14] A visual reminder of poverty and inequality is to be found in the urban slums that have sprouted up and around the metropolitan area. In 2011, around 7 percent of the population was living in informal settlements, defined as settlements that occurred as a result of land invasion in the1980s and 1990s (Programa Estado de la Nación 2013b:96). Most of these land invasions were due to the government's inability to create affordable housing to meet the demand of a growing population, much of which could ill afford the high cost of housing in Costa Rica (Pujol, Pérez, and Sánchez 2009).[15] Not all of these early squatters (*precaristas*) were the poorest of Costa Rica's poor. Many were otherwise lower middle- and working-class women who were experiencing downward mobility on account of economic crisis and spousal abandonment. They became part of organized movements to obtain land, housing, electricity, water, and pavement in vacant lots throughout the metropolitan area. As such, they viewed themselves as part of a popular urbanization project rather than impoverished squatters per se.[16] Regardless, most of these informal settlements suggest a spatially concentrated poverty that has increased over time (Pujol et al. 2009).

Some 17 percent of the individuals living in these informal settlements are Nicaraguan immigrants, many undocumented, who make their way to the Central Valley in search of work.[17] Despite threats of deportation, sexual and physical abuse by immigration authorities, and a proposed 900-meter-long wall along the Costa Rica–Nicaragua border, such immigrants provide the bulk of the seasonal labor in agriculture and a good portion of the construction workforce in the Central Valley (Mora and Hernandez 2001). The immigration of undocumented workers into Heredia was of concern to a number of middle class families, who nevertheless admitted that Nicaraguans did the work that they themselves would never do. But opposition also came from native-born men in neighborhoods such as Guararí. In a context of contracting formal employment, employers used educational qualifications to sift through the large number of applicants, a hiring strategy that was problematic for *Heredianos* such as Marco because poverty pushed them out of school at early ages. Even some unskilled positions in the factories required at least some secondary school education. Their lack of success in competing in low-wage labor markets forced many men such as Marco into informal work, chronic unemployment, and in some cases, drug and alcohol addiction. But to Marco and his contemporaries, it was the Nicaraguans who were to blame for taking all the jobs in Costa Rica.

In addition to a deep resentment toward Nicaraguan immigrants, the men in this group expressed a disdain for the city. In addition to Marco, all the native-born men younger than age 45 in this group expressed a desire to move to the countryside and out of the city. Given the nature of the neighborhoods in which Marco and his counterparts lived, their desire was not unwarranted. Like the working-class communities described in the last chapter, the urban slums surrounding Heredia were not necessarily tight-knit neighborhoods that nurtured and sustained workers in the face of precarious, low-wage work. But unlike individuals in Heredia's formal working class, *Heredianos* such as Marco could not depend on natal families and households either. To be sure, Marco lived at home with his mother, and he depended on her for financial support. But there was no pooling of resources and no mutual assistance in this household, just a tired woman working while her son wallowed in drugs and despondence. There *were* meaningful social ties and obligations for this group. They simply did not have the privilege to attend to them. Esperanza, for example, knew that leaving her children behind in Nicaragua was not a sign of "good" mothering. And Marco knew that failing to help his mother financially was not a sign of "manhood." But neither felt like they had much choice.

The detachment of this group of *Heredianos* from the social fabric of family, neighborhood, and community life is striking when we consider the case of Melissa. A thin woman with long straight brown hair, Melissa was born into a poor, rural family in the Central Valley. Her mother was a domestic worker and her father a casual farm laborer. Separation, remarriage, and alcoholism would cause both to abandon Melissa and her two younger siblings when Melissa was just 16. Having dropped out of school at 11, Melissa had already been working for five years at the time of her parents' abandonment, collecting coffee during the annual coffee harvest and working on neighboring farms. So she took over the care of her younger siblings, taking a job at an agroindustrial factory to support them. Her boyfriend, a security guard at a nearby factory, moved in to help them financially. When Melissa was 19, she became pregnant and gave birth to a baby girl. Her boyfriend abandoned them just eight months later. Unlike Vanessa, who was featured in the previous chapter, Melissa did not have much, if any, family support, and it was nearly impossible to care for her baby daughter while working at the factory. So Melissa did something she had promised that she would never do: she took a job at a bar, where she could work the nightshift. Melissa considered the job among the lowest of occupations because it was associated with prostitution and a lack of decency. But she had little choice. Her younger siblings watched over the infant at night while Melissa worked.

Eventually, the task of supporting and caring for a family became too much. Melissa searched for her mother, found her living in Heredia Central with a boyfriend, and sent her two younger siblings to live with her. In turn, Melissa and her baby moved in with friends in a small house in the neighborhood of Mercedes Sur. Her roommate, a Nicaraguan immigrant, used to work at the bar where Melissa had worked. They had both since quit—her roommate because she was pregnant and Melissa because she found a new job as a cook. Her roommate's husband, also a Nicaraguan immigrant, worked in construction. He and Melissa supported the household financially while Melissa's roommate looked after her own 3-year-old son and Melissa's daughter. By this point, Melissa was working at a small *soda* (lunch stand) in Heredia's Municipal Market. At the time of our interview, Melissa had also just started dating the father of her daughter again. He had been working at a *pulpería* and was giving her some money for the baby. But his financial support was erratic, and Melissa doubted that their relationship would last. As for her siblings, Melissa had some contact. But she did not have enough money to buy them presents for Christmas, and her shame prevented her from calling them.

Melissa had managed not to fall into a growing underclass characterized by unemployment, crime, and addiction. Indeed, she had succeeded in obtaining work and providing for herself and her daughter. But it was a precarious existence that rested on some of the lowest paying, socially "indecent," and precarious jobs available. In her case, gender norms could not be honored, social obligations could barely be met, and family ties could not be counted on. If she could not count on the support of her natal family, she certainly could not count on the support of her baby's father. Like five of the other eleven women in this group, Melissa was a single mother struggling to survive, which primed her to take undesirable jobs in the informal sector. The dirty work to which she was relegated may have stigmatized her in the eyes of the larger community, but Melissa could still cling to a popular script among the women in this group: she did what she had to do to feed and clothe her child. Unable to provide steady financial support to their children and given the informal jobs available to them, the men in this group had a difficult time even doing this. This might help explain why detachment from family and work was so common among the men in this group, especially those native-born men who struggled to compete with low-wage immigrants for jobs in construction and agriculture. The result was growing cynicism not simply over the meaning of work and mobility, but over the meaning of family and marriage.

Pedro's Request

If the workers in the last chapter were part of families on the "verge of breakdown" (Chant 2002), the workers in this chapter were part of families that never quite got off the ground. Of the 70,550 births registered in Costa Rica in 2013, 50 percent were to unwed women. In 8 percent of the cases, no father was named.[18] It is not possible to say definitively why out-of-wedlock childbearing is on the rise in Costa Rica. But it is reasonable to suspect that this trend is at least in part related to the inability of poor men to secure stable employment and achieve the resources necessary to provide for a family (Chant 2000). Regardless of its cause, the resulting rise in single-mother households exacerbates poverty and reproduces it over time. Because single working mothers are overrepresented among the self-employed and part-time workforce, because they alone are responsible for childcare, and because they often lack the financial support of fathers, single mothers and their households are much more vulnerable to poverty (Gindling and Oviedo 2008).[19] Alongside the rise in out-of-wedlock childbearing, then, has been an increase in the proportion of poor households headed by single mothers—from a little over 13 percent in 1990 to 29 percent in 2011 (Gindling and Oviedo 2008:7; Programa Estado de la Nación 2013a:97).

What do these trends look like when we examine the lives of Heredia's poor up close? It is hard to say. This group was the least accessible to me as a researcher, embedded as I was in a lower middle-class neighborhood and family. To some extent, I was able to connect with the women in this group. But with the men in this group, the differences in gender, class, nationality, and, in some cases, perceived racial status made it difficult for me to probe the relationship between poverty and family life. Nowhere was this more evident than in my relationship with Pedro. Born in 1980 in Matagalpa, Nicaragua, Pedro was one of thousands of undocumented immigrants living in Costa Rica at the time of my fieldwork. His origins were humble. The son of a miner and one of ten children, Pedro dropped out of primary school to work as a farm hand just before he reached the age of 12. As most boys and young men in Nicaragua knew, migration to neighboring Costa Rica provided more opportunities for those with few skills. So at the age of 14, he made his first of many treks to Costa Rica. Along with two friends and a brother, he migrated without papers into the country's northern frontier, where he found work picking vegetables. It was hard work but easy to secure. Indeed, the expansion of new agricultural exports associated with neoliberal restructuring has led to a proliferation of low-wage farm work in Costa Rica's countryside. To keep costs at a minimum in the competitive world of fresh produce exports, Costa Rican farmers rely heavily on Nicaraguan labor (Lee 2010).

Pedro would make three more migrations to Costa Rica over the next five years. Sometimes he worked on farms; sometimes he worked in construction. His migrations were always temporary, lasting six to nine months. But during his last migration, at the age of 19, his experience turned out to be much different. He had been working the annual coffee harvest in the hills surrounding Heredia. There, he met a Costa Rican woman with whom he became romantically involved. Just days before he was scheduled to return to Nicaragua, he learned she was pregnant with his child. Rumors were widespread in Costa Rica that Nicaraguan immigrants intentionally became involved with Costa Rican women with the hopes of securing a marriage or bearing a child, both of which would provide a familial link to establish permanent residency. Whether Pedro did this or not, I cannot say. It had taken me weeks just to get him to talk to me, nervous as he was to have some strange *gringa* asking him questions about his life history. What was clear was that he understood the requirements of permanent residency and had been pursuing this status through bureaucratic channels. His 4-month-old son, a citizen of Costa Rica, was his link to legal status because he declined to marry the mother of his child.

To apply for permanent residency, Pedro needed a good deal of money and patience. The processing of these applications was notoriously long and expensive. As an undocumented immigrant working in construction, Pedro was earning very low wages, and only when he had work; this hardly provided enough money to help support his child, let alone pay the fees associated with applying for permanent residency. His situation was, in a word, precarious. And it was not long before Pedro asked me for money. It was our first meeting, and I was accompanying him to his bus stop after a long day of work. The sun was setting rapidly as we wound our way through the crowded streets of Heredia. Pedro, a short man of medium build, carried a cloth backpack over a shoulder. "My child is going to bed hungry," he offered after a moment of silence. I nodded as I imagined his home life in Guararí. "His mother is trying to find work cleaning houses. But we struggle," he continued. Another heavy moment of silence slipped between us as I considered his impending request. "Is there any way you can help?" he finally asked.

When I recounted the story to Margarita and Ricardo later that evening, Margarita sighed heavily as she searched the refrigerator for eggs. "Susie," Ricardo began, "we've told you. *Nicas* are like this." Here, Ricardo used an oft-cited term for Nicaraguans, one that is derogatory in that it signifies what Sandoval-García (2004b:xiii) calls an "undesirable otherness." "Susie," Margarita began, "it's just that they're poor. They'll ask for money from whomever. How did the conversation end?" "I gave him our phone number and told him to call next week," I admitted. "You did what?" Margarita screamed. "Susie, you can't just give a person like that our phone number! We have no idea who this guy is! He could hurt us! He doesn't know where we live, does he?" My heart began to race. I had no idea if he knew where our house was. But the construction site at which we met was only six blocks away, so he could certainly find out. "No, Margarita," I said with feigned calm. "When he calls next week, I'll take care of it. Don't worry."

Pedro did call—many times. The first time he called, during the week that followed our interview, I offered to meet him at the *pulpería* near the construction site. In his hand, he held an application for permanent residency, upon which was taped a passport-sized picture of himself. Awkwardly, I offered him a sealed envelope with 7,000 *colones* (roughly US $28 at the time). Although he took the envelope, he did not open it. Instead, he stared at his shoes and asked if there was any way I could help him get to the United States to work. "No, Pedro," I said quietly. "This is all I can do to help." We parted ways shortly thereafter. The following day, Margarita reported that Pedro had called again. He explained to her that I had promised to give him 3,000 more *colones* to help feed his baby. "Why would you promise something like that?" Margarita demanded. "I didn't!" I explained. "When he calls back, and he *will*, I'm going to tell him you left the country due to an emergency. This is getting ridiculous," she declared. Pedro called the following day and, as promised, Margarita told him firmly that I had left the country due to a family emergency. But even as Margarita tried to resolve the situation, her frustration at me rose. In her mind, I had admitted an unsavory character into the sphere of her family.

Tension had already been brewing between Margarita and me during the spring of 2002. We were conflicting over a number of issues. Margarita thought that I was becoming too moody and she was, of course, right. The longer I lived in Costa Rica, the more frustrated and exasperated I became. It was as if the deeper I probed *Herediano* society, the more complex and overwhelming it became. My emotions aside, there was something more to Margarita's criticism—something that illuminated the fault lines that divided this rapidly changing city. She was not simply frustrated with me; she was resentful toward the turn my field work had taken. During the fall of 2001, when my interviews and observations had focused on middle class *Heredianos*, she had been proud to tell others that I was "writing a book about Heredia." As I reached out to working-class and poor *Heredianos*, her disapproval emerged and grew. "Why in the world you are wasting your time with those people is beyond me," she muttered one night. "Margarita," I began, "they're part of Heredia, too." "Susie," Ricardo piped in, "most of them are actually Nicaraguan. They're not *Herediano*." "What you need to do is call your professors and explain that you need to end this project now. What they're asking you to do is too risky. Walking around at night. Talking to these men. You're lucky you haven't been raped," she exclaimed.

It was not so much that Margarita worried about my safety, although I knew she did. It was that I was peeling back a layer of *Herediano* society that she and other middle class *Heredianos* had worked carefully to hide, or at least ignore. In the process, I was constructing a story about Heredia that was not "decent." In short, I was sullying the white, middle-class image of her household and her Heredia. By Margarita's calculation, there were no slums surrounding the city, no single-mother households, and no population of uneducated and poor *Heredianos*. There were simply Nicaraguans, who were not and never would be *Herediano*. Pedro was, to her and Ricardo, a perfect example of what was wrong with Costa Rica— something that originated *outside* the country, encroaching inward to erase all that made this nation exceptional. It was not the neoliberal project—something that was put into place *inside* the country, spreading outward to chip away at a reputation that had won the nation international acclaim and foreign investment. As for myself, I felt caught between indignation over Margarita's and Ricardo's xenophobic response and frustration over Pedro's overbearing requests for assistance. Try as I might, I could not turn my analytic lens to investigate these responses while I was in the field. I just became anxious.

On the Saturday before Easter, Pedro called four more times. I was out of the house for most of the day, and he left no number for me to call back. When he called Easter Sunday, after everyone but me had left for church, I answered. After he said that he needed more money, I firmly explained that I had already given what I could give. Silently, I wondered why I didn't just e-mail friends and raise money for him. But I barely knew him, and I felt uncomfortable with the prospect. After hanging up the phone, I decided to just accept the awkwardness of the situation and the ambivalent feelings it aroused in me and move on. But that evening, as Margarita and I sat talking at the dining room table, he called the house again, this time collect. Cecilia answered. "What kind of son-of-a-bitch calls a family he doesn't know *collect*?" Ricardo demanded getting red in the face with anger. "I'll take care of this," Margarita said with some determination. "Listen," she began on the phone with Pedro, "I don't know what you want. But if it's money, Susie doesn't have any to give you. Plus, she's already left the country. I'm going to tell you this once and, then, I do not want to hear from you again: you are going to have to solve this problem on your own. May God be with you." At this, she hung up. With that, the case was closed. Pedro never called again. Margarita never spoke of him again. And I never again suggested that this group of immigrants and their poor Costa Rican neighbors was as much a part of Heredia as the native-born elders who populated the Central Plaza on lazy afternoons.

The Racial Politics of Social Exclusion

During my year of living in Heredia, an acclaimed theatrical production called *El Nica* (*The Nicaraguan*) debuted in theaters throughout the Central Valley. The play consisted of a monologue by a character named José, a Nicaraguan immigrant in Costa Rica who works in construction. In the monologue, José talks to Jesus about his immigrant experience in Costa Rica, focusing on the hardship, prejudice and discrimination he faces each day. As the character tours the various stigmas that plague Nicaraguan immigrants in Costa Rica, audience members—mostly middle-class Costa Ricans—must confront their own stereotypes and prejudices. They are also compelled to consider the ways in which their national identity is wrapped up in notions of whiteness, Central American exceptionalism, and a sense of middle class belonging. José asks the audience to forgive him his Nicaraguan accent, his dark skin color, and his "Indian" hair. But he also reminds them that immigrants such as himself clean their houses and watch after their homes, helping to protect and even enhance notions of decency so central to many households in Costa Rica.[20]

It was not simply the middle class that challenged the Nicaraguan presence in Costa Rica. Marco, the native-born young man featured earlier in this chapter, had especially harsh words for Nicaraguan immigrants, who he blamed for most of his economic problems. According to Marco, *Nicas* were taking all the good jobs from Costa Ricans by accepting lower wages. Absent from his analysis was any discussion of the way in which neoliberalism and global capitalism more generally hinged on targeting the lowest-paid and most vulnerable sectors of the labor force—immigrants and women in particular. In the gender-segregated world of

Heredia's informal sector, however, Marco faced less competition from women than he did from immigrant men. Women were channeled into "domestic" services—caregiving, cooking, and cleaning. Men were channeled into construction and agriculture. Thus, for the native-born men in this group, it was immigrant men who were to blame for the declining job opportunities. The irony in Marco's contempt for Nicaraguans was that Marco and other native-born members of Heredia's poor were more or less lumped in with Nicaraguan immigrants by the city's middle class, who banished both from their narratives of *Herediano* society. Ricardo demonstrated this powerfully when he quipped that Heredia's poor were "actually Nicaraguan." Regardless of their nationality, they were rendered "not *Herediano*" by virtue of their poverty and lack of education.

To cast out the poor from their story of Heredia, middle-class *Heredianos* used a racial calculus that the country's elite had honed over two centuries. Historical research suggests that whiteness is central to Costa Rica's national mythology. Indeed, it might be seen as the hallmark of Costa Rican exceptionalism. The idea of whiteness was constructed carefully by the country's elite as Costa Rica's economy grew and expanded around coffee (Edelman 1992; Gudmundson 1984, 1986; Paige 1997; Sandoval-García 2004b). By the late 1800s, the economic dynamism of the Central Valley, where the ideal and appearance of whiteness was most firmly entrenched, became connected to small farmers of supposed European decent (Paige 1997). In contrast, the more stagnant economies of the north and northwest, where racial mixture and indigenous origins were more pronounced, became associated with dark-skinned peasants of "Nicaraguan" stock (Gudmundson 1984; Sandoval-García 2004b). Thus, to be from the Central Valley was to be white—and hence entrepreneurial, democratic, and civilized. To be from the north or northwest was to be nonwhite—and hence uneducated, violent, and uncivilized.[21] Nonwhiteness was not simply shorthand for social indecency and economic stagnation but something that was of probable Nicaraguan origin—something that was fundamentally *not* Costa Rican. As such, Sandoval-García (2004b) argues that the exclusion and racialization of Nicaraguans has been central to the construction of Costa Rica's identity as an "exceptional" country.[22]

Given that the construction of the Nicaraguan "other" has deep historical roots in Costa Rica, one would be mistaken to take the contemporary scapegoating of Nicaraguan immigrants as a mere by-product of neoliberal restructuring. In that the migration of Nicaraguans into Costa Rica intensified in an era of dramatic economic restructuring, however, one could argue that anti-Nicaraguan sentiment has escalated over the past few decades as Costa Ricans have grappled with what they see as their deteriorating state of exceptionalism. My 2014 revisit suggested that such prejudice has hardly waned. My fourth day back in Heredia, I left Margarita and Ricardo's house to walk downtown. Crossing the street, I heard a woman scream from around the corner. Within seconds, a small group of men rounded the corner in pursuit of a man whose shirt had been torn in two. Catching him, they threw him to the ground where they kicked him savagely, one of them brandishing, although not using, a rusted machete in his right hand. I watched alongside a growing group of neighbors, who were spilling out of homes to witness the melee. When one of the attackers pulled out a gun and shot in the air, we scrambled indoors for cover. Taking refuge in one of the neighbor's homes, I remarked that never had I seen violence in this corner of the city. "Susie, it's the Nicaraguans," said the neighbor. "Didn't you see the machete? Only Nicaraguans carry machetes." When we re-emerged, the attackers had dispersed, the victim was nowhere to be seen, and the streets had returned to their previous calm. My subsequent inquiries resulted in no real information on the attack and certainly no confirmation of the "foreign" status of the attackers. In the end, I was less interested in the truth than in the perception, which was that anything violent, dark, and uncivilized was simply "not Costa Rican." This turned out to be a very effective way of maintaining the country's well-guarded exceptionalism no matter how far economic change had altered social patterns in the country.

Immigrants and the poor were not simply written out of middle class narratives of *Herediano* society. They were also made invisible by the neoliberal project. Their work was performed "under the table" or in spaces where they were less visible—inside darkened municipal markets, behind the closed doors of middle class households, and on city outskirts where new housing developments were being constructed. This invisibility allowed most *Heredianos* to forget or even dismiss the central contributions of this group to the city's new economy. This invisibility is reminiscent of the kind of treatment from which women have long suffered in their role as mothers, wives, and caregivers. Although women's unpaid labor is crucial to household survival, its unpaid nature and its social meaning renders women's work a mere expression of their biological nature and maternal devotion, not an actual form of work. Likewise, immigrant and informal workers who provide key services to this city are viewed as non-workers. Immigrants look for handouts; informal workers simply get by;

and *vagabundos* literally do nothing. Constructed as a nonproductive drain on the country's economy, Nicaraguan immigrants especially become a ready target for the problems associated with neoliberal restructuring, such as the deterioration in public services and the rising level of economic insecurity (Sandoval-García 2004b).

Although almost all of the *Heredianos* in this impoverished group were treated as a dark secret, something to be hidden in the city's shadows, the experiences of men and women in this group were profoundly different. The men were disconnected from most forms of social support, but they were not tied down in the way their female counterparts were. The women, abandoned by partners and beholden to children, were forced into "indecent" work, treacherous migrations, and household poverty. Costa Rica, it turns out, was (and is) a classic case of the "feminization of poverty," even as its government has made efforts to assist low-income women (Chant 2009). Since 1995, the country's Social Welfare Institute (*Instituto Mixto de Ayuda Social* [IMAS]) has provided financial assistance and employment training for women in poverty, especially those who head households of their own (Chant 2009). Relatedly, the 2001 Law for Responsible Paternity (*Ley de Paternidad Responsible*) requires men who do not voluntarily register themselves on a child's birth certificate to submit to a paternity test. If paternity is established, these men are required to contribute to the cost of pregnancy and childbirth, as well as the child's expenses during their first year of life. The law was intended to improve the economic conditions of mother-headed households, but as Chant (2009:25) points out, indicators of women's poverty suggest that the law has had limited success. For the Melissas of Heredia, economic security will remain elusive for women so long as it remains elusive for men and so long as women are forced to shoulder the consequences of out-of-wedlock childbearing.

I was struck by both the powerlessness of the men in this group and the resignation of the women. Both left me with more questions than answers. During my ordeal with Pedro, for example, I thought often about his *compañera* (companion) and tried to imagine her life. What did her biography look like and how did it land her as the mother of a poor immigrant's child? Did she feel like a mere ticket to Pedro's permanent residency? And what would become of her and their child if and when Pedro gave up in his quest to obtain residency? She was as mysterious to me as Pedro—a fleeting character whose motivations and emotions I could not unpack. That I remained so disconnected from this group, which was defined by its disconnectedness to the social fabric of this city, was unsurprising. This alienated group was accustomed to floating unseen through the city streets. Without a basis for friendship, Pedro and I had little choice but to succumb to the stale script of the foreign benefactor and poor immigrant. We were both uneasy with our parts—Pedro because he could not escape his low social status, me because I could not come to terms with my high social status. My privilege as a middle class *gringa*—this was *my* dark secret. And I packaged it up like the *colones* I handed to Pedro in a sealed envelope, something to consider long after the collect calls from Pedro had stopped.

CHAPTER 7

The Ethnographic Imagination Revisited

Cecilia's *quinceañera* (fifteenth birthday party) occurs on a Friday evening in mid-April of 2002, just weeks before I would leave Heredia to make my way back to the United States.[1] Although many such coming-of-age parties take place in reception halls, Margarita plans a smaller, more intimate gathering at home. She decorates the backyard with pink and white balloons and arranges two rows of tables covered with white plastic tablecloths. Carefully, she positions pots of fresh flowers atop each table. On the night of the party, Cecilia wears tight blue jeans, a pink tank top, and high-heeled sandals. Her hair is worn down in thick black curls. Aunts, uncles, and cousins begin arriving just after 7:00 in the evening, making their way through the front door and toward the back door to return to the cool evening air. As Margarita works furiously in the kitchen, Cecilia's Aunt Marta doles out large servings of chicken and rice from two stainless steel tubs in the back patio. Salsa music plays loudly on a stereo held together with duct tape on a makeshift bar that Ricardo has made atop the washing machine. Ricardo wears an affable smile as he hands out cans of beer, stirs rum and cokes, and pours ice-cold lemonade.

Forty-five minutes after the food has been served, the sound of trumpets can be heard from the house's interior. Within seconds, a *mariachi* (Mexican folk music) band is descending down the patio steps, playing music loudly. Cheers go up from the guests, who make room for the band on the back patio. Someone shouts for Cecilia to come forward, and she does so timidly. She smiles appreciatively as the band plays in her honor. They finish the song, and the guests erupt in loud applause. Before starting a second song, the band leader directs Ricardo onto the dance floor, where he is expected to dance with his daughter. At 15 years of age, Cecilia, known affectionately in the family as Ceci, is already taller than Ricardo. And in her high-heeled sandals, she towers over him. But she leans in to place her head on his right shoulder and they dance closely for the remainder of the song. Watching from the sidelines, I struggle to hold back tears as I think back to that humid afternoon in 1994 when I first met Ceci, then just 6 years old and clinging to her mother's left leg.

Ceci is still considered a child and, as the younger of two daughters, she is certainly still considered the baby of the family. She has never had a boyfriend, but frequently young men come calling on her, sitting outside the front stoop to talk with her under her mother's close supervision. She has not completed secondary school, but already she and her mother discuss Ceci getting a certificate in cosmetology and opening up her own hairdressing business. One could say that her future is an open book. But it might be more apt to say that it is a collection of probable scenarios that will unfold from her biography and her country's history. As such, we might venture some guesses as to who she will become and where her journey will lead. Likewise, we might guess what will happen to the *Heredianos* among whom I lived and worked at the dawn of the twenty-first century. And so I end on three simple questions. What will become of the people who call Heredia home? What will happen to Heredia and Costa Rica more generally? And why should we care?

Economic Change Retold

In Chapter 1, I suggested that real people are implicated by trends such as market liberalization and government restructuring. This may seem obvious, but it is a fact that often gets lost in the overly statistical and theoretical accounts of economic restructuring in the social sciences. Students and scholars of neoliberalism learn more about fluctuations in exchange rates than they do about the complicated strategies and identities that individuals construct in times of rapid change. Even ethnographic accounts that take us into the lives of people coping with economic restructuring have the habit of banishing the intimate details of daily life to footnotes and a few descriptive paragraphs, as if the human story is not *the* central story to tell of liberalization. To the extent that neoliberalism reduces individual workers to raw inputs, neoliberalism is not simply a political and economic project; it is a dehumanizing project. Ethnographers arguably have a responsibility to counter that dehumanization by highlighting how individual biographies unfold against the backdrop of this profound economic transformation.

Focusing on human lives under neoliberal restructuring is not just important in a humanistic sense. As I have argued throughout this book, it enriches our understanding of the economic processes we are studying. To date, scholarly accounts have been overly focused on the workplace and the household as key sites where neoliberalism is constructed and enacted. By putting individual biographies at the center of my analysis, I tried to show how economic change is not just about changing institutions but about an intense wrestling over old and new ideas of what it means to be middle and working class, a man and a woman, a citizen and an immigrant. People make sense of changes in the macroeconomic environment in the intimate spaces of their daily life and it is here, in these everyday spaces, where individuals construct livelihood strategies and cultural lifeways that accommodate and/or challenge the prevailing economic ideology. This more biographical approach helps us grasp how people act within a particular economic context, not simply how they are acted *on* by larger economic forces. Hence, I urged readers in Chapter 1 to cultivate an "ethnographic imagination," which, like the "sociological imagination," helps make this connection between the individual life and the larger history in which that life is embedded.

Chapters 3 through 6 laid bare the ethnographic and biographical details that help illuminate how economic change translates into the lives of individuals in one Costa Rican city. I organized these details loosely around the country's different social classes. In Chapter 3, I showed how an emerging professional class of *Heredianos* harnessed the opportunities introduced under neoliberal restructuring to construct individualistic lifeways, cosmopolitan identities, and new middle-class livelihoods. A 2011 State of the Nation report confirmed the advantages enjoyed by this group, reporting that the professional class has enjoyed higher wages and more opportunities given their skill sets (Programa Estado de la Nación 2011:351). As the case of Violeta suggests, the material comfort and leisured lifestyle of this class softened the impact of the "stalled revolution" experienced by many of the women in this group. So, too, did material gain assuage the social isolation that individuals such as Luis experienced as a result of their social mobility. This privilege gave this group a kind of investment in the neoliberal project that made them unlikely to challenge its many side effects such as income inequality.

For the lower middle-class group featured in Chapter 4, social and work life were rooted in the patriarchal bargain that men and women made with each other and with the state in the "golden" years of Costa Rica's social democratic experiment. As a group, these *Heredianos* formed a modest middle class around public sector jobs and stable small businesses. Less global and more national in scope, this class helped forge a national identity around economic prosperity, social moderation and political stability. This identity is gendered in that it was grounded in a breadwinner-homemaker model that associated masculinity with labor force participation and femininity with unpaid domestic work. Neoliberal restructuring has undermined the basis of this middle-class sensibility to the extent that it has pushed many lower middle-class men out of work and many of their wives into the market in search of income. Therefore, individuals in this group have contested the neoliberal project, but these contestations have typically become confused with marital conflict or been confined to the ballot box. In some cases, as with public sector unions that have been active in protesting state restructuring, these contestations have taken on a more open and critical character.

Like its lower middle class, Heredia's working class faced a rapidly changing economic landscape. As Chapter 5 suggests, feminized jobs in the new economy have afforded working-class women some ability to rewrite traditional gender scripts, allowing them to leave abusive husbands and head households of their own. But the lives of single working mothers such as Vanessa were not exactly enviable because they entailed endless hours of paid and unpaid work. In turn, men such as Jose Luís were emasculated in a workplace where labor regulations and minimum wages were routinely flouted—an emasculation that translated back into the household, where wives used their newfound economic power to renegotiate household hierarchies. In comparison to the previous two groups, this group has had less room to maneuver economically or politically because their power is so limited. But we do see some strategizing here, from attempts to outmigrate in search of higher wages to the formation of extended-family households. Given the low rates of unionization among the men in this group and the ways in which they confuse embattled gender relations with the larger feminization of labor, however, we have not seen a consistent and articulate critique of the neoliberal project from the group most vested in transforming it.

A final piece of neoliberal restructuring is the informalization of labor markets, which has drawn poor women, immigrant workers, and older *Heredianos* into an unregulated sphere of the economy. In Chapter 6, their less visible lives come into view. Through their labor, subdivisions and shopping malls are built, the working class is fed at reasonable prices, and inexpensive clothes are sewn and sold to subcontractors. In spite of their centrality, the workers in this group are underpaid and unprotected, their daily lives relegated to the city's slum-like periphery. They are considered Heredia's dark secret, a sliver of the community that is invisible not simply because they work "under the table," but because their darker skin, migrant status, and enduring poverty counter prevailing narratives of Costa Rican nationhood. However powerless, they have not been passive. Their migratory movements, land invasions, and informal enterprises have, in a sense, embodied globalization and a free market ethos. But these acts also challenge the neoliberal project to the extent that each is undertaken outside the existing legal framework. Here, in this group, we see perhaps the most subversive challenge to the legitimacy of neoliberalism, because its "borders" are so routinely flouted.

In Chapter 1, when I asked what an ethnographic analysis might look like if ethnographers were more "parent-like than physician-like," I wanted to get at how economic change is not just about economic forces bearing down on individuals and communities. It is about how career pathways and cultural lifeways are constructed by everyday people that work with and against those forces. As a parent might remind a physician that the child is not defined by the illness, so, too, might ethnographers remind the world that everyday people are not determined by their economic circumstances. In both cases, of course, they are constrained by their situation. Hence, prevailing economic forces will shape an individual's evolving understanding of themselves and the possibilities that lay before them. But they will not change the fact that people are sentient beings capable of determining a course of action and imagining alternative futures. As a parent might imagine an infant capable of confronting and overcoming an illness, so might an ethnographer imagine a "subject" capable of confronting and even shaping a macroeconomic context. And this is precisely what I mean when I speak of an "ethnographic imagination"[2] and a "book of one's own." But what does all this suggest about the future of Heredia and Costa Rica more generally? It is to this question that I now turn.

Patriotism, Protest, and the Neoliberal Project

When I arrived in Costa Rica in May of 2001, the country was seen as a case of "gradual" neoliberal reform (Clark 2001). Instead of slashing social spending, the government slowly contracted public programming and its expansive state apparatus.[3] It promoted investment and employment in the nontraditional export sector, such that workers ejected from a shrinking older economy might be reabsorbed into new economic sectors. On the whole, and in comparison to other Latin American countries, its gradual approach was seen as more successful, or at least less deleterious to citizens and workers (Clark 2001; Itzigsohn 2000). Statistics seem to bear this out. Apart from the downturn associated with the global recession in 2008 and 2009, the Costa Rican economy has grown by an average of 4 percent per year over the past ten years. The country's life expectancy remains one of the highest in the region and its infant mortality rates one of the lowest. In 2011, literacy stood at 98 percent, access to clean water at 97 percent, and access to electricity at 99 percent, suggesting near universal coverage in each respect (Programa Estado de la Nación 2011). Finally, the country continues to have the highest healthcare coverage in Latin America, with more than 90 percent of its population covered by health insurance (Vega 2012:18). Costa Rica, it appears, remains a regional leader in social welfare.

These statistics notwithstanding, there are also indicators that suggest that the country is becoming a little more like its Central American neighbors. As I documented in the previous chapter, inequality reached historic highs in 2001 and 2012. And the country's poverty rate has not declined despite a growing economy. Adding to these problems has been a seemingly endless barrage of corruption scandals, which have suggested an increasingly cozy relationship between government officials and private investors. In 2004, former president Miguel Angel Rodríguez (1998–2002) stepped down as secretary-general of the Organization of American States and returned to San José to face charges of accepting a bribe from a French telecommunications company interested in winning a government contract to provide cell phone lines (Lehoucq 2005:141).[4] Just one week later, another former president, Rafael Angel Calderón (1990–1994), was taken to jail on corruption charges.[5] In addition to these cases, there have been less internationally known scandals, including a 2009 case in which the Ministry of Labor, ignoring blatant violations of labor law, approved the inspection of a 700-room beach resort being constructed by a Spanish firm. The inspections uncovered rampant use of undocumented Nicaraguan workers and overcrowded and unsafe living conditions for workers. The Ministry of Health was forced to intervene after one of the workers died after four days of vomiting (Ramírez 2009).

Due in part to deteriorating social conditions and high-profile corruption cases, there has been a steady decline in support for the country's traditional two parties, which have, in recent decades, advocated neoliberal reforms (Seligson 2002; Seligson and Martínez 2009).[6] After the historic runoff election of 2002, which I documented in Chapter 4, the Citizen Action Party (PAC) challenged the traditional two parties again in the 2006 elections. This election ended in a virtual tie between the PAC candidate, Ottón Solís, and Óscar Arias of the National Liberation Party (PLN). The results forced a recount, which Arias won by just a few thousand votes (Frajman 2012:124).[7] Seligson and Martínez (2009:331) argue that the declining support for Costa Rica's traditional two parties is indicative of a growing mismatch "between elites in favor of neoliberal reforms and masses of citizens who, to varying degrees, appreciate and remain attached to benefits derived from welfare state institutions." Nowhere did this growing mismatch reveal itself more starkly than in the unprecedented challenge that erupted in the country over passage of the Central American Free Trade Agreement (CAFTA). The aim of CAFTA is to create a free trade area between the United States and most of Central America, much like the North American Free Trade Agreement (NAFTA) did between the United States, Canada, and Mexico.[8] As such, CAFTA can be understood as the final bolt of a neoliberal machine that has been in the making for some three decades. That the strongest challenge to CAFTA erupted in Costa Rica is instructive. If it was in Costa Rica that neoliberalism was at its most gradual, why would it be in Costa Rica that neoliberalism was fought most fiercely? In 2007, CAFTA had been ratified by every country except Costa Rica, where debate over the agreement had defined the 2006 presidential elections between Solís, who opposed CAFTA, and Arias, who embraced the agreement. Cupples and Larios (2010:96) suggest that the anti-CAFTA movement emerged strongest in Costa Rica because it was Costa Rica that had the most to lose. Its social programs and public services were what made Costa Rica so exceptional and what gave the anti-CAFTA movement its drive.

When it was clear that opposition to CAFTA was going to stall its passage in the National Assembly, newly elected President Óscar Arias called for a public referendum. By most accounts, Arias was confident of a victory (Cupples and Larios 2010; Willis and Seiz 2012). At his disposal were state resources, financial support from the business sector, and a pro-CAFTA media.[9] Almost immediately after Arias called the referendum, a coalition of labor unions, student groups, PAC leaders, environmental groups and agricultural groups formed a loose coalition called the Patriotic Movement for No (*Movimiento Patriótico Contra el TLC*) (Cupples and Larios 2010; Frajman 2012; Willis and Seiz 2012).[10] Although many in the anti-CAFTA movement were against free trade, opposition to free trade was not a defining feature of the movement. Rather, it was the erosion of Costa Rica's strong welfare state. "What is bad about CAFTA," noted one opposition leader, "is that it is 80 percent transformation of the State, and 20 percent free trade" (quoted in Willis and Seiz 2012:138). At stake here was a vision of what Costa Rica was and what it might become. The pro-CAFTA camp envisioned a country with a modern, dynamic economy that was committed to growth; the anti-CAFTA camp envisioned a country with a transparent public sector that was committed to equity (Cupples and Larios 2010; Willis and Seiz 2012).

On September 30, 2007, the "No" (anti-CAFTA) campaign held a mass demonstration in San José. An estimated 150,000 people participated, making

In 2007, the Central American Free Trade Agreement (CAFTA) had been ratified by every country except Costa Rica, where the population remained bitterly torn over the issue. In 2007, then President Óscar Arias called for a public referendum on the issue. A coalition of labor unions, student groups, environmental groups, and agricultural groups formed to protest its passage. Their movement, the Patriotic Movement for No (*Movimiento Patriótico Contra el Tratado de Libre Comercio*), nearly succeeded in stopping CAFTA's passage in Costa Rica. In this picture, a reminder of these protests can be seen on the side of a building in Heredia in 2014. The graffiti reads "No al TLC"—TLC being the Spanish acronym for CAFTA.

it the largest political demonstration in the country's history (Cupples and Larios 2010:98; Willis and Seiz 2012:133). On the eve of the referendum, polls suggested that the "No" movement had pulled ahead, pushing the pro-CAFTA camp into last-minute acts of desperation.[11] A press release from Washington, DC warned that if CAFTA was not ratified, Costa Rica would lose its trade benefits and privileges under the Caribbean Basin Initiative, the existing preferential trade agreement that granted Costa Rica special access to the US market (Cupples and Larios 2010:97; Willis and Seiz 2012:143–4). Many foreign companies told their workers that they would abandon their Costa Rican operations if CAFTA was not approved; other companies provided free transportation to the polls and half a day's pay to all "Yes" voters (Cupples and Larios 2010:97). Thus, the final results of the referendum were decidedly close. CAFTA was approved by just 51.6 percent of the voters. The difference was fewer than 50,000 votes (Willis and Seiz 2010:141). The agreement became effective on January 1, 2009.

In the months following the referendum, the "No" movement largely disbanded as disagreements over strategy and philosophy emerged (Frajman

2012:128; Willis and Seiz 2010:135). But the sentiments that fueled the anti-CAFTA movement did not disappear. In the 2014 elections, not one, but *two* populist political parties challenged the PLN and the Social Christian Unity Party (PUSC). In addition to PAC, which was trying a fourth time to present a viable alternative to the country's traditional two parties, there was the far more left-leaning *Frente Amplio* (Broad Front), which ran on a progressive and human rights platform. In the months before the election, polls showed the Broad Front virtually tied in first place with the long-standing PLN. After another runoff election, both parties lost to the center-left PAC candidate, Luis Guillermo Solís, who is now the president of Costa Rica.[12]

These election results do not suggest that Costa Rica is embracing some radical socialist agenda. On the contrary, Costa Rica remains politically moderate and decidedly capitalist. As I have suggested, many *Heredianos* have embraced aspects of the free-market philosophy because it dovetails with their varied survival strategies, small-business ethos, and historic integration into the global economy. In 2014, for example, Luis, the new professional discussed in Chapter 3, scoffed at the anti-CAFTA movement and the Latin American Left in general. "What's a little country like Costa Rica going to do if it cuts itself out of trade?" he asked in defense of his voting "yes" in the CAFTA referendum. But many *Heredianos* also articulated a sense of frustration with the free market and its troublesome side effects. Between these two viewpoints lay the Costa Rican state, which was expected by most to soften the rough edges of global capitalism. Margarita's comments in 2014 articulated this understanding. As she scrubbed clothes in an outdoor sink, she lamented the arrival of Walmart in Costa Rica and the instability of the country's export model. "Women used to be able to open a small *bazar* out of their house, earn a little money," she explained. "Now they can't compete! They can't even get jobs because the cost of labor is too expensive in Costa Rica; all the businesses are running off to Nicaragua and China! What happened to Intel? Gone! Levi's? Gone!" She ticked off multinational companies that had come and gone on pruned fingers as water ran out of the hose in the sink below. "Who knows? Maybe this new guy Solís will be different. Maybe he'll change things. *Ojalá*," she concluded, using one of the most oft-repeated phrases in Costa Rica that means "God willing."

A Nation Reimagined

I opened this chapter with the story of Cecilia, or Ceci, who never made it into my original study due to her age. But her case illuminates in so many ways the complicated future that lays ahead of Heredia and Costa Rica more generally. Ceci continues to reside in Heredia, although she had moved out of her parents' house just a few months before my 2014 revisit. The twists and turns her life took were startling to me, a welcome reminder that sociological predictions are almost always just good (and sometimes bad) guesses. In 2002, I predicted that Ceci would remain with her parents well into her 20s as a result of delayed marriage and childbearing, that she would become a hair stylist who received clients in a room out of her parents' house, and that she would dabble in classes at the university but never quite finish her degree. My predictions were based largely on her laid-back character and her very close relationship with her parents. They were also based on my understanding of trends in Heredia's middle class, such as delayed marriage, self-employment, and university education. But Ceci surprised me.

Ceci did remain in her parents' house well into her 20s and she did delay marriage and, to some extent, childbearing. In these respects, my predictions proved correct. But her work and family life in 2014 looked nothing like I had imagined back when Ceci was just beginning her adult life. It turns out that Ceci rejected a possible career in hairstyling, choosing instead to attend a private university, where she received her bachelor's degree in journalism. In that her final semester coincided with a surprise pregnancy, she had to fight hard to complete that degree. By the time she had the baby, she and the father, Freddy, had long broken up. They had been dating on and off for years, much to her parents' dismay. As Margarita would confide in me later, "Freddy was not exactly what we had imagined for Ceci." This admission was arguably a polite understatement. Freddy was not a well-educated professional with long roots in the Central Valley. He was from the coastal province of Limón, he was a singer, and he was black. Ceci and he had met at a club when Ceci was in her early twenties. She had e-mailed me often about him, describing him as not exactly to her parents' liking but a very decent man nonetheless. Eventually, they broke up and Ceci continued her university studies. But they still saw one another on occasion, which is how Ceci found herself at age 25, single and carrying his child.

"How did you learn about Ceci's pregnancy?" I wanted to know of Margarita when I visited in 2014. "She went to Violeta first. She was terrified of what we might say. Violeta and she came together to tell Ricardo and me," Margarita explained. "How did you react?" I asked. Margarita sighed and shifted in her chair. "You see, Ceci and Freddy had been long broken up. And I don't mean they had *just* broken up. They had *been* broken up for almost a year!" she exclaimed. "So when she told us she was pregnant, our first question was, 'Who is the father?' Imagine, just imagine, our surprise when she said Freddy." As Margarita recalled, Ricardo was so angry he spoke not one word. Later, in the privacy of their bedroom, Margarita had to counsel him on how to handle it. Margarita explained: "'Ricardo,' I said, 'What's done is done. Accept it and move on.' As for Ceci, I said, 'This is your life now, the result of your decision. Now you have to live it.' But I did give her one piece of advice. I told her 'Do not marry just for the sake of this baby. And if you do marry and leave this house, you're gone for good. There will be no returning.'"

Had Margarita not wanted her daughter to marry because she did not want Ceci to feel trapped? Or because Margarita, herself, did not want to welcome a black man into the family? This is hard to say. If it was the latter, the birth of Jason less than a year later left her little choice but to accept that her family had become racially mixed. Jason, a darling 2-year-old boy with boundless energy in 2014, was the mirror image of his father. Months before his birth, Ceci made the decision to have him on her own and, with her parents help, turned Violeta's old bedroom into a nursery. It was Margarita and Ricardo who went with Ceci to the hospital when it came time for Jason to be born; and it was Margarita and Ricardo who helped Ceci raise him in his first year of life. "That little Jason," Margarita said with a smile. "He is the light of his Tito's life." Tito is Ricardo, who, when I saw him in 2014 after an eight-year absence, gave me just a quick hug and kiss before searching the house for Jason. Finding him in the back bedroom, he wrapped his arms around him, showered him with kisses all over his tiny face, and whispered, "Who is Tito's favorite *negrito*?[13] You are, my love. You are."

When Jason was a year old, Ceci and Freddy began dating again. Margarita admits that he made a good effort to become part of Jason's life, giving Ceci money for diapers and formula. Just eight months before my arrival in 2014, they wed under a park gazebo in Heredia surrounded by close friends and family. By the time of my visit, they had moved into a small apartment some three blocks from Margarita and Ricardo's house. Ceci had by this time secured part-time work as a public relations officer for a small nongovernmental organization. She worked out of her apartment, with Jason underfoot, not because she had requested to telecommute, but because her part-time status did not afford her office space in the organization's downtown San José office. Unlike many young mothers who seek out part-time work to balance work and family obligations, Ceci would have preferred full-time. "This whole idea of part-time, *por favor* (please)!" she exclaimed to me on my first night in town. "It's full-time work with part-time benefits. Susie, I just want you to imagine, too, what it's like to work with your two-year-old child in the house. There have been times when I'm cooking Jason's lunch over the stove while on a conference call, with Jason screaming at my feet. I can't do this much longer."

On occasion, Ceci brought Jason over to Margarita's house so she could attend a meeting or get some work done. But both Ceci and Margarita agreed that what Ceci needed was work *afuera de la casa* (out of the house). They had their sights set on a government job that provided good benefits. The irony in all of this was not lost on me. Just one generation before, Margarita had prayed to God for an opportunity to quit her government job so that she could earn money while staying at home with her children. In part, economic restructuring made government jobs a kind of scarce resource, something for middle-class professionals to covet rather than expect. In part, gender restructuring had transformed married women's full-time work from something once exceptional to something now expected. But we only have to consider Violeta's middle-class life of privatized mothering to see that class also has some explanatory power here. Although raised in the same household with similar levels of education, Violeta and Ceci ended up in very different middle-class locations. Again, I cannot generalize from Ceci's situation, reading Heredia's future like tea leaves in the life of this woman. But her case provides in broad brushstrokes a suggestion of what it means to be *Herediano* at this moment in time—more racially heterogeneous, more educated and professionally savvy, but also more "feminized" in terms of economic insecurity. Perhaps Ceci cannot stand in for Heredia. But in that she is a native *Herediana*, middle class, and mestizo, she could arguably stand in for its exceptionalism. And in this sense, she is no longer the sheltered young girl who ventured no further than the front stoop of her parents' home, but a young woman forming an adult life out of the rubble of her family's middle-class mores, Heredia's racial anxiety, and Costa Rica's evolving state.

I find in Ceci's life, in this one poignant moment of becoming, an Heredia transformed. My last day in Heredia, Ceci invited me and Margarita over for lunch. Freddy took a break from his music to join us, while Jason, exhausted from a full-blown temper tantrum, slept soundly on a worn blue sofa. Over a lunch of spaghetti, we debated Costa Rican history and its meaning for the present. "My people came from St. Lucia, London, and Jamaica; became Costa Rican in the plains of Guanacaste; migrated to Limón to work for almost nothing on the railroad; and arrived in the Central Valley where we made our home," Freddy bellowed in his booming baritone voice. "This is not just my history; this is *our* history. A history that *we* are retelling. It is a kind of revolution." Margarita shifted uncomfortably in her chair, although she smiled politely. Ceci looked across the table at me and, quickly, before anyone noticed, winked at me in playful recognition of the hilarious incongruity of the scene. Margarita, who once contested every mention of racial others in discussions of *Herediano* society, was forced to contend with not simply a new family, but a new Heredia. When we stood to leave, Margarita stood on tiptoes to hug Freddy's large frame. "*Suegra* (mother-in-law)," he said, "next time you come, I'll make you some good Caribbean food." Freddy was right; this was nothing short of revolutionary.

The Ignoble Ethnographer

In 2014, Margarita and I celebrated 20 years of friendship. Although it had been some eight years since I had last seen her, we slipped back into a comfortable routine of mutual teasing and affection. It was as if no tension had ever existed between us. But tension had defined our relationship many times over the years. Back in 2002, as I prepared to leave the field and return home to the United States, my bedroom in Margarita's house was stripped to its bare bones. I took down maps and photographs from the walls, pulling off chunks of bright blue paint with the tape as I did so. The scarred walls became a visual testament to all the messiness I left behind after a year of fieldwork. After the incident with Pedro, tensions between Margarita and I came to a head, ending in a tense standoff over a breakfast of soggy cereal and stale bread. A year's worth of minor misunderstandings and hurt emotions were laid bare, as Margarita and I alternated between indignation and defensiveness. Exhausted by the end of the conversation, I wiped salty tears from my cheeks and said, "I'm sorry, Margarita. I'm sorry I didn't communicate better with you this past year. But I'm very thankful for having you in my life." Margarita looked taken aback, as if she had never received an apology and was not sure what to say next. Her own eyes welled up with tears and, as she dabbed the corner of her eyes with a wilted napkin, said finally, "Well, there's no point in crying about it." And with that, she stood up, walked to the kitchen sink, and began washing dishes. Later that day, upon returning home from the Internet café, I found a vase of fresh yellow flowers in my bedroom with a note from Margarita that said, "*Siempre amigas*" (always friends).

It was not simply Margarita with whom my relationship was strained. Walking into downtown Heredia was like an arcade game in which I had to dodge individuals with whom I had some issue. Everywhere I turned, complicated social relationships lurked. There was Roberto, the Colombian who managed an Internet café and whose excessive romantic advances were too uncomfortable to bear; Alvarado, who lived in Barrio Cleto Gonzalez and whose greetings always seemed to morph into long conversations about accepting Jesus as my savior; and Alejandra, who cleaned a corner grocery store and who would pause for long stretches of time to complain about her "worthless" ex-husband. On days that I had errands to run and appointments to keep, and even on days when I wanted to take a leisurely walk through town, I picked my routes carefully, taking side streets and circuitous pathways as I marveled at how field work can end on such complicated terms.

Ethnographers have long recognized the trope of the noble savage— that idealized indigenous "other" who anthropologists and sociologists have pursued, constructed, and romanticized in research around the world. But it struck in me in my final weeks in Heredia that we might also speak of the "noble ethnographer." The noble ethnographer observes the cultural world around them dispassionately and analytically, never reacting, and certainly not over-reacting, to the events and people that form the basis of their research and writing. They track down sources and quotes with the finesse of a seasoned journalist and have unlimited tolerance for whatever environmental conditions and individual personalities that they encounter. Indeed, they love getting wet during the rainy season; engaging in conversations that stretch endlessly into the night; and spending countless hours in the sun with paper, pencil, and camera. In short, the noble ethnographer is a *good* ethnographer and a *happy* ethnographer (Smith 2009). But the noble ethnographer is not me.

My first fieldwork experience took place in Kenya, where I barely survived the stresses of qualitative research. When I returned to the University of Michigan and described these stresses to my anthropology professor, he looked at me and scoffed, "You weren't even in the 'bush.'" According to his version of fieldwork, ethnographers were supposed to be remotely located, emotionally detached, and decidedly rugged. They were not supposed to have a culture of their own, personal problems, or bad days. Nor were they to tire, cry, or lose hope and perspective. In contrast, I was in a well-traveled field site and was more apt to wear high heels than hiking boots. I was also introverted and had a need for unusual amounts of personal space and quiet time. I found the whole ethnographic enterprise emotionally, mentally, and physically exhausting, even as it satisfied my intellectual curiosities and humanistic impulses. In these earlier years, I had the distinct feeling that I was the world's worst ethnographer. But as I have gained fieldwork experience, I have come to the conclusion that ethnographers can and do feel many things beyond interest, affection, and joy in field work. They just are not supposed to write about it.

If the noble ethnographer is an idealized abstraction of what a "good" ethnographer should be, then I am quite comfortable calling myself an ignoble ethnographer. Ignoble ethnographers are as excited as they are exhausted, at once interested and irritated, and decidedly analytical but also emotional. In short, ignoble ethnographers are human, just like their research "subjects." In that I now have two children of my own, I can say that being an ethnographer is a lot like being a parent. And this was perhaps my greatest ethnographic discovery. My old anthropology professor no doubt understood ethnographers to be more physician-like than parent-like. But my own experience was far too intimate and far too personal to ever resemble anything clinical and scientific. In the end, then, my ethnographic experiences are human experiences—never dispassionate, always a little messy, and at once painful and joyful. Perhaps the best thing that we can do as ethnographers is to admit and accept that human element. It is, after all, the one genuine connection that ties us to the people we are studying, that makes us care for them and not simply gaze at them.

On May 9, 2002 at 5:00 in the morning, Margarita, Ricardo, and I left for the airport where a plane bound for the United States waited. Ceci got up to hug me goodbye before returning, half asleep, to bed. At the airport, Margarita hugged me tightly and between tears said, "Forgive me, Susie, for anything I did wrong. You know you mean a great deal to me." I hugged her back and then hugged Ricardo, saying nothing because I was too exhausted to think of something meaningful to say. But as I walked away, I thought back to when I had first arrived to do my fieldwork. Margarita and Ricardo had picked me up from the airport and we drove to their home, talking quickly and smiling madly. When we got to the house, the girls were sound asleep in their bed. Margarita threw on all the lights in the house and woke them up. "Our Susie is home!" she screamed, "Our Susie is home!" The memory brought tears to my face but also a quiet smile. In the years that followed my return home that day in 2002, I would finish my dissertation, become a professor, get married, and give birth to two children. By the time I returned to Margarita's house in 2014, I would be the same age as she was when I first met her in 1994 and in remarkably similar circumstances—raising two young daughters, married to a government worker, and living in tumultuous economic times. The experience would make me all the more sympathetic to the angst and frustration that hung throughout Margarita and Ricardo's house like a thick fog that year. Margarita and Ricardo were never "labor inputs" or "middle class workers." They were never research "subjects" or "cases." And they were never some oppressed or romantic "other." They were human. And so was I.

Sample Characteristics

	MEN (n = 52)	WOMEN (n = 48)	TOTAL (n = 100)
Age			
15–24	14	14	28
25–44	14	13	27
45–64	14	18	32
65+	10	3	13
Place of Birth			
Heredia province	32	33	65
Other Costa Rican province	15	11	26
Outside Costa Rica	5	4	9
Civil Status			
Single	22	26	48
Married/unión libre	24	16	40
Divorced/separated/widowed	6	6	12
Number of Children			
0	21	21	42
1–2	15	14	29
3+	16	13	29
Educational Level			
Primary or less	13	19	32
Some or all secondary	27	16	43
At least some post-secondary	12	13	25
Economic Condition			
Economically active	39	28	67
Economically inactive	13	20	33

GLOSSARY OF SPANISH TERMS

....

Ama de casa Housewife

Amigos con derechos Literally, friends with privileges; usually refers to two people in a sexual relationship without an emotional or romantic commitment to one another

Área metropolitana Metropolitan area surrounding a major city

Barrio(s) Neighborhood(s)

Bazar Small store, usually selling gifts and small novelties

Beneficio(s) Coffee-processing plant(s)

Cabildo(s) Administrative council(s) that governed municipalities in early postcolonial Costa Rica

Callejera Colloquial term for a woman, usually a prostitute, who works the streets

Cantina Bar

Cantón (pl. *cantones*) Administrative subdivision(s) in Costa Rica; slightly smaller than a county

Carnicería Butcher shop

Chiquilla Term of endearment for a younger girl; Margarita used it with all her daughters

Colón (pl. *colones*) Official currency in Costa Rica

Compañero(a) Partner; in some contexts, refers to a romantic partner

Dependiente Store clerk or salesperson (in Costa Rica)

Diplomado 2-year college degree; akin to an associate's degree in the United States

Doctorado Doctoral degree

Encomienda Labor system in the Spanish empire in which the Spanish crown awarded a person the legal right to exploit indigenous labor in exchange for their protection; this system had limited applicability to colonial Costa Rica due to the small indigenous population

Finca Farm or ranch

Gallo pinto Dish of black beans and rice often eaten at breakfast in Costa Rica

Gringo(a) Person who is not Hispanic or Latino; usually refers to a non-Hispanic white from the United States

Guapo(a) Handsome; can be used in reference to men or women in Costa Rica

Herediano(s) Resident(s) of Heredia, Costa Rica

Hija Daughter; in Costa Rica, it can also be used when referring to a young woman

Licenciatura 4- to 5-year college degree; akin to a bachelor's degree in the United States

Los Estados Unidos (The) United States

Macho Term used to describe very traditional, masculine men in Costa Rica

Maestría 2-year postgraduate degree; akin to a master's degree in the United States

Maicero(s) Maize grower; in Costa Rica, maize growing predominates in the country's northwest

Malcreada Person who is ill-bred, spoiled, and/or rude

Maquiladora Export factory usually operated by a multinational corporation in a free-trade zone in Mexico, Central America, or the Caribbean; also referred to simply as a *maquila*

Meseta Central Literally, the "Central Table;" the central plateau that characterizes Costa Rica's topography

Mestizaje Process of racial mixing

Mestizo(s) Person(s) of mixed racial ancestry

Metiche A nosy person (usually a woman) who gets into other people's business

Movilidad laboral Literally, labor mobility; refers to government workforce reduction programs that began in the 1990s

Muchacha Young woman

Nica Derogatory term used in Costa Rica to refer to Nicaraguans or, in some cases, any person who is dark-skinned and poor

Ojalá Common phrase in Costa Rica meaning "God willing"

Pirata(s) Unlicensed taxi driver in Costa Rica

Precario Dilapidated shack made of sheet metal, cardboard and/or pieces of wood; the landless individuals who inhabit these dwellings are referred to as *precaristas*

Profesorado 2- to 3-year college degree, mostly for teacher training

Pulpería Small neighborhood store that provides families with basic necessities, such as tortillas and eggs, which can be bought on credit from the *pulpero*, or store owner

Quinciñiera Fifteenth birthday party and a major coming-of-age moment for young women in Latin America; often celebrated with an elaborate party for family and friends; akin to the "sweet sixteen" birthday in the United States

Siesta Afternoon nap usually taken after lunchtime

Soda Small low-priced food stand catering to workers

Solidarismo Alternative to unionization that developed in Costa Rica in the late 1940s; the *solidarista* association acts as an employee savings fund, to which both labor and management contribute

Suegra Mother-in-law

Tamales Dish of seasoned meat wrapped in cornmeal dough and steamed or baked in corn husks

Tico(a) Colloquial term for a native Costa Rican; used by Costa Ricans when referring to themselves

Unión libre Union in which a couple cohabitates but does not marry; akin to a common law marriage in the United States, but not legally binding

Vagabundo Colloquial term in Costa Rica that means a do-nothing, or a person who does not work, study, or contribute to society; often refers to drug-addicted, unemployed, male youth in Costa Rica

Zonas francas Territorially bound industrial parks where nontraditional export production and processing are concentrated in Costa Rica; companies in these zones enjoy fiscal incentives and proximity to urban labor markets

NOTES

....

Chapter 1

1. Scholars contest almost all of the terms used in reference to low- and middle-income countries, most with a history of colonization. Many terms, such as "Third World," are outdated, misleading, and insensitive. Hence, when I use the term "Third World," I will put it in quotes. Likewise, I will use other terms, such as global South and developing world, with the acknowledgment that they are imperfect and problematic.

2. The first of these—state protection of domestic industries—was a key component of the "import-substitution industrialization" approach. In this approach, domestic industries were protected from foreign competition through state subsidies and tariffs. The purpose was to overcome the developing world's positioning in the world economy as an exporter of primary goods and to nurture indigenous industrial development.

3. There are important variations in this respect within Latin America. Costa Rica is generally considered the most equal and Brazil among the most unequal (Portes and Hoffman 2003:60).

4. According to Grugel and Riggirozzi (2012), one of the things accommodating the post-neoliberal turn is increased demand for natural resource exports from Latin America, which have helped subsidize new welfare programs for the poor.

5. The philosophy behind conditional cash transfer programs, most of which are modeled after Brazil's *Bolsa Familia* program, is that the intergenerational cycle of poverty can be broken by investing in the human capital of children. Some form of these programs has been implemented in almost every Latin American country since the 1990s. Examples include

Mexico's *Progresa/Oportunidades* program, Chile's *Solidario* program, and El Salvador's *Red Solidaria* program. Of these, Mexico's *Progresa/ Oportunidades* program has been the most widely studied (Cecchini and Madariaga 2011). Costa Rica's version of this program, known as *Avancemos*, will be discussed in Chapter 6.

6. Another critique is that because many of these programs pivot on the role of mothers in ensuring that children go to school and/or get health checks, they have the effect of retraditionalizing gender roles in Latin America (Molyneux 2007).

7. Early research in this area debated whether such work was a positive or negative development for women in the developing world. Lim (1990) and Tiano (1994) argued that women's factory work had at least some positive aspects. Fernandez-Kelly (1983) and Ward (1990) disagreed, pointing to women's subjugation within the workplace and the home. By the mid-1990s, the consensus was that the answer was somewhere in between. As low-wage factory workers, women become a source of highly exploited labor, but they also find new sources of autonomy within the world of work and home (Salzinger 2003; Sassen 1998).

8. When interviewed, managers in the new export factories have explained that they recruit women workers because women are more biologically suited to routine assembly work. Women supposedly have more "nimble" fingers and a more docile disposition on the shop floor (Elson and Pearson 1981; Fernandez-Kelly 1983; Ong 1987; Safa 1981). Scholars discount such explanations, arguing instead that employers prefer female workers because they are unorganized, can be paid lower wages, and can be hired and fired with ease (Fernandez-Kelly 1983; Safa 1981).

9. In response to economic insecurity, many households also altered their consumption patterns (Benería and Feldman 1992) and engaged in sideline economic activities (González de la Rocha 1994, 2001).

10. For more on how women protest the erosion of household survival at the neighborhood and community level, see Chant and Craske (2003), Craske (1999), and Molyneux (1998, 2003).

11. See also special issues of the *European Journal of Development Research* (2000, vol. 12, no. 2) and *Men and Masculinities* (2001, vol. 3, no. 3).

12. There are a couple of noteworthy exceptions in this regard. Carla Freeman's *High Tech and High Heels in the Global Economy* (2000) details how women working in high-tech informatics jobs in Barbados come to distinguish themselves from ordinary factory workers through dress and the adoption of "pink-collar identities." Here, we get a sense of how women become "modern" female subjects and not simply low-wage labor inputs. Likewise, Pun Ngai's *Made in China*

(2005) provides rich detail about young women working at a factory in Shenzhen, China. She documents how the bodies and psyches of these women resist the dehumanization of the global assembly line. But she also shows how women romanticize modern city life, which keeps them migrating into China's "special economic zones" in search of work. Both ethnographies are among my favorites because they give a sense of the everyday lifeworlds of workers.

13. To be sure, many studies demonstrate the ways in which workers have become historical agents in the neoliberal era. Mendez (2005), for example, investigates the collective efforts of women in Nicaragua to better their working conditions (see also Bandy and Mendez 2003). But the starting point of these studies is a grass-roots mobilization that has already delineated a critique of the neoliberal model. It is not the story of how individuals make sense of their changing economic realities and arrive at what turns out to be very diverse political and social outcomes.

14. Mills died of a heart attack in 1962 at the age of 45.

15. Costa Rica is organized into seven provinces and 81 *cantones* (roughly, counties), within which are several districts. Heredia is the name given to one of these provinces. Within this province, there is also a *cantón* by the name of Heredia, and within this central *cantón* a district by the name of Heredia. It is this central district that serves as the provincial capital. Although Heredia is my focus in this study, I did not want to cast my net to include the whole province. It is both too big and extends all the way into the north, where economic conditions are completely different. At the same time, I did not want to limit my study to Heredia's central district, which holds a decreasing portion of the area's population as people move outward into suburban neighborhoods. Therefore, I encircled an area on a map large enough to include many of these population movements and close enough to the city center to be part of the same labor market and social milieu. Ultimately, I chose eleven districts, which correspond to four different *cantones*, all in the province of Heredia and part of the San José metropolitan area.

16. Because I had not originally planned to revisit my study site, the original human subject's protocol for my research project required that I destroy the list of study participants, which included full names and addresses. Therefore, I had no systematic way of following up on each study participant. Instead, I contacted those participants with whom I had kept in touch—about 15 percent of my sample. Hence, the data for my revisits are very limited in nature.

17. I will delve into this issue much more in Chapters 2 and 6.

18. There is much debate about being an insider versus an outsider in qualitative research. It is fair to say that there are advantages and disadvantages associated with each. Insiders may not be detached enough to analyze their

social world effectively, and outsiders may be too detached to really understand it. I would describe my own relationship as one that constantly shifted between emotional attachment ("insider") and scientific detachment ("outsider").

19. Portes and Hoffman identify three types of elite classes in Latin America: capitalists, executives, and professionals. I did not interview any capitalists or executives for this project. So professionals are the only "elite" individuals I studied.

20. In addition to these social classes, Portes and Hoffman (2003) identify a petty bourgeoisie class made up of own-account professional workers (i.e., independent consultants) and small business persons (i.e., microentrepreneurs). But the ways in which the cultural lifeways, social networks, and economic trajectories were patterned in my sample, I combined independent consultants with professional workers and microentrepreneurs with white-collar, middle class workers.

21. Table 1.1 includes the category "Retired/not included," which refers to the retired individuals in my sample who are not featured in the empirical chapters. Some of these retired individuals are discussed in the next chapter, which sketches out key moments in Costa Rican history.

Chapter 2

1. A *unión libre* is akin to a common law marriage in the United States.

2. This was possibly stomach cancer, of which Costa Rica has one of the highest rates in the Western world.

3. Because of its topography and location near the equator, temperatures in Costa Rica do not vary by season but by altitude. The central mountain ranges interact with trade winds to produce a distinct dry season (January–April) and rainy season (May–December).

4. During most of the colonial period, Costa Rica was not its own colony but the southernmost province of the Captaincy General of Guatemala, an administrative division of the Spanish empire that consisted of most of Central America.

5. This migration outward from Cartago was technically in its second phase by this point. The first phase occurred in the 1600s and involved migration to such hamlets as Barva and Curridabat, where indigenous populations concentrated and colonial officials attempted to establish an *encomienda* system. The contemporary Catholic Church in Barva, a small town to the north of Heredia, for example, sits atop an old indigenous burial ground. The name of the town was borrowed from the indigenous chief of this area. Largely as a result of the failure of the *encomienda* system to resolve the labor

problems of the time, the second phase of settlement favored areas that were independent of indigenous populations (Gonzalez 1997:21–2).

6. The strike was led by Carlos Luis Fallas, among Costa Rica's most important labor leaders and novelists. Fallas began his work life on a banana plantation, and his novel, *Mamita Yunai* (1941), depicts brutal working conditions on banana plantations under the domineering control of North American managers. Fallas would later migrate to the Central Valley, where he became a shoemaker and joined the Communist Party.

7. Figueres' abolishing the army was done largely to prevent an armed insurrection against himself rather than for any peaceful motives on his part (Paige 1997:148–50).

8. The Party would not be legalized again until 1972.

9. By the 1940s, Universidad de Costa Rica in San José had already been established. Later, Universidad Nacional (UNA) in Heredia, a technical college in Cartago, and a distance learning university were also established (Miron 1989:150).

10. One of the problems was that coastal land was being taken up in ever larger portions by plantations. The other factor was the massive population explosion throughout the country after 1950. Between 1950 and 1973, the population skyrocketed from 800,000 to 2,000,000 (Molina and Palmer 2000:99).

11. In addition to banning the Communist Party, Figueres banned the Costa Rican Workers Confederation (CTCR in Spanish), which represented 125 unions and had close ties with the Communist Party (Donato and Rojas 1989).

12. *Solidarismo* was an idea developed by an associate of Figueres by the name of Alberto Martén. In an incredibly ironic twist of fate, I became friendly with Martén's son during my field work. Like his father, Martén junior is an ardent anticommunist, who studied medicine in the United States. In 2002, he was a plastic surgeon and ran a successful private practice in San José.

13. Many scholars argue that it tends to work to the advantage of management (Rojas 1989:158).

14. Technically, there were three structural adjustment programs implemented in Costa Rica under the auspices of the World Bank. They were initiated in 1985, 1989, and 1995, respectively (Marois 2005:111).

15. Such assistance came with a price. The country was expected to give US military operatives full use of its northern territory to launch an offensive against the socialist revolution in Nicaragua (Clark 2001:49–51).

16. These zones are also referred to as "export free zones," "industrial export zones," and "industrial parks" in Costa Rica.

17. In 2014, Intel announced it was closing most of its operations in Costa Rica, a topic to which I turn in a later chapter.

18. In 1983, opposition to Figueres' National Liberation Party (PLN) allied under the Social Christian Unity Party (PUSC), which has since alternated power with PLN.

19. These revisits were much shorter in length, each lasting approximately one month.

Chapter 3

1. Located in between cocaine producers in South America and drug cartels in Mexico, Costa Rica is something of a way station for drug smugglers and money launderers. Although violent crimes against US citizens are not committed frequently, there has been an increase overall in drug-related and violent crime in the country, especially in coastal areas and in downtown San José. As such, the US Department of State has given Costa Rica a high crime rating and it recommends that walking alone at night be avoided. For more on these trends, see the Organismo de Investigacion Judicial (2013), US Bureau of Diplomatic Security (2014), and US Bureau of International Narcotics and Law Enforcement Affairs (2014).

2. In the group of 100 *Heredianos* that I interviewed (85 of whom were not retired), 15 were part of this professional class. Given my sampling technique, we cannot take this group as representative of all professional workers in Heredia. But some of the basic characteristics of this subsample may be of interest. These 15 individuals were more or less equally divided between men (n = 7) and women (n = 8). As a group, they were relatively young, with 12 of the 15 younger than age 45. All but three of the individuals in this group boasted a university degree, and the remaining three were either attending the university full-time or planning to do so. On the whole, the group was made up of more public sector workers (n = 8) than either private sector workers (n = 5) or independent contractors (n = 2). About half of the individuals in this group (n = 7) were married. A smaller number of women (n = 1) than men (n = 4) had children.

3. This was up from 5 percent in 1973 and 15 percent in 2000. Education statistics were retrieved from the Fourth Report on the State of Education, published by the Programa Estado de la Nación. (Retrieved on August 14, 2014 at http://www.estadonacion.or.cr/estadisticas/compendio-estadisticas/compendio-costa-rica/compendio-costa-rica-educacion.)

4. By comparison, the professional workers I interviewed represent a little less than 18 percent of the nonretired individuals in my sample.

5. Higher education in Costa Rica is provided by public and private universities, as well as various private postsecondary institutions ("para-universities"). The latter typically award technical and business certificates. Higher education in the country is generally divided into three stages. The first stage, which consists

of two to three years of university training, results in the *diplomado* (akin to an associate's degree in the United States) or the *profesorado* (an intermediary degree between the associate's and bachelor's degree; mostly for teacher training). The second stage, which consists of four to five years of school, results in the *licenciatura* (akin to a bachelor's degree). The third stage, which consists of two to four years of school, results in the *maestría* (akin to a master's degree) or the *doctorado* (akin to a doctorate degree).

6. More recently, a special fund for public universities was negotiated between the state and public universities, but the fund has been riddled with problems due to the global financial crisis.

7. In 2008, for example, 62 percent of university diplomas were awarded from private universities, compared to 28 percent from state universities (Programa Estado de la Nación 2008:87).

8. The Fourth State of Education Report found that students attending private universities are more likely to hail from technical and evening high schools, both of which are less academically rigorous (Programa Estado de la Nación 2013a:23).

9. During my 2014 follow-up, at least two of the professional men in this group had switched from the private sector to the public sector. So it could be that this gender difference became less pronounced over time. Both men mentioned that the government offered better benefits than did the private sector.

10. This was even true for Ana Lucía, whose salary would go down at ICE if she started her own consulting business. This is due to a salary incentive the agency has to keep its workers from competing with the agency for contracts.

11. When I was conducting the bulk of my fieldwork in 2001 to 2002, most commuters traveled to San José by bus or car. By 2014, most commuters were traveling to the capital by train. Costa Rica established a commuter train system in 2005, in response to the gridlock experienced during rush hour.

12. The previous three urban-planning attempts were: (1) the establishment of a national institute for housing and urban planning (*Instituto Nacional de Vivienda y Urbanismo*) in 1954, (2) the first law regulating urban development (*Ley de Planificacíon Urbana*) in 1968, and (3) an urban development plan for the greater metropolitan area (*Plan para la Gran Área Metropolitana*) in 1982 (Avalos 2001).

13. See Hite and Viterna (2005) for an in-depth discussion of the indicators of gender parity among professional workers in Latin America.

14. It is still the case that the higher the education, the lower the incidence of single motherhood. In other words, single motherhood is more pronounced among less educated women. But as Esteve et al. (2012) demonstrate, the relationship between education and single motherhood is reversed when

we consider women who are already mothers. Among mothers, single motherhood is actually more frequent among those with advanced education than among those with a primary school education or less.

15. Among social scientists, economists have been the most attentive to the growth of Latin America's middle class. See, for example, Birdsall (2012).

16. Research on women's activism in Latin American suggests an historic divide between feminist activism, which has been dominated by elite, middle-class women, and grassroots activism, which has been dominated by nonelite women involved in community and consumption issues rather than women's issues per se (Molyneux 1998; Safa 1990).

17. Currently, abortion in Costa Rica is illegal, even in cases of rape or incest, unless to preserve the life or physical health of the woman.

18. A striking example can be found in former President Laura Chinchilla. In 2010, Chinchilla became the first woman elected President of Costa Rica, but her official position on abortion was that she would fight any legislative attempt to legalize it in the country.

Chapter 4

1. As is typical of countries that have industrialized and experienced an increased standard of living, Costa Rica has undergone a demographic transition in which birth rates have fallen over time. As such, we see a huge difference in the number of children that Rosalina's mother had (twelve children who lived to be at least age 2) and the number of children that Rosalina had (two children). Costa Rica's fertility rate is now below the replacement level, which is the level at which a population exactly replaces itself from one generation to the next. For most developed countries, the replacement level is 2.1 children per woman. In Costa Rica, the fertility rate is around 1.8 children per women.

2. Again, because I did not take a random sample of Heredia's population, the characteristics of this group are not representative of all members of Heredia's lower middle class. Even so, some basic description of this group is in order. In the group of 100 Heredianos that I interviewed (85 of whom were not retired), 6 men and 8 women (n = 14) were part of this lower middle-class group. The group was predominantly middle age, with 12 out of the 14 individuals between the ages of 45 and 64. The majority (n = 10) were married with children. All but 2 individuals were native *Heredianos*, with an average of twenty-two years living in their then current residence. Among the 8 economically active men and women, 5 were in the public sector and 3 were self-employed.

3. A select few found their way into the professional class described in the previous chapter.

4. As such, many of these individuals will be the subject of the next two chapters.

5. By comparison, the individuals who I describe in this chapter represent around 16 percent of the nonretired individuals in my sample.

6. According to the 2011 census, 64 percent of women age 15 and over in Costa Rica were economically inactive. Statistic obtained from *Instituto Nacional de Estadística y Censos* at http://www.inec.go.cr/Web/Home/ GeneradorPagina.aspx, accessed on August 20, 2014.

7. Specifically, five of the seven women I interviewed were married to a state worker or small businessman.

8. Health insurance through the Costa Rican Social Security Fund extends to all dependents of workers. The only groups left out of these social programs are the self-employed and seasonal workers, although there are strong government incentives for these groups to join voluntarily. By virtue of being outside the fold of government regulation, informal workers are necessarily excluded from these social welfare programs.

9. Clark (2001:33) points out that because the state provides free health insurance to the uninsured poor, the remaining 10 percent of people lacking health insurance do so because they voluntarily seek medical care through private doctors rather than enroll in the state healthcare system. In this sense, there are virtually no Costa Ricans who involuntarily lack access to healthcare.

10. By law, public sector workers in Costa Rica who leave as part of a state employment reduction program are entitled to one month's salary for each year they were employed by the government (Clark 2001:164). The costs associated with these severance packages stalled initial efforts to reduce the government workforce. In 1991, the US Agency for International Development contributed $12 million to help defray these severance costs, allowing the program to move forward (Clark 2001:73).

11. In this chapter, I use "microenterprise" and "self-employment" interchangeably. Technically, "self-employment" is the broader of the two terms, encompassing both sole proprietors and owners of businesses that employ less than five people.

12. Costa Rica celebrates Mother's Day on August 15. *El Dia de las Madres*, as the day is known, is a national holiday.

13. Three of these four women left the labor force to care for children, and one left to care for aging parents. Of the remaining two women featured in this chapter, one had never married and was employed by the state at the time of our interview. The other woman was married to a state worker and had never worked outside of the home.

14. Among these enterprises were those in sugar refining, fertilizer, cotton, and aluminum.

15. My interpretation resembles that of Benería and Roldán (1987), who found in their study of homeworkers in Mexico City that it was not so much men's lack of help around the house but their failed efforts in the economic sphere that disappointed their wives.

16. Public sector unions have been quite active in resisting state cutbacks, which explains in part why Costa Rica has been so slow to reduce its government workforce (Clark 2001).

17. Relatively liberal divorce laws have been on the books in Costa Rica since 1974. Under the Family Code (*Código de familia*) of that year, individuals may petition for a divorce for a variety of reasons. Since that time, divorce rates have gone up in the country, from 9.9 to 21.2 per 100 between 1980 and 1996 (Chant 2002:111). Nonetheless, divorce is still a stigma among many middle-aged and middle-class *Heredianos*.

18. According to a 2012 US Department of Agriculture (USDA) report on the Costa Rican retail food sector "some customers are known to visit their favorite neighborhood 'pulperia' as often as four times a day. And while middle-class Costa Ricans enjoy their biweekly visit to a large supermarket, many supplement the large weekly purchase with visits to these popular traditional markets . . ." (USDA Foreign Agricultural Service 2012).

19. The election turned out to be an historic one. For the first time in Costa Rica's modern history, no candidate received a majority of the votes. With the fewest votes of all three major candidates, Solís conceded defeat. But the challenge he had posed to Costa Rica's entrenched two-party system served as a wake-up call to PUSC and the PLN, who would go on to compete in an historic runoff on April 7, 2002. The PUSC candidate, Abel Pacheco, won.

20. In 2012, Walmart owned more than 80 percent of supermarkets in Costa Rica. Its 214 retail outlets include Walmart stores but also other brands such as Palí and Mas x Menos. A study conducted in 2013 found that these are the most visited supermarkets in Costa Rica.

Chapter 5

1. When I returned to Heredia for my follow-up research, I was unable to track down Mario.

2. In the group of 100 *Heredianos* that I interviewed (85 of whom were not retired), 33 were part of this formal working class or tied to this formal working class through family. Again, this group cannot be taken as representative of the formal working class in Heredia due to my sampling method. But some of the characteristics of this group may be of interest. Of these 33 individuals, there were 15 men and 18 women. As a group, they were predominantly between the ages of 15 and 24 (n = 10) or 25 and 44 (n = 15),

with fewer than one-fourth between the ages of 45 and 64 (n = 8). Reflecting these ages, a little less than half of the group had never married (n = 15) and some two-thirds had no children (n = 12). Ten of the individuals in this group were economically inactive (students, homemakers, and/or the disabled). Of the 23 economically active individuals, 8 were self-employed, 13 were employed in the private sector, and 2 were employed in the public sector. The majority of the individuals in this group had completed their secondary education (n = 6) or had some secondary school education (n = 18). A sizable minority had not completed primary school (n = 7). Of these 7 individuals, 6 were women.

3. By comparison, the individuals who I describe in this chapter represent around 39 percent of the nonretired individuals in my sample. The elevated figure is probably due to the fact that I include a handful of economically inactive students, disabled workers, and unemployed workers in this group. Were I to exclude these individuals, the workers described in this chapter would represent around 27 percent of the nonretired individuals in my sample, which would be more in line with the estimates provided by Portes and Hoffman (2003).

4. In a couple of cases, the students that I interviewed had no formal work history, but their family's class background and their social location were likely to place them in the formal working class once they completed school.

5. Comparable estimates for the manual formal working class can be found in Chile and Venezuela.

6. In 2000, there were more than 245,000 immigrants living in Costa Rica, and some 87,000 Costa Rican immigrants living abroad (OECD 2009). Even so, Kordick (2012) cautions against viewing Costa Rica as a mere receiving country, because this understates the importance of emigration for particular Costa Rican communities. The bulk of Costa Rica's emigrants come from two areas: the Los Santos–Pérez Zeledón region and the area around Grecia, Sarchí, and Palmares along the eastern edge of the Central Valley (Kordick 2012). As Kordick (2012) points out in her study of emigrants from the coffee-growing region of Los Santos–Pérez Zeledón, emigration became popular among men in the 1980s when declining coffee prices made it nearly impossible for landless workers or small farmers to achieve mobility in the local economy. For these areas, emigration has become standard—for men in particular. Thus, although numerically, Costa Rica does receive more migrants than it sends, emigration is critical to many communities in the country.

7. The majority of Costa Rican immigrants in the United States live in California (especially Los Angeles), Florida (especially Miami and Fort Lauderdale), New Jersey (especially Trenton and Paterson), New York

(especially New York City), and Texas (especially Houston and Galveston). For an in-depth and fascinating study of Costa Rican immigrants from the canton of Tarrazú who have settled in and around Paterson, New Jersey, see Kordick (2012).

8. Those immigrants sent an estimated 110,000 million *colones* in remittances back to Costa Rica in 2004, more than the country's coffee export earnings from that year (Feigenblatt 2005). Kordick (2012) takes these figures as a clear sign that the immigrants Costa Rica does send have an important effect on many local economies in Costa Rica.

9. Indeed, some 70 percent of Costa Rican immigrants have at least a secondary school education (OECD 2009).

10. By 2013, unemployment remained at 8 percent, the second highest in Latin America (ECLAC 2014).

11. It is customary in *maquiladoras* not to hire pregnant women and/or to let workers go once they become pregnant.

12. This pattern is also typical of households throughout Latin America, where single mothers have a very high incidence of living in extended households (Esteve, García-Román, and Lesthaeghe 2012).

13. All figures are from the online database of Comision Economica para America Latina y el Caribe (CEPAL), Centro Latinoamericano y Caribeno de Demografia (CELADE), Division de Poblacion (http://www.eclac.cl/migracion/migracion_interna/seleccion.asp?parametro=DAM_Costa_Rica_2000.prn|Costa Rica 2000|DAM). Accessed on March 7, 2011.

14. See Esteve, García-Román, and Lesthaeghe (2012), who find very high rates of coresidence in extended family households for much of Latin America's population.

15. By 2014, they had repainted the church a light shade of peach.

16. José Luis' decision to move in with a friend is an exception to the more common practice of men and women returning to their natal family after marital dissolution.

17. Data obtained from World Bank (http://databank.worldbank.org/Data/Views/reports/tableview.aspx, accessed on September 11, 2014). See also the 2013 State of the Nation report on youth unemployment in Costa Rica (http://www.estadonacion.or.cr/files/biblioteca_virtual/019/Pacheco_2013.pdf). As this report makes clear, rates for youth unemployment are particular high for youth in urban areas, for youth with an incomplete secondary school education or less, and for female youth.

18. The working-class men in this group shared a remarkably similar job trajectory as Carlos. Nine of the 17 men in this group started off as *dependientes* (store clerks) or assistants during their mid-teens. Carlos, David,

Victor, José, and Bernardo started off in grocery stores, and Rafael, Jonathan, Joaquin, and José Luis in their father's small businesses. After their first job, 8 of the 17 went to work at a factory. Carlos worked at a factory producing nuts and bolts, Rafael at a chemical factory, José Luis at a textile factory, Bernardo at a fruit export packing plant, Alvaro at a leather exporting plant, Joaquin at an electronics factory, José at a ceramics factory, and Mariano at a plant packaging Speedstick deodorant for export. As their employment history developed, 7 of the 17 took on jobs in the most traditionally masculine of areas: cars. Carlos became a trained mechanic; David worked at a used car lot; José Luis took a job at an auto parts store; Gerardo bought and sold used cars; and José Luis, Ernesto, and Bernardo became taxi drivers. At this stage, two of the men migrated to North America to work for a year—Rafael to Florida where he worked as a maintenance man and David to Texas where he worked in construction. In both cases, these men returned to Costa Rica to invest in small businesses. Rafael started his own Internet café, while David began importing and reselling used cars from the United States. The rest of the men in this group were no less entrepreneurial. In addition to Carlos' sidelines *pirata* business, José Luis partnered with a friend importing auto parts and Alvaro started his own leatherworking shop.

19. Economic insecurity had led many young men to do likewise. Indeed, *piratas* had become so common that licensed taxi drivers staged a work stoppage in June of 2001, parking their cars in the middle of the streets in San José to block traffic and draw attention to their plight. Chanting in front of San José's Supreme Court, they demanded that the government penalize pirate taxi drivers who, they argued, were stealing their business without having to pay for licensing fees (Wolkoff 2001). Less than a week later, *piratas* staged their own demonstration, demanding that the government give them temporary licenses (Murillo 2001). As one demonstrator remarked, "People need the money" (Feigenblatt 2001). In August, the government attempted to resolve the standoff by offering a limited number of licenses to unlicensed drivers while also instituting fines for those taxi drivers found driving without a permit (Golcher 2001).

20. The crude divorce rate is the number of divorces occurring in a particular population per 1,000. Statistics were obtained from the United Nations on September 12, 2014 at http://www.un.org/esa/population/publications/WMD2008/Data/UNPD_WMD_2008_DIVORCES.xls and http://unstats.un.org/unsd/demographic/products/dyb/dyb2011/Table25.pdf.

21. As Molina and Palmer (2000:106) point out, the rise of a mass production system also undercut the artisanal basis of the country's vibrant working-class culture.

Chapter 6

1. The Sandanistas took over the Nicaraguan government in 1979 after the Nicaraguan Revolution.

2. In the group of 100 *Heredianos* that I interviewed (85 of whom were not retired), 23 were informal workers. Of these workers, 12 were women and 11 were men. In terms of age, this group tended to be either younger (14 individuals between the ages of 15 and 24) or older (8 individuals between the ages of 45 and 64). More than one-fourth of the individuals in this group (n = 6) were single or widowed women with children. Almost one-third were immigrants (n = 7), most of them from Nicaragua. More than half (n = 12) had dropped out of primary school. In terms of work, most were own-account workers (n = 8) or unprotected wage workers (n = 6), although a sizable number were domestic workers (n = 2) or unpaid family workers (n = 3). Two of the individuals were unemployed, and 2 were housewives.

3. First, Portes and Hoffman (2003:52) tally the sum total of own-account workers (minus professionals and technicians), domestic servants, unpaid family workers, workers in small rural enterprises, and workers in urban microenterprises. This approximation results in the lower end estimate of 34 percent, which, they argue, does not fully include all informal workers because it excludes workers in large enterprises who are paid off the books. Using social security coverage as a proxy for formal employment, they adjust for this undercount by calculating the number of workers who are not covered by social security benefits. Using this second method, they arrive at the higher-end estimate of 39 percent (Portes and Hoffman 2003:52). By comparison, the individuals described in this chapter represent 27 percent of the nonretired individuals in my sample. Thus, it appears that I undersampled informal workers, which was likely given that informal workers perform "hidden" work and are difficult to find.

4. Using this definition, they estimate that the group constituted around 40 percent of the Costa Rican population in 2009 (Birdsall et al. 2014).

5. In 2012, the unemployment rate for individuals between the ages of 15 and 24 was almost 19 percent (Programa Estado de la Nación 2013a:108).

6. In 2009, "strugglers" in Costa Rica averaged six years of education, compared to eight years for the population as a whole (Birdsall et al. 2014:134).

7. Costa Rica's high school desertion rate among 15- to 19-year-olds (25 percent) is far above that of Chile (11 percent), the Dominican Republic (15 percent), and Venezuela and Brazil (19 percent) (Programa Estado de la Nación 2011:5).

8. *Avancemos* was modeled after similar "conditional cash transfer" programs elsewhere in Latin America (see Chapter 1). The program involves a cash transfer to poor families on the condition that a youngster remains in secondary school. The cash transfer increases as the age of the student increases, with the idea being that the older the student, the more likely he or she would be able to earn in the labor market. The average monthly stipend per person in 2008 was $52 (Molina and Fallas 2009:222).

9. This is not to say that men did not participate in street vending. At least two of the men I interviewed were working as street vendors at the time of my interview with them. My point here is simply that self-employed men are more likely to be found in construction and self-employed women in street vending.

10. Heredia has slightly more foreign-born Costa Ricans than the national average, with a little over 10 percent of its population born outside of the country in 2011. By way of comparison, 9 percent of my sample (9 out of 100) was foreign-born. Unless otherwise noted, statistics on Costa Rica's foreign-born population were obtained from the 2011 Costa Rican Census on September 14, 2014 at http://www.inec.go.cr/Web/Home/GeneradorPagina.aspx.

11. Some 78 percent of the immigrants in my sample were Nicaraguan. Given the precarious position of undocumented workers and the sensitive nature of the question, I did not ask research participants to reveal their immigrant status. Only one participant offered this information. Unsurprisingly, she had secured permanent residency through an amnesty program. My best guess is that three of these immigrants had the legal right to work in Costa Rica, whereas four did not.

12. To work legally in Costa Rica, a foreign-born individual must have permanent residency or a temporary work visa. Generally, Nicaraguans are not eligible for temporary work visas in Costa Rica, meaning that the only way they can obtain the legal right to work in Costa Rica is to obtain permanent residency through amnesty or a familial link to a Costa Rican citizen (marriage or a child born in Costa Rica). There are some 200,000 documented Nicaraguan immigrants in Costa Rica, most of whom obtained permanent residency through one of the three amnesty programs in the 1990s (Lee 2010:323–4).

13. Policy makers and social commentators use the term "nini" when referencing the Costa Rican population that neither studies nor works. (In Spanish, "neither studying nor working" translates as *ni estudia ni trajaba*—hence the term "nini.") The group, notes the 2013 State of the Nation report, is a diverse one and includes young people who simply cannot find decent work given low levels of education and those who have left school and labor market due to domestic responsibilities in the home. These "nini" profiles

are gendered to the extent that the former is overwhelmingly male and the latter overwhelmingly female. In 2000, some 24 percent of the Costa Rican population age 12 to 24 was considered a "nini," a percentage that had dropped to 19 percent by 2011 (Programa Estado de la Nación 2013b:92).

14. The highest Gini Coefficient during this time period was in 2001, when the coefficient was 0.519. The Gini Coefficient ranges from 0, which represents complete equality, to 1, which represents complete inequality. For comparative purposes, the Gini Coefficient in the United States was 0.477 in 2011; in Honduras it was 0.570 in 2009; and in the Dominican Republic it was 0.472 in 2010. Accordingly, Costa Rica has a relatively higher level of income inequality than the United States and the Dominican Republic but a lower level of income inequality than Honduras. Note that a country may have a higher poverty rate but a lower Gini Coefficient. Thus, the Dominican Republic may have a lower level of income inequality than Costa Rica, but it has a higher poverty rate (around 40 percent compared to Costa Rica's 20 percent.) Note, too, that Costa Rica is one of the few countries in Latin America wherein income inequality is rising and not falling (Programa Estado de la Nación 2012). Statistics obtained from the World Bank on September 16, 2014 at http://data.worldbank.org/indicator/SI.POV.GINI.

15. Pujol et al. (2009) argue that in the context of structural adjustment, the state all but abandoned the construction of affordable housing, although it did formalize many of the informal settlements created through land invasion during the 1980s and 1990s.

16. In a fascinating study of the squatter movements that developed in the 1980s, Badilla and Cerdas (2013) find that many of these women were in fact uncomfortable with being associated with the poor and in such impoverished conditions. They were accustomed to indoor plumbing and electricity; thus, they experienced these subpar living conditions as a diminution of their middle-class social status. Perhaps as a result of their class location, many of the more radical squatter movements were vulnerable to cooptation. Badilla and Cerdas (2013) document how the National Liberation Party (PLN) helped organize some of these early land invasions as a way to garner votes in the elections of the 1980s. It appears that these efforts were decisive in the PLN electoral victories of 1982 and 1986. This is, of course, ironic, because the PLN platform during and after this decade has been one of reduced government intervention and social assistance. From 1986 onward, housing assistance would be coordinated through the National Housing Finance System (*Sistema Financiero Nacional para la Vivienda*), which stimulated private sector investment in housing construction, and the Housing Mortgage Bank (*Banco Hipotecario*), which provided housing subsidies to lower income families

through a Family Housing Voucher (*Bono Familiar*). Often, these housing vouchers went toward the construction of new homes, from which private developers naturally profited. From 2000 to 2005, these housing vouchers accounted for some 45 percent of all newly constructed homes in Costa Rica (Ministerio de Vivienda y Asentamientos Humanos 2006).

17. As this figure suggests, the majority of residents in these informal settlements (83 percent) are native Costa Ricans.

18. Statistics were obtained on September 16, 2014 at the website of Costa Rica's Instituto de Instituto Nacional de Estadística y Censos: http://www.inec. go.cr/bincri/RpWebEngine.exe/Portal?BASE=VITNAC. See also Budowski and Bixby (2003) for an analysis of paternity, child acknowledgment, and lone mothers in Costa Rica.

19. The proportion of working women in poor households who were self-employed increased from 22 percent in 1990 to 42 percent in 2003 (Gindling and Oviedo 2008:4).

20. In her study of the coffee-growing canton of Tarrazú, Kordick (2012) finds a similar dynamic. Here, the migration of native-born men out of the region led to a labor shortage in the area's coffee industry. This labor shortage prompted the seasonal migration of thousands of indigenous Ngöbe-Buglé laborers, whose reservation straddles the border of Costa Rica and Panama. The migration of indigenous peoples to work the seasonal coffee harvest effectively racialized coffee picking as a demeaning form of labor. However, it also allowed working-class Tarrazúceños to reimagine themselves as part of a "white" middle-class nation in a way that they could not when they were "just" laborers in the coffee industry.

21. As Sandoval-Garcia (2004b) points out, this distinction became further pronounced during the socialist revolution in Nicaragua and the armed conflicts that ensued.

22. This "nonrecognition" extends to internal others, such as indigenous peoples, Afro–Costa Ricans, and peasants, who are seen as not quite belonging in a modern, progressive Costa Rica (Sandoval-Garcia 2004b).

Chapter 7

1. A *quinceañera* is a fifteenth birthday party and a major coming-of-age moment for young women in Latin America. It is akin to a "sweet sixteen" birthday in the United States and is often celebrated with an elaborate party for family and friends.

2. In outlining an ethnographic imagination, I am drawing deliberately on the work of C. Wright Mills. Mills argued that when individuals developed a sociological imagination, they would be able to overcome their constraints

and act on the historical forces bearing down on them. In his understanding, this critical consciousness was the primary motor of social change.

3. More recently, Clark (2010) has documented the reversal of even some of these gradual public sector reforms. Examining the country's Social Security Institute, she finds that the government backed away from experiments with decentralization and privatization. Again, this suggests that Costa Rica has long avoided full privatization, holding fast to the public sector institutions that extend benefits to a larger portion of Costa Ricans.

4. Rodríguez's trial began in 2010. He was found guilty of bribery and sentenced to five years in prison. Later, an appeals court overturned the conviction and acquitted him of all charges.

5. Calderón was accused of taking $450,000 in kickbacks from a government contract awarded to a Finnish firm. Calderón's trial began in 2008. He was found guilty and sentenced to five years in prison. In 2011, his appeal was rejected, but his sentence was reduced from five to three years.

6. Throughout the 1980s and 1990s, the PLN and PUSC accounted for more than 90 percent of all votes in Costa Rican elections. In the election of 2002, they garnered just 63 percent of the vote. See Lehoucq (2005) for an analysis of these trends.

7. Arias won 40.9 percent of the vote and Solís 39.6 percent of the vote.

8. The agreement includes Guatemala, El Salvador, Honduras, Nicaragua, and Costa Rica. Eventually, CAFTA came to include the Dominican Republic—hence the name CAFTA-DR, which is now the official abbreviation of the agreement.

9. The pro-CAFTA camp spent an estimated US $58 million in contrast to the $4 million spent by the anti-CAFTA camp (Cupples and Larios 2010:96).

10. One of the defining features of the "No" movement were the *comités patrióticos*, which were geographically based committees that organized towns, neighborhoods, and workplaces at the grassroots level. By the time the referendum took place, there were more than 160 such committees hard at work around the country (Willis and Seiz 2012:133).

11. A poll released four days before the referendum put the "No" vote at 55% and the "Yes" vote at 43% (Cupples and Larios 2010:101).

12. In the runoff to the 2014 elections, Solís won by 78 percent of the votes. This landslide was unprecedented in the country's history. Ultimately, PAC's broad appeal may be its downfall. It has tried to rally voters disgusted by the country's corruption scandals while catering to a socially conservative but politically left-of-center group that favors a strong social welfare state. This broad base of support may be difficult to sustain in the long run.

13. Translated into English and in this context, this term means "little dark-skinned one."

REFERENCES

Alvarenga Venutolo, Patricia. 1997. "Los productores en la Costa Rica precafetalera (1750–1840)." *Nuestra Historia* 8. San José, Costa Rica: Editorial Universidad Estatal a Distancia.

Arias, Omar. 2001. "Are Men Benefiting from the New Economy? Male Economic Marginalization in Argentina, Brazil, and Costa Rica." World Bank Policy Research Working Paper. Washington, DC: The World Bank.

Arroyo, Beatriz. 2001. "Columna fuera de casa." *La Nación*, August 20.

Ávalos, Ángela. 2001. "Ciudades atraen mas gente." *La Nación*, August 23.

———. 2002. "Tras mas orden en ciudades." *La Nación*, April 23.

Babb, Sarah. 2005. "The Social Consequences of Structural Adjustment: Recent Evidence and Current Debates." *Annual Review of Sociology* 31:199–222.

Badilla Gómez, Patricia and José M. Cerdas Albertazzi. 2013. "Movimientos pro vivienda en San José: una clientela movilizada (1980–1990)." *Revista de Historia* no. 67:121–56.

Bandy, Joe, and Jennifer Bickham Mendez. 2003. "A Place of Their Own? Women Organizers in the Maquilas of Nicaragua and Mexico." *Mobilization: An International Journal* 8(2):173–88.

Barley, Stephen R., and Gideon Kunda. 2004. *Gurus, Hired Guns, and Warm Bodies: Itinerant Experts in a Knowledge Economy*. Princeton, NJ: Princeton University Press.

Barquero, Marvin, and Edgar Delgado. 2001. "Frenados los negocios ticos." *La Nación*, September 13.

Benería, Lourdes, and Shelley Feldman, eds. 1992. *Unequal Burden: Economic Crisis, Persistent Poverty and Women's Work*. Boulder, CO: Westview Press.

Benería, Lourdes, and Marta Roldán. 1987. *The Crossroads of Class and Gender: Industrial Homework, Subcontracting, and Household Dynamics*. Chicago: University of Chicago Press.

Birdsall, Nancy. 2012. "A Note on the Middle Class in Latin America." CGD Working Paper 303. Washington, DC: Center for Global Development. Retrieved June 17, 2015, http://www.cgdev.org/files/1426386_file_Birsdall_Note_on_Middle_Class_FINAL.pdf.

Birdsall, Nancy, Nora Lustig, and Christian J. Meyer. 2014. "The Strugglers: The New Poor in Latin America?" *World Development* 60(1):132–46.

Boddiger, David. 2001. "Hotels, Airlines Plan Blitz." *The Tico Times*, October 5, 2001.

———. 2002. "C.R.'s Central Valley's Still Top Choice for Most." *The Tico Times*, March 22.

Budowski, Monica, and Luis Rosero Bixby. 2003. "Fatherless Costa Rica? Child Acknowledgement and Support Among Lone Mothers." *Journal of Comparative Family Studies* 34(2):229–54.

Burawoy, Michael. 2003. "Revisits: An Outline of a Theory of Reflexive Ethnography." *American Sociological Review* 68(5):645–79.

Burdick, John, Philip Oxhorn, and Kenneth M. Roberts, eds. 2009. *Beyond Neoliberalism in Latin America: Societies and Politics at the Crossroads.* New York: Palgrave Macmillan.

Cambronero Vindas, Roberto. 2001. "Años de infancia, siglos de guerra." In *Niñas y niños del 48 escriben,* edited by Mercedes Muñoz. San José: Editorial de la Universidad de Costa Rica.

Cantero, Marcela. 2001a. "Busco empleo." *La Nación,* May 29.

———. 2001b. "Mama, y mucho mas." *La Nación,* August 15.

———. 2002. "Alumnos de noches completas." *La Nación,* February 7.

Castells, Manuel, and Alejandro Portes. 1989. "World Underneath: The Origins, Dynamics and Effects of the Informal Economy." In *The Informal Economy: Studies in Advanced and Less Developed Countries,* edited by Alejandro Portes, Manuel Castells, and Lauren A. Benton. Baltimore: Johns Hopkins University Press.

Cecchini, Simone, and Aldo Madariaga. 2011. "Conditional Cash Transfer Programmes: The Recent Experience in Latin America and the Caribbean." Cuadernos de la CEPAL No. 95. Santiago, Chile: Comisión Económica para América Latina y el Caribe. Retrieved June 17, 2015, http://repositorio.cepal.org/bitstream/handle/11362/27855/S1100263_en.pdf?sequence=1.

Cerrutti, Marcela. 2000. "Economic Reform, Structural Adjustment and Female Labor Force Participation in Buenos Aires, Argentina." *World Development* 28(5):879–91.

Chant, Sylvia. 2000. "Men in Crisis? Reflections on Masculinities, Work and Family in North-West Costa Rica." *European Journal of Development Research* 12(2):199–218.

———. 2002. "Families on the Verge of Breakdown? Views on Contemporary Trends in Family Life in Guanacaste, Costa Rica." *Journal of Developing Societies* 18(2–3):109–48.

————. 2009. "The 'Feminisation of Poverty' in Costa Rica: To What Extent a Conundrum?" *Bulletin of Latin American Research* 28(1):19–43.

Chant, Sylvia, with Nikki Craske. 2003. *Gender in Latin America*. New Brunswick, NJ: Rutgers University Press.

Chant, Sylvia, and Matthew C. Gutmann. 2001. *Mainstreaming Men into Gender and Development: Debates, Reflections, and Experiences*. Oxford: Oxfam Publishing.

Clark, Mary. 1995. "Non-traditional Export Promotion in Costa Rica: Sustaining Export-Led Growth." *Journal of Interamerican Studies and World Affairs* 37(2):181–224.

————. 1997. "Transnational Alliances and Development Policy in Latin America: Nontraditional Export Promotion in Costa Rica." *Latin American Research Review* 32(2):71–97.

————. 2001. *Gradual Economic Reform in Latin America: The Costa Rican Experience*. Albany: State University of New York Press.

————. 2010. "The Recentralization of Health Care Reform in Costa Rica." CIPR Occasional Paper, July 10, 2010. New Orleans, LA: Center for Inter-American Policy and Research. Retrieved June 30, 2015, http://stonecenter.tulane.edu/uploads/THE_RECENTRALIZATION_OF_THE_CCSS_IN_COSTA_RICA.pdf.

Craske, Nikki. 1999. *Women and Politics in Latin America*. New Brunswick, NJ: Rutgers University Press.

Creamer, Winifred. 1987. "Mesoamerican as a Concept: An Archaeological View from Central America." *Latin American Research Review* 22(1):35–62.

Cupples, Julie, and Irving Larios. 2010. "A Functional Anarchy: Love, Patriotism, and Resistance to Free Trade in Costa Rica." *Latin American Perspectives* 37(6):93–108.

Dobles, Fabián. 1994. "The Targuá Tree." In *Costa Rica: A Traveler's Literary Companion*, edited by Barbara Ras. San Francisco: Whereabouts Press.

Donato, Elisa M., and Manuel Rojas Bolanos. 1989. "Problems and Prospects of the Costa Rican Trade Unions." In *The Costa Rica Reader*, edited by Marc Edelman and Joanne Kenen. New York: Grove Weidenfeld.

Economic Commission for Latin America and the Caribbean (ECLAC). 2010. "Costa Rica." In *Preliminary Overview of the Economies of Latin America and the Caribbean 2009*. Retrieved September 9, 2014, http://www.cepal.org/publicaciones/xml/3/38063/costa_rica.pdf.

————. 2014. "Costa Rica." In *Preliminary Overview of the Economies of Latin America and the Caribbean 2013*. Retrieved September 9, 2014, http://www.cepal.org/publicaciones/xml/1/51821/BPI-CostaRica.pdf.

Edelman, Marc. 1992. *The Logic of the Latifundio: The Large Estates of Northwestern Costa Rica Since the Late Nineteenth Century*. Stanford, CA: Stanford University Press.

Edelman, Marc, and Joanne Kenen. 1989. "The Origins of Costa Rican Exceptionalism—Colonial Period and the Nineteenth Century." In *The*

Costa Rica Reader, edited by Marc Edelman and Joanne Kenen. New York: Grove Weidenfeld.

Elizondo Mora, Victor Manuel. 1997. "La Plaza de Flores y los 'pioneros' de nuestro foot-ball." In *Heredia . . . Historia, tradiciones, y vivencias*, edited by Carlos Melendez. Heredia, Costa Rica: Editorial de la Universidad Naciónal.

Elson, Diane, and Ruth Pearson. 1981. "'Nimble Fingers Make Cheap Workers': An Analysis of Women's Employment in Third World Export Manufacturing." *Feminist Review* 7(1):87–107.

Esteve, Albert, Joan García-Román, and Ron Lesthaeghe. 2012. "The Family Context of Cohabitation and Single Motherhood in Latin America." *Population and Development Review* 38(4):707–27.

Esteve, Albert, Ron Lesthaeghe, and Antonio López-Gay. 2012. "The Latin American Cohabitation Boom, 1970–2007." *Population and Development Review* 38(1):55–81.

Fallas, Carlos Luis. 1941. *Mamita Yunai*. San José, Costa Rica: Soley y Valverde.

Feigenblatt, Hazel. 2001. "Taxis piratas: negocio de muchos." *La Nación*, September 3.

———. 2005. "Consulados estiman que unos 220.000 costarricenses viven en EEUU." *La Nación*, March 13.

Fernandez-Kelly, Maria Patricia. 1983. *For We Are Sold, I and My People: Women and Industry in Mexico's Frontier*. Albany: State University of New York Press.

Frajman, Eduardo. 2012. "The People, Not the Movement: Opposition to CAFTA in Costa Rica, 2002–2007." *Latin American Perspectives* 39(6):116–32.

Freeman, Carla. 2000. *High Tech and High Heels in the Global Economy: Women, Work, and Pink-Collar Identities in the Caribbean*. Durham, NC: Duke University Press.

Garcia, Brigida, and Orlandina de Oliveira. 1994. "Motherhood and Extradomestic Work in Urban Mexico." *Bulletin of Latin American Research* 16(3):367–84.

Gereffi, Gary, and Miguel Korzeniewicz, eds. 1994. *Commodity Chains in Global Capitalism*. Westport, CT: Praeger.

Gindling, T. H. 1991. "Labor Market Segmentation and the Determination of Wages in the Public, Private-Formal, and Informal Sectors in San José, Costa Rica." *Economic Development and Cultural Change* 39(3):584–605.

———. 2009. "South-South Migration: The Impact of Nicaraguan Immigrants on Earnings, Inequality and Poverty in Costa Rica." *World Development* 37(1):116–26.

Gindling, T. H., and Luis Oviedo. 2008. "Single Mothers and Poverty in Costa Rica." Discussion Paper No. 3286. Bonn, Germany: Institute for the Study of Labor. Retrieved November 11, 2011, http://ftp.iza.org/dp3286.pdf.

Golcher, Raquel. 2001. "Gobierno entregaria concesiones de taxis." *La Nación*, August 14.

González de la Rocha, Mercedes. 1994. *The Resources of Poverty: Women and Survival in a Mexican City*. Oxford: Blackwell.

———. 2000. "Private Adjustments: Household Responses to the Erosion of Work." Social Development and Poverty Alleviation Division, UNDP (SEPED) Conference Paper Series #6. New York: United Nations Development Programme (UNDP). Retrieved June 30, 2015, http://www.chs.ubc.ca/lprv/PDF/lprv0483.pdf.

———. 2001. "From the Resources of Poverty to the Poverty of Resources? The Erosion of a Survival Model." *Latin American Perspectives* 28(4):72–100.

González Salas, Edwin. 1997. "Evolución histórica de la población de Costa Rica (1840–1940)." *Nuestra Historia* 9. San José, Costa Rica: Editorial Universidad Estatal a Distancia.

Grugel, Jean, and Pia Riggirozzi, eds. 2009. *Governance after Neoliberalism in Latin America*. Basingstoke, UK: Palgrave Macmillan.

———. 2012. "Post-neoliberalism in Latin America: Rebuilding and Reclaiming the State after Crisis." *Development and Change* 43(1):1–21.

Gudmundson, Lowell. 1984. "Black into White in Nineteenth Century Spanish America: Afro-American Assimilation in Argentina and Costa Rica." *Slavery and Abolition* 5:34–49.

———. 1986. *Costa Rica Before Coffee: Society and Economy on the Eve of the Export Boom*. Baton Rouge: Louisiana State University Press.

———. 1995. "Peasant, Farmer, Proletarian: Class Formation in a Smallholder Coffee Economy, 1850-1950." In *Coffee, Society, and Power in Latin America*, edited by William Roseberry, Lowell Gudmundson and Mario Samper Kutschbach. Baltimore: The Johns Hopkins University Press.

Gutmann, Matthew C. 1996. *The Meanings of Macho: Being a Man in Mexico City*. Berkeley: University of California Press.

———. 2003. *Changing Men and Masculinities in Latin America*. Durham, NC: Duke University Press.

Hall, Carolyn. 1976. *El café y el desarrollo historico-geografico de Costa Rica*. San José: Editorial Costa Rica y Universidad Nacional.

Heimer, Carol A. 2001. "Cases and Biographies: An Essay on Routinization and the Nature of Comparison." *Annual Review of Sociology* 27:47–76.

Herrera Rodriguez, Rodrigo. 2001. "Mi experiencia en 1948." In *Niñas y niños del 48 escriben*, edited by Mercedes Muñoz. San José: Editorial de la Universidad de Costa Rica.

Hite, Amy Bellone, and Jocelyn S. Viterna. 2005. "Gendering Class in Latin America: How Women Effect and Experience Change in the Class Structure." *Latin American Research Review* 40(2):50–82.

Hochschild, Arlie, with Anne Machung. 1989. *The Second Shift: Working Parents and the Revolution at Home*. New York: Viking Books.

Hoffman, Kelly, and Miguel Angel Centeno. 2003. "The Lop-Sided Continent: Inequality in Latin America." *Annual Review of Sociology* 29:363–90.

Hondagneu-Sotelo, Pierrette. 2001. *Doméstica: Immigrant Workers Cleaning and Caring in the Shadows of Affluence.* Berkeley: University of California Press.

Instituto Naciónal de Estadística y Censos (INEC). 2001. *IX Censo Naciónal de Población y V de Vivienda: Resultados Generales.* San José, Costa Rica.

————. 2012. *X Censo Naciónal de Población y VI de Vivienda: Resultados Generales.* San José, Costa Rica.

Itzigsohn, José. 2000. *Developing Poverty: The State, Labor Market Regulation, and the Informal Economy in Costa Rica and the Dominican Republic.* University Park: The Pennsylvania State University Press.

Kandiyoti, Deniz. 1988. "Bargaining with Patriarchy." *Gender & Society* 2(3):274–90.

Kordick, Carmen. 2012. "Tarrazú: Coffee, Migration, and National Building in Rural Costa Rica, 1824–2008." PhD Dissertation, Department of History, Yale University, New Haven, CT.

Korzeniewicz, Roberto Patricio, and William C. Smith. 2000. "Poverty, Inequality, and Growth in Latin America: Searching for the High Road to Globalization." *Latin American Research Review* 35(3):7–54.

Láscaris, Constantino. 2004. "In Defense of the Corner Store." In *The Costa Rica Reader: History, Culture, and Politics*, edited by Steven Palmer and Ivan Molina. Durham, NC: Duke University Press.

Lee, Ching Kwan. 1998. *Gender and the South China Miracle: Two Worlds of Factory Women.* Berkeley: University of California Press.

Lee, Sang E. 2010. "Unpacking the Packing Plant: Nicaraguan Migrant Women's Work in Costa Rica's Evolving Export Agriculture Sector." *Signs* 35(2):317–42.

Lehoucq, Fabrice Edouard. 2005. "Costa Rica: Paradise in Doubt." *Journal of Democracy* 16(3):140–54.

Leiton, Patricia. 2001. "Hoteles: 2.500 despidos." *La Nación,* September 29.

————. 2002. "Construccion domina en zona central." *La Nación,* January 19.

Lim, Linda. 1990. "Women's Work in Export Factories: The Politics of a Cause." In *Persistent Inequalities: Women and World Development.* Edited by Irene Tinker. New York: Oxford University Press.

Lustig, Nora. 1995. "Introduction." In *Coping with Austerity: Poverty and Inequality in Latin America,* edited by Nora Lustig, 1–41. Washington, DC: The Brookings Institution.

Lustig, Nora, Luis F. Lopez-Calva, and Eduardo Ortiz-Juarez. 2012. "Declining Inequality in Latin America in the 2000s: The Cases of Argentina, Brazil, and Mexico." CGD Working Paper 307. Washington, DC: Center for Global Development. Retrieved June 30, 2015, http://www.cgdev.org/files/1426568_file_Lustig_et_al_IneqLA_FINAL.pdf.

MacDonald, Laura, and Arne Ruckert, eds. 2009. *Post-Neoliberalism in the Americas.* New York: Palgrave Macmillan.

Marois, Thomas. 2005. "From Economic Crisis to a 'State' of Crisis? The Emergence of Neoliberalism in Costa Rica." *Historical Materialism* 13(3):101–34.

Martínez Franzoni, Juliana, and Koen Voorend. 2012. "Black, Whites or Greys? Conditional Transfers and Gender Equality in Latin America." *Social Politics* 19(3):383–407.

Martínez, Ricardo, and Isabel Ducca, eds. 2001. *Tertulias de Barrio*. Heredia, Costa Rica: Ministerio de Cultura, Juventud y Deportes.

McKay, Steven C. 2006. *Satanic Mills or Silicon Islands?: The Politics of High-tech Production in the Philippines*. Ithaca, NY: ILR Press.

Melendez Chaverri, Carlos. 2001. *Añoranzas de Heredia*. Heredia, Costa Rica: Editorial Universidad Naciónal.

Melendez, Carlos, and Quince Duncan. 1977. *El negro en Costa Rica*. San José: Editorial Costa Rica.

Mendez, Jennifer Bickham. 2005. *From Revolution to the Maquiladoras: Gender, Labor and Globalization in Nicaragua*. Durham, NC: Duke University Press.

Menjívar Ochoa, Mauricio. 2010. "La masculinidad a debate." *Cuaderno de Ciencias Sociales* 154. San José, Costa Rica: FLACSCO.

Meza-Cordero, Jaime A. 2011. "The Effects of Subsidizing Secondary Schooling: Evidence from a Conditional Cash Transfer Program in Costa Rica." Working paper. Retrieved May 26, 2013, https://dornsife.usc.edu/assets/sites/1/docs/The_Effects_of_Subsidizing_Secondary_Schooling_Evidence_from_a_Conditional_Cash_Transfer_Program_in_Costa_Rica.pdf.

Mills, C. Wright. 1959. *The Sociological Imagination*. New York: Oxford University Press.

Ministerio de Vivienda y Asentamientos Humanos (MIVAH). 2006. *Compendio de Estadísticas del Sector Vivienda y Asentamientos Humanos 2005*. MIVAH: San José, Costa Rica.

Minujin, Alberto. 1995. "Squeezed: The Middle Class in Latin America." *Environment and Urbanization* 7(2):153–66.

Miron, Louis F. 1989. "Costa Rican Education: Making Democracy Work." In *The Costa Rica Reader*, edited by Marc Edelman and Joanne Kenen. New York: Grove Weidenfeld.

Molina Jimenez, Ivan. 1995. "Comercio y comerciantes en Costa Rica (1750–1840)." *Nuestra Historia* 7. San José, Costa Rica: Editorial Universidad Estatal a Distancia.

Molina, Ivan, and Steven Palmer. 2000. *The History of Costa Rica*. San José: Editorial de la Universidad de Costa Rica.

Molina, Maria, and Yessenia Fallas. 2009. "Transferencias monetárias condicionadas en Costa Rica: el caso del Programa AVANCEMOS." *Revista Políticas Públicas* 13(2):219–29.

Molyneux, Maxine. 1998. "Analyzing Women's Movements." *Development and Change* 29:219–45.

———. 2003. Women's Movements in International Perspective: Latin America and Beyond. Chapel Hill, NC: Institute for the Study of the Americas.

———. 2007. "Change and Continuity in Social Protection in Latin America: Mothers at the Service of the State?" Gender and Development Programme Paper No.1. New York: United Nations Research Institute for Social Development.

Monge Alfaro, Carlos. 1980. *Historia de Costa Rica*. 16th ed. San José, Costa Rica: Imprenta Trejos.

Mora, Emilia, and Carlos Hernandez. 2001. "Detectan maltrato a ilegales nicas." *La Nación*, August 12.

Morales, Natalia. 2013. "Aspectos relevantes en desigualdad y pobreza al 2012. In *Decimonoveno Informe Estado de la Nación en Desarrollo Humano Sostenible*. San José, Costa Rica: Programa Estado de la Nación. Retrieved June 30, 2015, http://www.estadoNación.or.cr/files/biblioteca_virtual/019/morales_2013.pdf.

Murillo, Alvaro. 2001. "Pais expuesto a sanción." La Nación, June 14.

Naim, Moises. 2000. "Fads and Fashion in Economic Reforms: Washington Consensus or Washington Confusion?" *Third World Quarterly* 21(3):505–28.

Nakano Glenn, Evelyn. 1992. "From Servitude to Service Work: Historical Continuities in the Racial Division of Paid Reproductive Labor." *Signs* 18(1):1–43.

Newson, Linda A. 1987. *Indian Survival in Colonial Nicaragua*. Norman: University of Oklahoma Press.

Ngai, Pun. 2005. *Made in China: Women Factory Workers in a Global Workplace*. Durham, NC: Duke University Press.

O'Dougherty, Maureen. 1999. "The Devalued State and Nation: Neoliberalism and the Moral Economy Discourse of the Brazilian Middle Class, 1986–1994." *Latin American Perspectives* 26(1):151–74.

Ong, Aihwa. 1987. *Spirits of Resistance and Capitalist Discipline: Factory Women in Malaysia*. Albany: State University of New York Press.

Organisation for Economic Co-operation and Development (OECD). 2009. "Migration Country Notes—Costa Rica." In *Latin American Economic Outlook 2010*. Retrieved June 11, 2014, http://www.oecd.org/dev/americas/latinamericaneconomicoutlook2010.htm#Content.

Organismo de Investigacion Judicial. 2013. "Reporte de Situacion, Costa Rica 2013: Tráfico de Drogas y Amenazas del Crimen Organizado en Costa Rica." Retrieved June 8, 2015, http://www.poder-judicial.go.cr/oij/index.php?option=com_phocadownload&view=category&id=90&Itemid=273.

Paige, Jeffery M. 1997. *Coffee and Power: Revolution and the Rise of Democracy in Central America*. Cambridge, MA: Harvard University Press.

Panizza, Francisco. 2009. *Contemporary Latin America: Development and Democracy Beyond the Washington Consensus*. London: Zed Books.

Portes, Alejandro. 1994. "The Informal Economy and Its Paradoxes." In *The Handbook of Economic Sociology*, edited by Neil J. Smelser and Richard Swedberg, 426–50. Princeton, NJ: Princeton University Press.

Portes, Alejandro, Manuel Castells, and Lauren A. Benton, eds. 1989. *The Informal Economy: Studies in Advanced and Less Developed Countries.* Baltimore: Johns Hopkins University Press.

Portes, Alejandro, and Kelly Hoffman. 2003. "Latin American Class Structure: Their Composition and Change During the Neo-Liberal Era." *Latin American Research Review* 38(1):41–82.

Pratt, Christine. 2001. "'Emergency' Tourism Plan." *The Tico Times,* September 28.

———. 2002. "'La Casona' Rebuilt, Reborn." *The Tico Times,* March 22.

Programa Estado de la Nación. 2005. *Primer Informe Estado de la Educación.* San José, Costa Rica: Programa Estado de la Nación.

———. 2008. *Segundo Informe Estado de la Educación.* San José, Costa Rica: Programa Estado de la Nación.

———. 2011. *Decimoséptimo Informe Estado de la Nación en Desarrollo Humano Sostenible.* San José, Costa Rica: Programa Estado de la Nación.

———. 2012. *Decimoctavo Informe Estado de la Nación en Desarrollo Humano Sostenible.* San José, Costa Rica: Programa Estado de la Nación.

———. 2013a. *Cuarto Informe Estado de la Educación.* San José, Costa Rica: Programa Estado de la Nación.

———. 2013b. *Decimonoveno Informe Estado de la Nación en Desarrollo Humano Sostenible.* San José. Costa Rica: Programa Estado de la Nación.

Pujol, Rosendo, Eduardo Pérez, and Leonardo Sánchez. 2009. "Hacia un cambio en la oferta de vivienda en la GAM: Una exploración desde los grandes desafíos planteados por la demanda potencial de vivenco de la region." In *Decimoquinto Informe Estado de la Nación en Desarrollo Humano Sostenible.* San José, Costa Rica: Programa Estado de la Nación. Retrieved June 30, 2015, http://www.estadonacion.or.cr/files/biblioteca_virtual/015/Pujol_et_al_2009.pdf.

Ramírez Aguilar, Lucía. 2009. "Guanacaste construye su riqueza con miles de manos pobres." *Seminario Universidad* January 13, 2009. Retrieved June 20, 2015, http://semanariouniversidad.ucr.cr/pais/guanacaste-construye-su-riqueza-con-miles-de-manos-pobres/.

Rodríguez, Eugenia. 2000. "Civilizing Domestic Life in the Central Valley of Costa Rica, 1750–1850." In *Hidden Histories of Gender and State in Latin America,* edited by Elizabeth Dore and Maxine Molyneux. Durham, NC: Duke University Press.

Rodrik, Dani. 1997. *Has Globalization Gone Too Far?* Washington, DC: Peter G. Peterson Institute for International Economics.

Rogers, Tim. 2001. "End to Poverty in C.R. Predicted." *The Tico Times,* November 30.

Rojas Bolanos, Manuel. 1989. "The *Solidarismo* Movement." In *The Costa Rica Reader,* edited by Marc Edelman and Joanne Kenen. New York: Grove Weidenfeld.

Safa, Helen. 1981. "Runaway Shops and Female Employment: The Search for Cheap Labor." *Signs* 7(2):418–33.

———. 1990. "Women's Social Movements in Latin America." *Gender & Society* 4(3):354–69.

———. 1995. *The Myth of the Male Breadwinner: Women and Industrialization in the Caribbean*. Boulder, CO: Westview Press.

Salzinger, Leslie. 2003. *Genders in Production: Making Workers in Mexico's Global Factories*. Berkeley: University of California Press.

Samper Kutchbach, Mario. 1978. "Los productores directos en el siglo del cafe." *Revista de Historia* 7:123–217.

———. 2003. "Tierra, trabajo y tecnoogía en el desarrollo del capitalism agrario en Costa Rica." *Historia Agraria* 29:81–104.

Sandoval-García, Carlos. 2004a. "Contested Discourses on National Identity: Representing Nicaraguan Immigration to Costa Rica." *Bulletin of Latin American Research* 23(4):434–45.

———. 2004b. *Threatening Others: Nicaraguans and the Formation of National Identities in Costa Rica*. Athens: Ohio University Research in International Studies.

———. 2007. "Football: Forging Nationhood and Masculinities in Costa Rica." *History of Sport* 22(2):212–30.

Sassen, Saskia. 1998. *Globalization and Its Discontents*. New York: The New Press.

Seligson, Mitchell A. 1980. *Peasants of Costa Rica and the Development of Agrarian Capitalism*. Madison: University of Wisconsin Press.

———. 2002. "Trouble in Paradise? The Erosion of System Support in Costa Rica, 1978–1999." *Latin American Research Review* 37(1):160–85.

Seligson, Mitchell A., and Juliana Martínez. 2009. "Limits to Costa Rican Heterodoxy: What Has Changed in 'Paradise'?" In *Democratic Governance in Latin America*, edited by Scott Mainwaring and Timothy Scully. Stanford, CA: Stanford University Press.

Shakow, Miriam. 2014. *Along the Bolivian Highway: Social Mobility and Political Culture in a New Middle Class*. Philadelphia: University of Pennsylvania Press.

Smith, Katherine L. 2009. "Is a Happy Anthropologist a Good Anthropologist?" *Anthropology Matters* 11(1). Retrieved August 19, 2013, http://www. anthropologymatters.com/index.php?journal=anth_matters&page=articl e&op=view&path%5B%5D=28&path%5B%5D=46.

Standing, Guy. 1999. "Global Feminization through Flexible Labor: A Theme Revisited." *World Development* 27(3):583–602.

Starcevic, Suzanna. 2002. "Safe, Select: World Behind Walls Beckons." *The Tico Times,* March 22.

Stepan, Nancy Leys. 1991. *'The Hour of Eugenics': Race, Gender, and Nation in Latin America*. Ithaca, NY: Cornell University Press.

Stiglitz, Joséph E. 2002. *Globalization and Its Discontents*. New York: W. W. Norton & Company.

Stone, Samuel Z. 1989. "Aspects of Power distribution in Costa Rica." In *The Costa Rica Reader*, edited by Marc Edelman and Joanne Kenen. New York: Grove Weidenfeld.

Sweetman, Caroline. 2001. *Gender, Development and Health.* Oxford: Oxfam Publishing.

Tardanico, Richard. 1996. "Employment, Restructuring, and Gender: The Case of San José, Costa Rica." *Studies in Comparative International Development* 31(3):85–122.

Tardanico, Richard, and Mario Lungo. 1995. "Local Dimensions of Global Restructuring: Changing Labour Market Contours in Urban Costa Rica." *International Journal of Urban and Regional Research* 19(2):223–49.

Tiano, Susan. 1994. *Patriarchy on the Line: Labor, Gender, and Ideology in the Mexican Maquila Industry.* Philadelphia: Temple University Press.

Twombly, Susan B. 1997. "Curricular Reform and the Changing Social Role of Public Higher Education in Costa Rica." *Higher Education* 33(1):1–28.

US Bureau of Diplomatic Security. 2014. "Costa Rica 2014 Crime and Safety Report." Retrieved June 10, 2015, https://www.osac.gov/pages/ContentReportDetails.aspx?cid=16121.

US Bureau of International Narcotics and Law Enforcement Affairs. 2014. "2014 International Narcotics Control Strategy (INCSR) Report." Retrieved June 8, 2015, http://www.state.gov/j/inl/rls/nrcrpt/2014/vol2/222699.htm.

USDA Foreign Agricultural Service. 2012. "Costa Rica: Retail Food Sector Report." Retrieved August 29, 2014, http://gain.fas.usda.gov/Recent%20GAIN%20Publications/Retail%20Foods_San%20Jose_Costa%20Rica_6-25-2012.pdf.

Vega, Isabel Román. 2012. *Social Protection Systems in Latin America and the Caribbean: Costa Rica.* Economic Commission for Latin America and the Caribbean (ECLAC) Project Document. Santiago, Chile: United Nations.

Vega, Mylena. 1989. "CODESA, Autonomous Institutions, and the Growth of the Public Sector." In *The Costa Rica Reader,* edited by Marc Edelman and Joanne Kenen. New York: Grove Weidenfeld.

Ward, Kathryn B., ed. 1990. *Women Workers and Global Restructuring.* Ithaca, NY: ILR Press.

Williamson, John. 2004. "A Short History of the Washington Consensus." Paper commissioned by Fundación CIDOB for a conference "From the Washington Consensus Towards a New Global Governance," Barcelona, September 24–25, 2004. Retrieved November 4, 2011, http://www.iie.com/publications/papers/williamson0904-2.pdf.

Willis, Eliza J., and Janet A. Seiz. 2012. "The CAFTA Conflict and Costa Rica's Democracy: Assessing the 2007 Referendum." *Latin American Politics and Society* 54(3):123–56.

Wolf, Diana. 1992. *Factory Daughters: Gender, Household Dynamics and Rural Industrialization in Java.* Berkeley: University of California Press.

Wolkoff, Lauren. 2001. "Taxi Drivers Block Traffic." *The Tico Times,* June 8.

Yashar, Deborah J. 1995. "Civil War and Social Welfare: The Origins of Costa Rica's Competitive Party System." In *Building Democratic Institutions: Party Systems in Latin America,* edited by Scott Mainwaring and Timothy R. Scully. Stanford, CA: Stanford University Press.

INDEX

....

Note: Page numbers followed by *f* and *t* refer to figures and tables respectively. Those followed by n refer to notes, with note number.